I0795939

Postcard History Series

Grove City

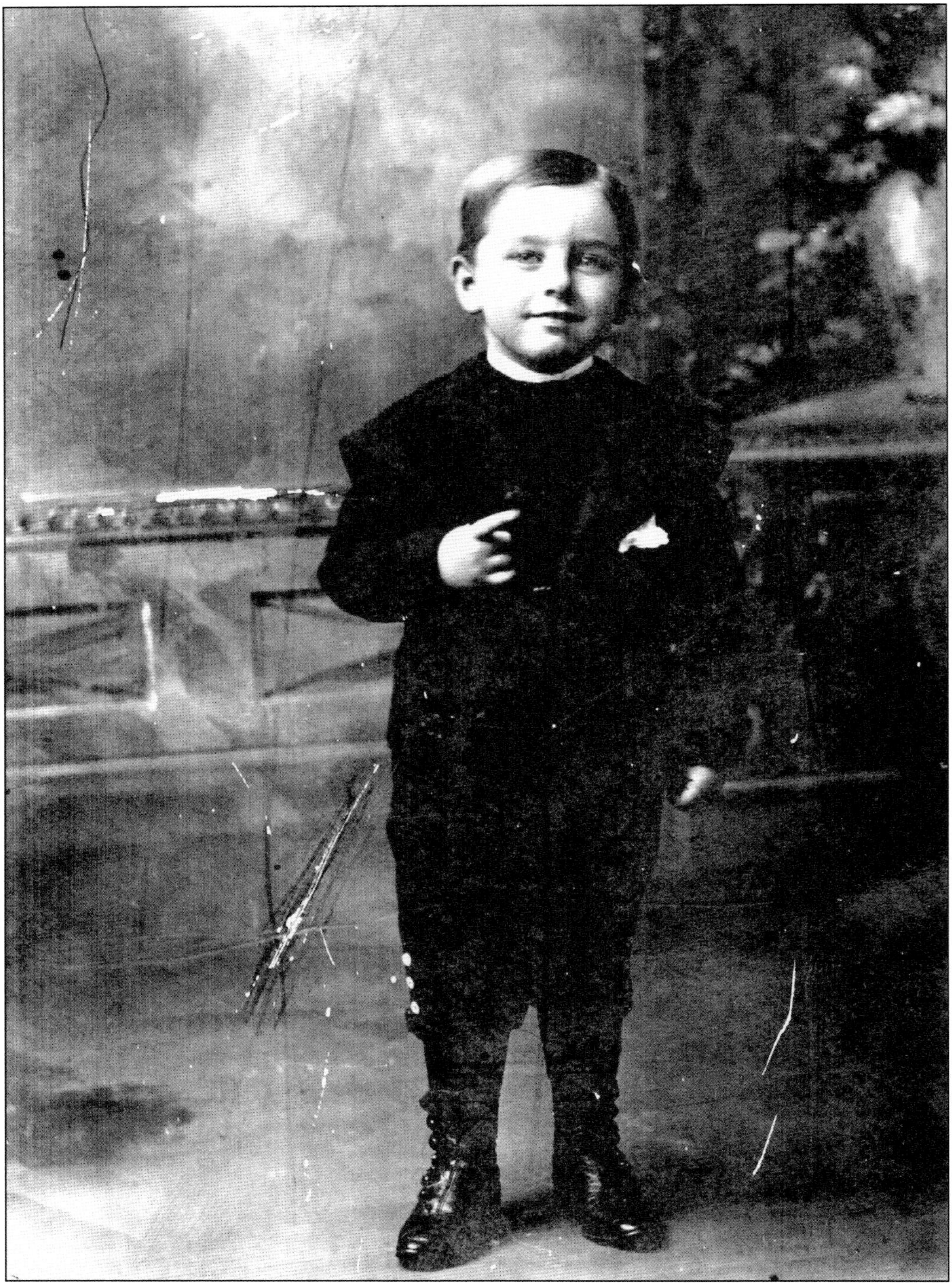

Charlie Ray is shown here as a young boy; he was photographed by Charles Daugherty in the early 1880s. After a childhood bout of polio, Ray was left without the full use of one arm. This, however, did not stop him from becoming Grove City's first chief of police in 1918, a position he held for the next 17 years.

POSTCARD HISTORY SERIES

Grove City

Mike S. Adams, John H. Hummel,
Marjorie J. Hummell, and Bradley C. Isles

ARCADIA
PUBLISHING

ISBN 978-0-7385-3555-5

Published by Arcadia Publishing
Charleston, South Carolina

Printed in the United States of America

Library of Congress Control Number: 2004100478

For all general information, please contact Arcadia Publishing:
Telephone 843-853-2070
Fax 843-853-0044
E-mail sales@arcadiapublishing.com
For customer service and orders:
Toll-Free 1-888-313-2665

Visit us on the Internet at www.arcadiapublishing.com

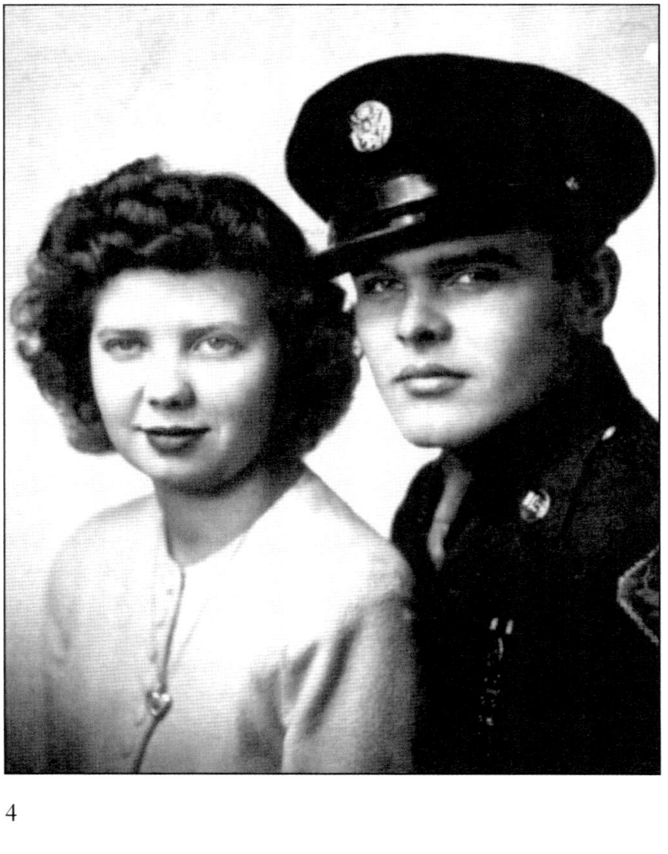

Newlyweds John and Marjorie Hummel, shown here in their wedding picture from 1943, have been on their honeymoon for more than 60 years. Avid postcard collectors and local historians, they contributed most of the material appearing in this book from their collection of more than 3,000 postcards and from their many recollections and stories about life in Grove City. Using original photographs from his own private collection, Mike Adams provided the few images shown here that are not part of the Hummel's extensive collected works.

CONTENTS

Acknowledgments

The authors would like to acknowledge Bonnie Adams, Amy McCamey, Brenda Hillard, Floyd McFarland, and others who wish to remain anonymous for their contributions to this book.

Of the many photographers who created the images used here, little is known for sure. Probably the work of professional photographers J. R. Vasbinder, Charles Daugherty, Mark Reynolds, Ralph E. Conner. and possibly Arthur Hewlett are included, as well as images captured by amateur photographers, such as Kathryn Deniker, who happened to photograph the aluminum craftsmen at Arthur Armour's workshop one warm day in 1938.

Likewise, these postcards would not exist if not distributed by companies, such as B. B. Montgomery, Harry H. Hamm, the Grove City View Company, Robbins and Son, Robert D. Young and Son, Richard T. Young, G. A. Rogaliner, International Post Card Company, and probably many others.

INTRODUCTION

When Valentine Cunningham arrived at the banks of Wolf Creek in a wooded section of western Pennsylvania in 1798, he immediately realized the potential of the meandering natural resource. He quickly went to work building a dam across its course, and the power it created from the flowing water was used to run a gristmill. Outward from the banks of Wolf Creek grew the village of Pine Grove, which would later be called Grove City.

Today, Grove City is a town of 8,000 residents and is located in southeastern Mercer County. It is widely considered the crossroads of western Pennsylvania since major interstates 79 and 80 intersect just five miles from downtown.

Grove City is home to a nationally recognized private Christian college that consistently ranks among the best in the United States. Founded in 1876 by Rev. Dr. Isaac C. Ketler, Grove City College prides itself on its independence while holding true to its mission of providing a quality education at an affordable price in a thoroughly Christian atmosphere.

Along with education, industry played an important role in Grove City's development. The Bessemer and Lake Erie Railroad bisects the town and connects key shipping ports in Erie to the north and Pittsburgh to the south. Along its rails and within the borough is the Cooper-Bessemer plant, which was the town's largest employer for much of the 20th century. Dr. Edwin J. Fithian, who in 1920 ran for the U. S. Senate on the Prohibition ticket, made his fortune after founding the Bessemer Gas Engine Company. It later became the Cooper-Bessemer Corporation and closed its doors in the late 1990s, leaving hundreds of blue-collar workers unemployed.

Were it not for Cunningham and his brother-in-law James Graham (who built his own dam a few miles upstream in the early 1800s), "the Bessemer," as locals called it, never would have become a reality. The college could not have existed without them either. For it was those dams and Wolf Creek itself that proved to be the foundation for the growing village.

Wolf Creek has offered recreation in the form of boating and fishing in the spring and summer and ice-skating in the winter. It was a source of power, of inspiration, and of romance. Prior to strict environmental regulations, it even served as a dump for raw sewage and waste. It has also been witness to tragedy.

The pictures in this book represent Grove City's history from its beginning in the late 1700s through its industrial and educational boom in the early 1900s. The authors chose the postcards carefully to represent different parts of the town and how they helped make Grove City what it is today. With Wolf Creek being a central focus, it is no surprise that bridges are a common theme. Like those spans, the authors are helping the reader get from one side of history to the other, while offering a beautiful view along the way.

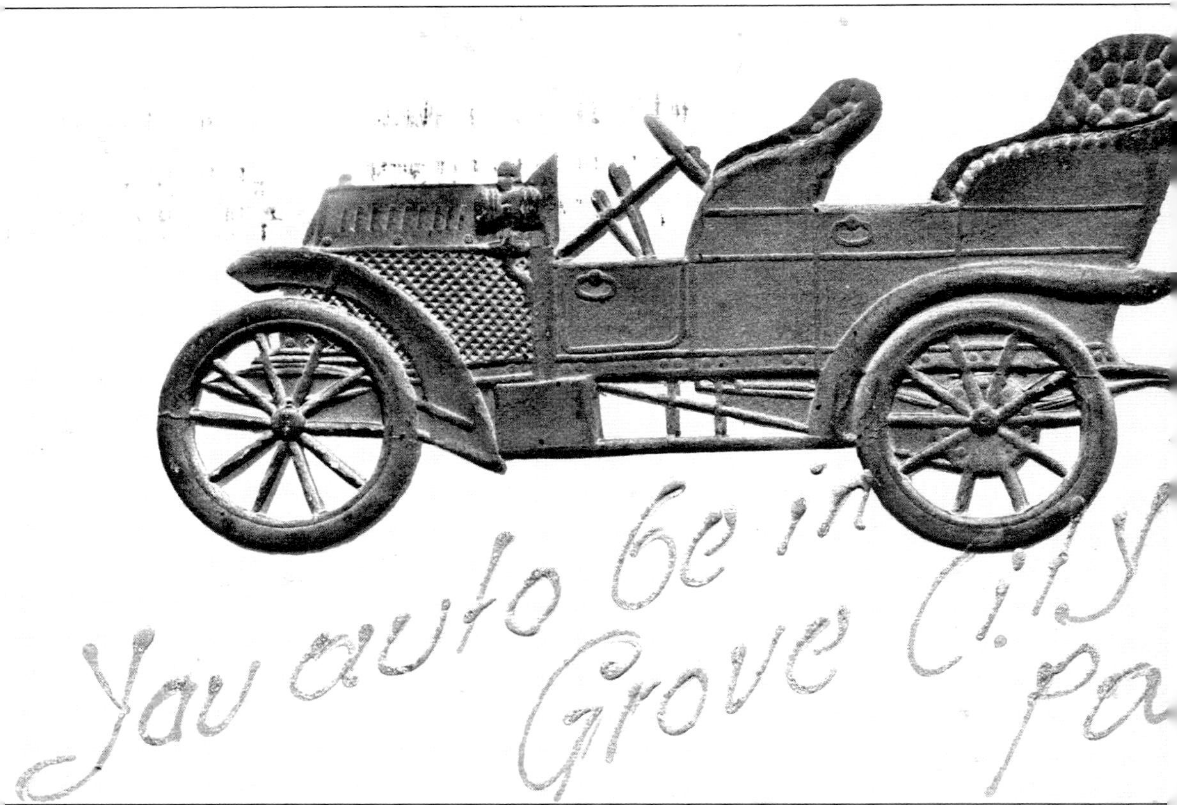

Postcard publishers in the early 20th century produced a variety of novelty cards. This embossed example with the text "You auto be in Grove City" shows a style of automobile from the earliest days of motorized transportation in town. Just a few years after this card was published, the automobile had almost entirely replaced the horse-drawn carriage as the main source of transportation.

One
Lower Dam and Lover's Lane

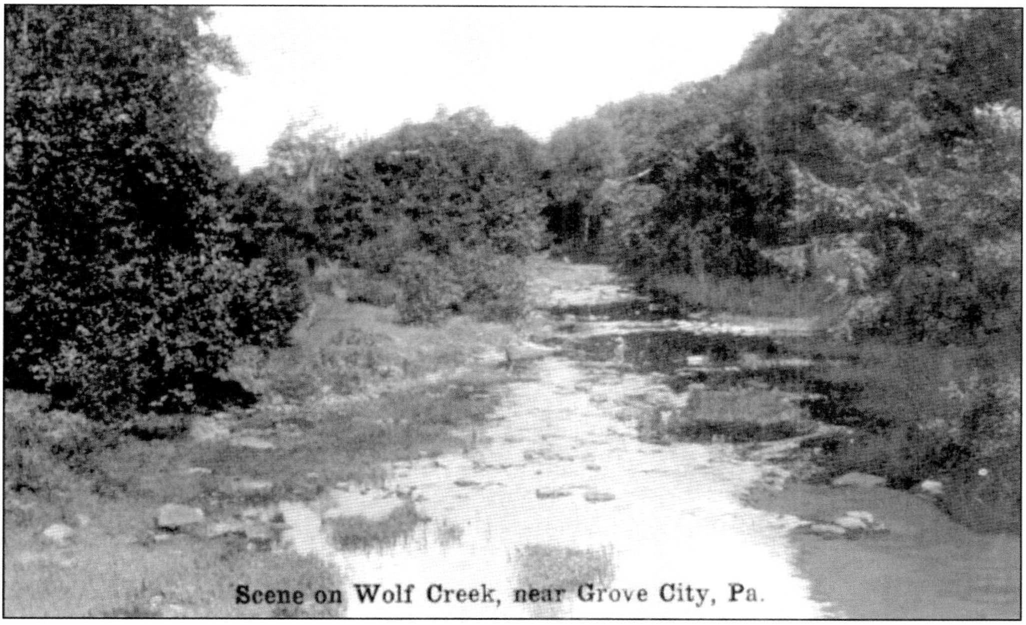

Valentine Cunningham arrived at Wolf Creek in Western Pennsylvania in 1798 and commenced building a dam across the creek. Water spilling over the dam powered his new gristmill. Grooves cut into hard, flat, round granite, known as "mill stones," crushed the grain poured into the center of the stones. Cunningham sifted the crushed grain through a deer hide perforated with a heated table fork. As his was the only mill for miles around, sometimes there was a considerable delay in getting feed ground. Farmers made "ash cakes" by mixing the ground flour with water and heating them over a fire while they waited.

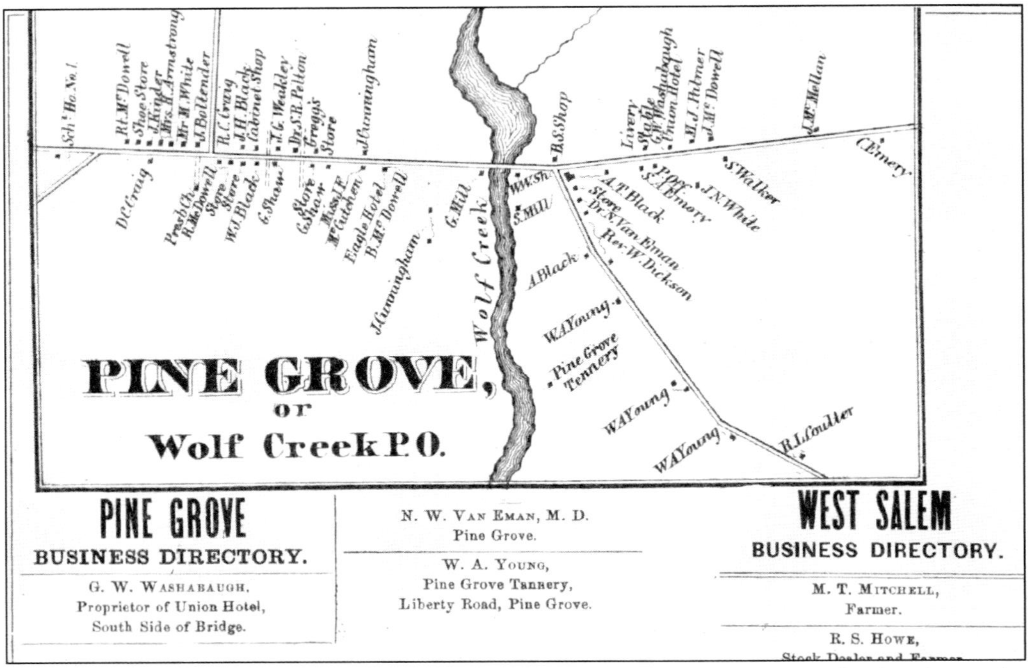

The above map from 1873, 75 years after the arrival of the Cunningham family, shows the development of a small town. In addition to a mill, Pine Grove had, at least, a tannery, a livery stable, two hotels, three stores, a cabinet shop, a shoe store, and a school.

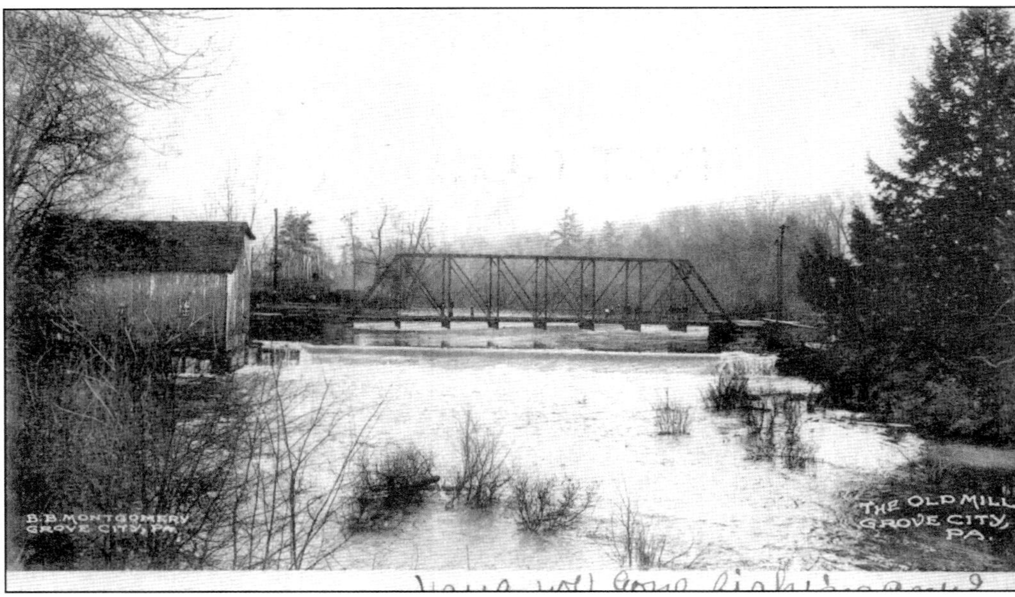

Cunningham's original mill site and dam were upstream from the Main Street Bridge, which is shown here, and currently lie submerged beneath the water behind the Lower Dam's impoundment. In this postcard called "The Old Mill," the building to the left was known as Locke's Mill and Locke's Dam. Locke operated the mill in the late 1800s.

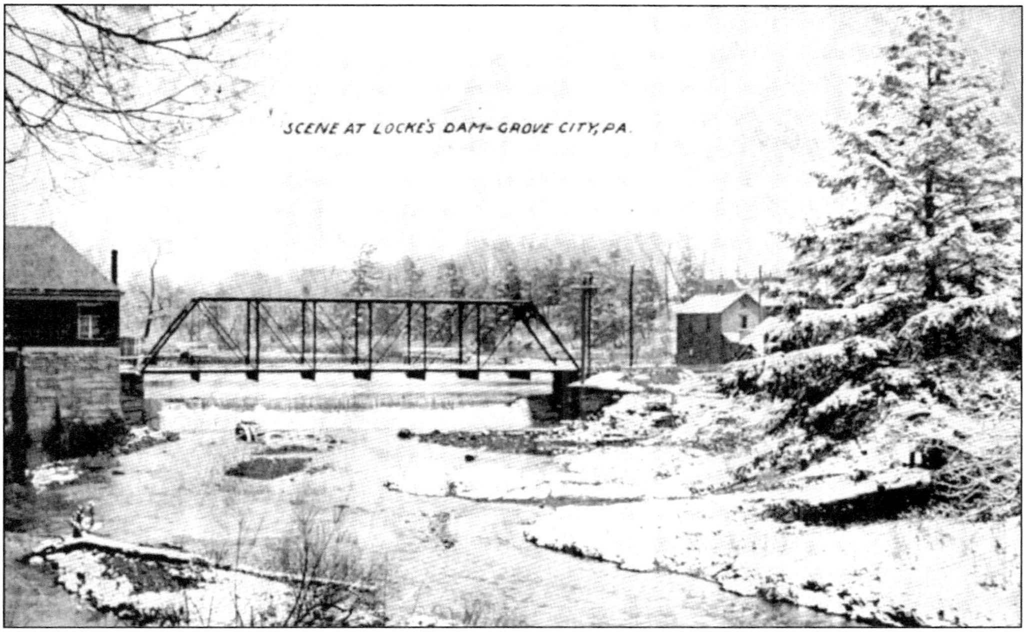

By the time this wintry photograph was taken in the early 1900s, Locke's Mill had been replaced by the Grove City Water Works. Although the building was torn down in the 1970s, the dam remained. The house to the right was Homer McMillin's candy store through the Great Depression. It is now the location of the Main Street entrance to Grove City College.

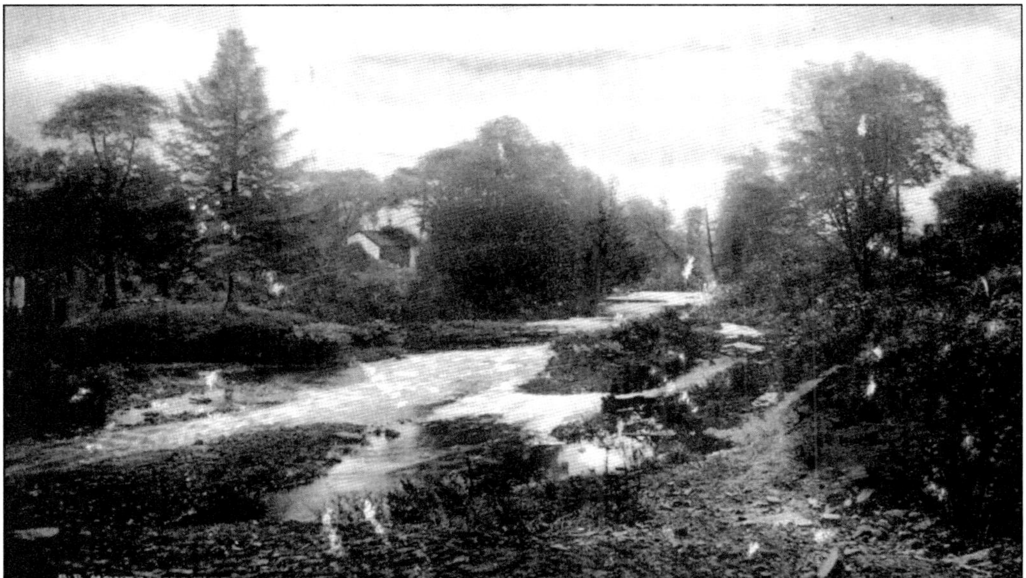

Standing on Main Street looking down stream, one can see houses along Liberty Street on the left and homes along what is now Greenwood Drive on the right. Greenwood has had many different names, two of which were Creek Street and Water Street. Two popular unofficial names were Cow Belly Bend and Lover's Lane. The oldest cemetery in town is along Greenwood Drive, where town founder Valentine Cunningham and his wife are buried.

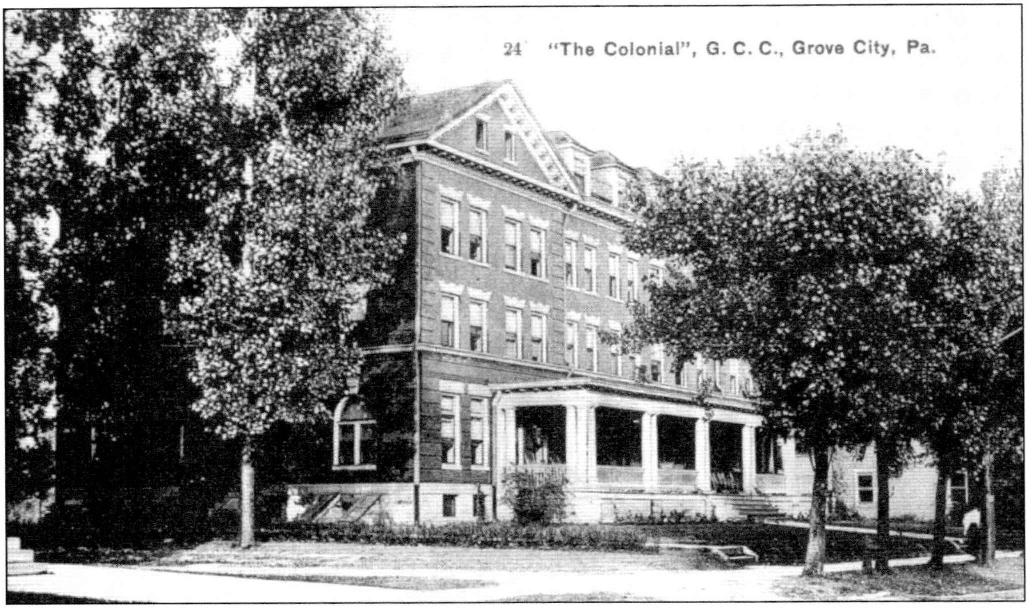

Less than one block up East Main Street, Grove City College gentlemen could pick up their dates at the college's Colonial women's dormitory and go for a stroll along Lover's Lane—properly known as Greenwood Drive. Today, even though the Colonial has been replaced by other women's dormitories on campus, college coeds continue this tradition at Hunter Farm Park.

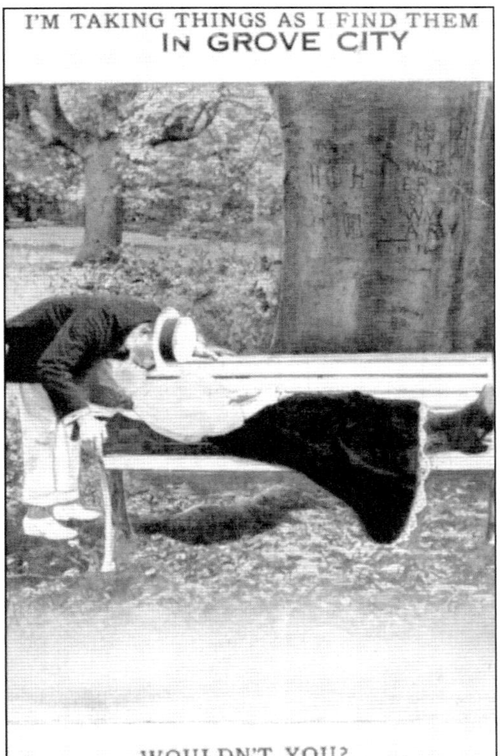

At the time of its printing, this racy card would have been pushing the envelope of propriety. For example, it would not have been acceptable behavior for a young woman to fall asleep on a park bench. It would have been even more inappropriate for a gentleman to kiss the "sleeping beauty."

Grove City College, founded by the Rev. Dr. Isaac C. Ketler, has strict rules of conduct for its men and women students. For example, the nationally recognized private Christian college has stern visitation rules, and no coed dormitories. Chapel attendance is compulsory, but Sunday attendance at a local church is usually a valid substitute for attendance on the campus.

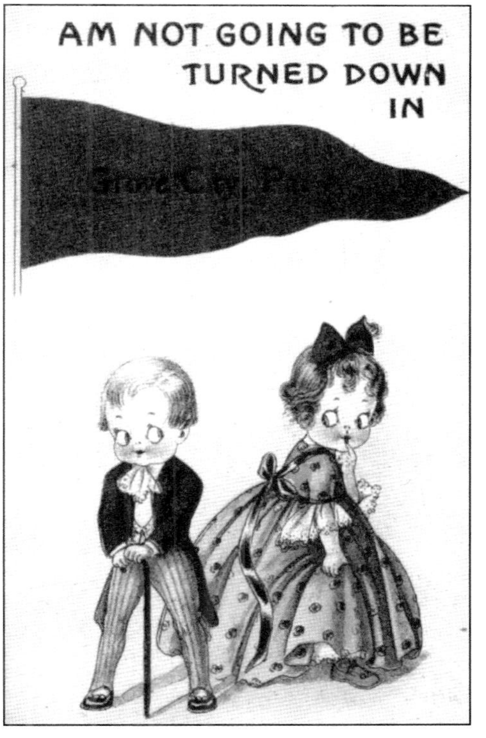

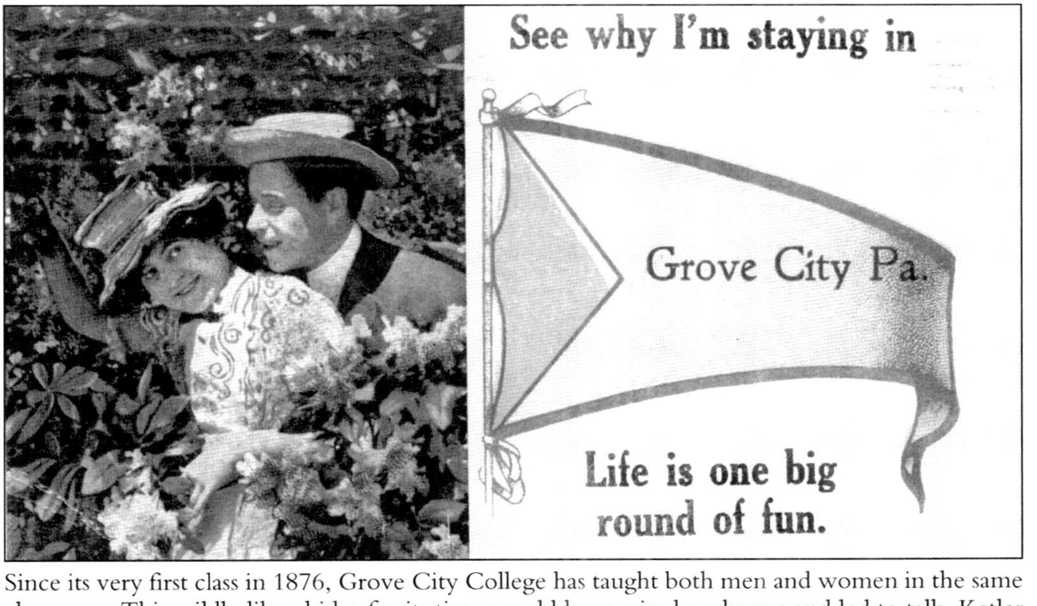

Since its very first class in 1876, Grove City College has taught both men and women in the same classroom. This wildly liberal idea for its time would have raised eyebrows and led to talk. Ketler would have undoubtedly been very sensitive to what people said about his new school, hence the strictly enforced code of conduct, emphasizing to both students and to the public that people went to Grove City College to learn. As late as the 1940s, students who married without permission could be expelled. Even between semesters, students had to have the college's permission to marry.

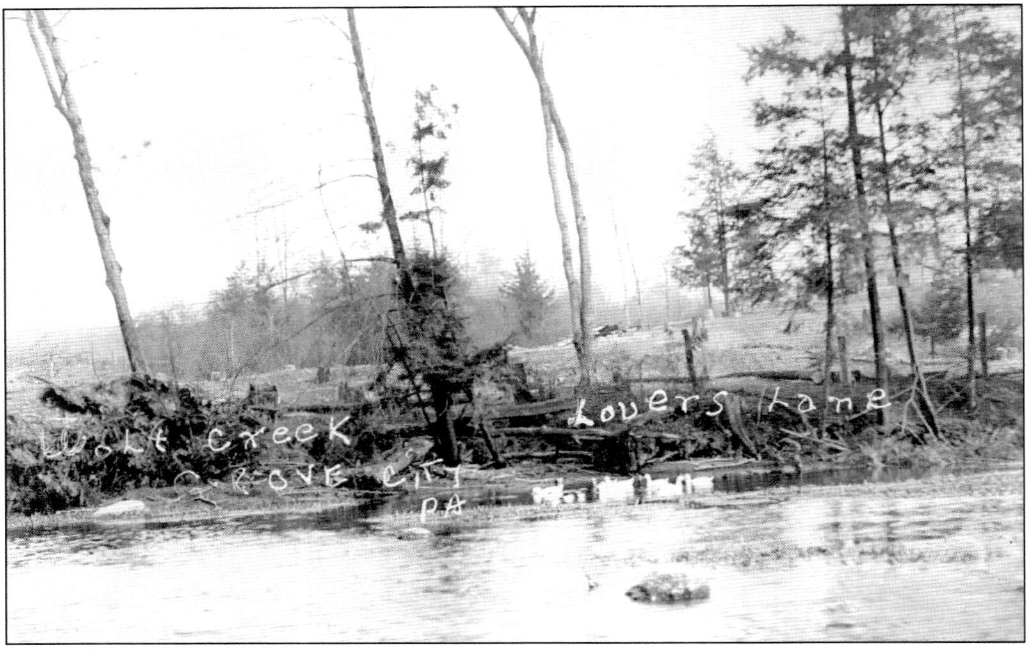

Nevertheless, it would be naive to imagine that couples went for picnics along Lover's Lane simply to behold its breathtaking natural beauty. At the turn of the 20th century, it would have been considered very naughty for a couple to visit Lover's Lane without a chaperone.

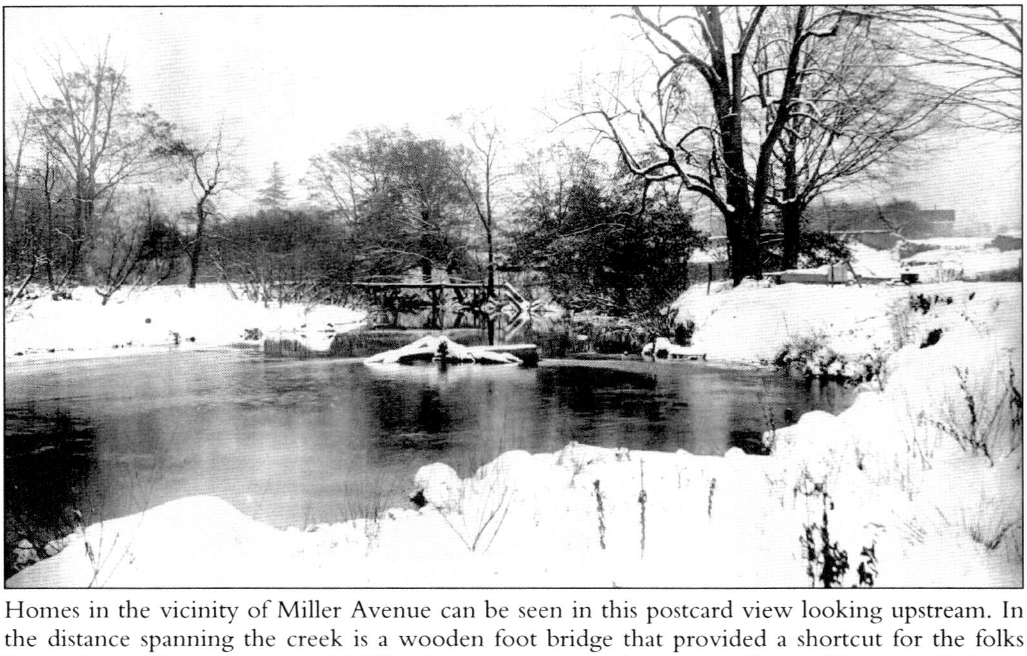

Homes in the vicinity of Miller Avenue can be seen in this postcard view looking upstream. In the distance spanning the creek is a wooden foot bridge that provided a shortcut for the folks living along Liberty Street and Miller Avenue to get to downtown Grove City. Lover's Lane, now known as Greenwood Drive, runs parallel to the left bank. The footbridge abutment can still be seen in the vicinity of the new Pennsylvania Fish and Boat Commission handicapped accessible fishing area along Wolf Creek.

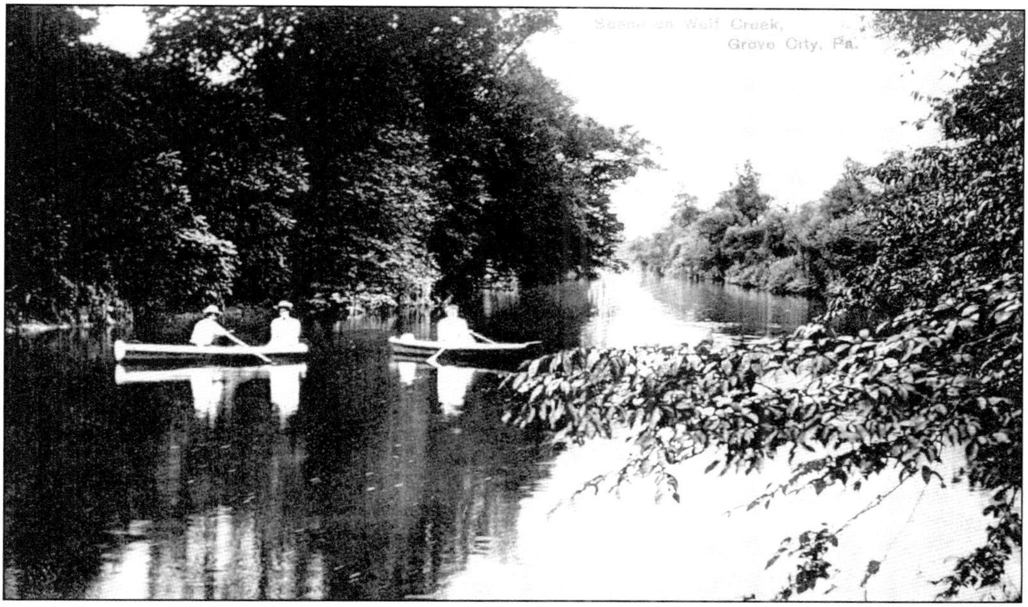

The Lower Dam, as it is now known, was originally built for the waterworks. It creates a "lake," backing up the water nearly to Chestnut Street through town. In the early 20th century, boating on Wolf Creek provided another relaxing summertime outing for Grove City College students and residents.

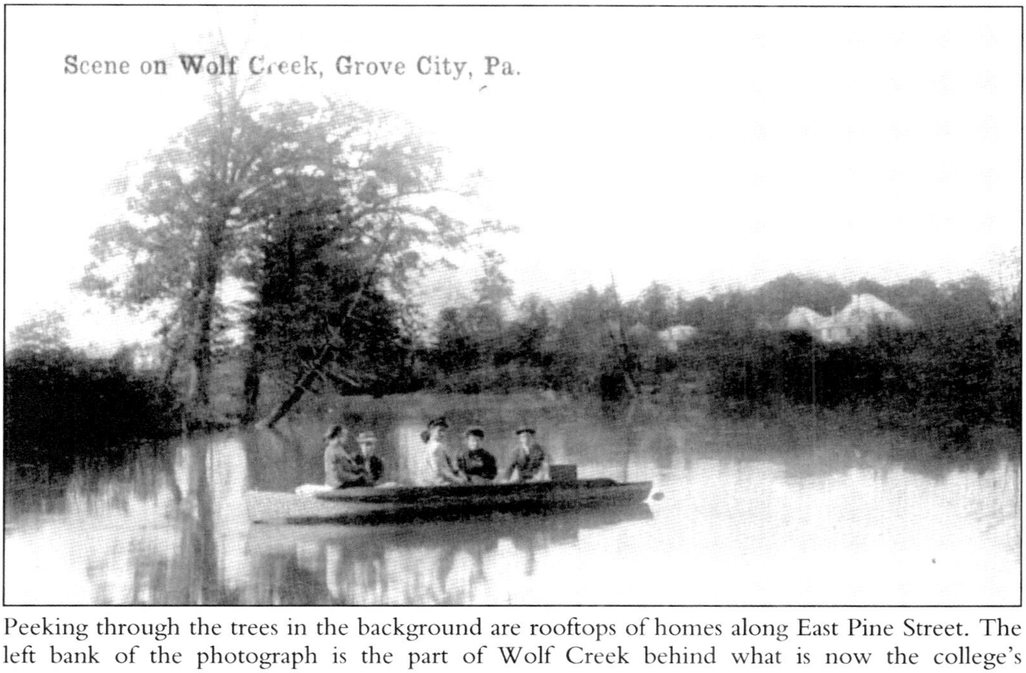

Peeking through the trees in the background are rooftops of homes along East Pine Street. The left bank of the photograph is the part of Wolf Creek behind what is now the college's athletic building and football field. The creek was a natural divider between the lower and upper campuses.

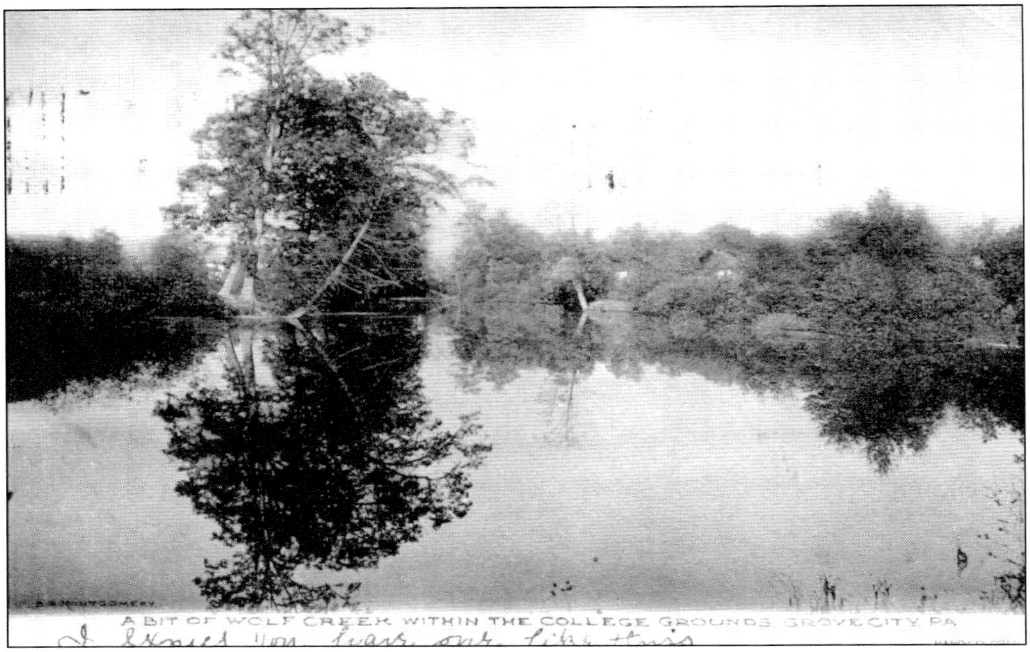

The photographer in this picture was probably standing where the college's Rainbow Bridge would later be constructed. After approximately 90 years of service, the Lower Dam is scheduled for removal in 2005. The lake shown in this picture, which has existed for more than 200 years (since Cunningham's dam was built), will be permanently drained.

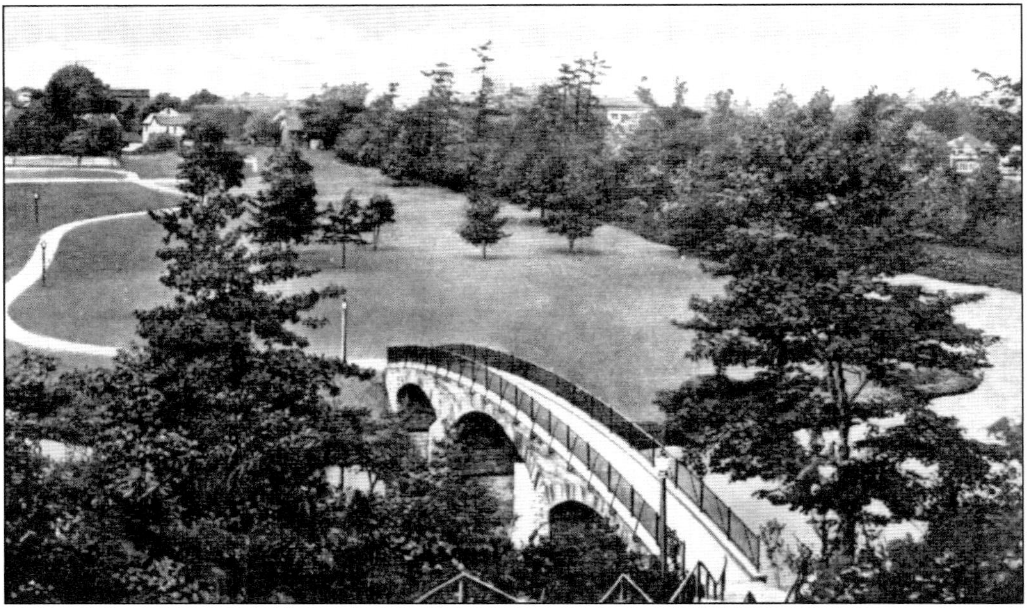

The Rainbow Bridge connects Grove City College's upper and lower campuses, which are separated by Wolf Creek. The bridge, which had been in service since the 1920s and in need of extensive repairs, was entirely demolished and replaced with a nearly exact replica in 2003. Many hopeful young men have proposed marriage to their sweethearts on this graceful span.

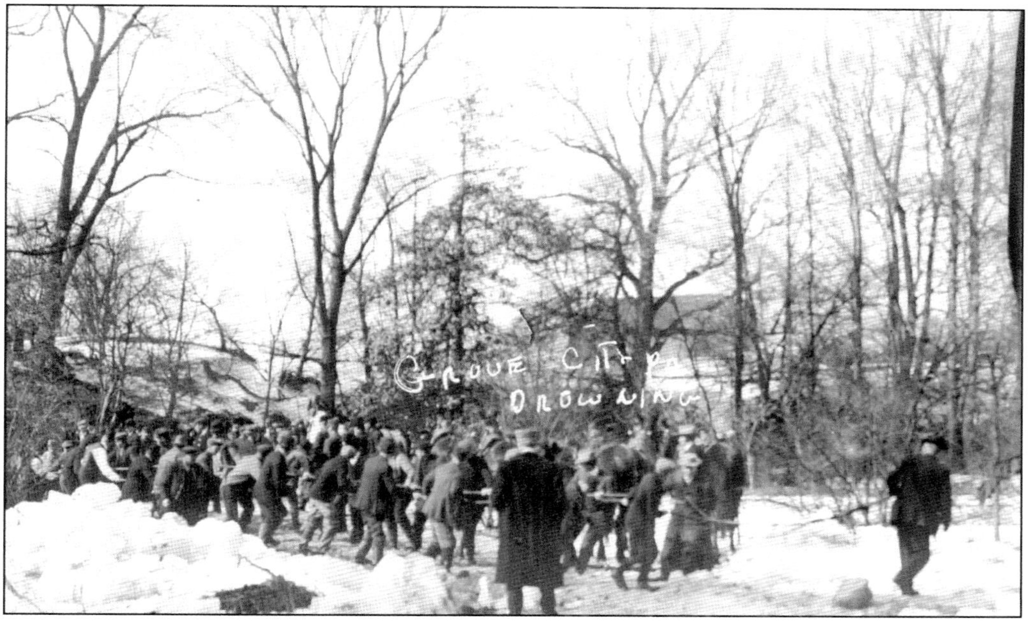

Boating provided an idyllic way to pass a summer's afternoon along Wolf Creek, and there was often ice-skating during cold winters. However, for much of the year the ice covering Wolf Creek is deceptively thin. This image shows town's people dragging the creek searching for the body of a drowned boy who fell through the ice.

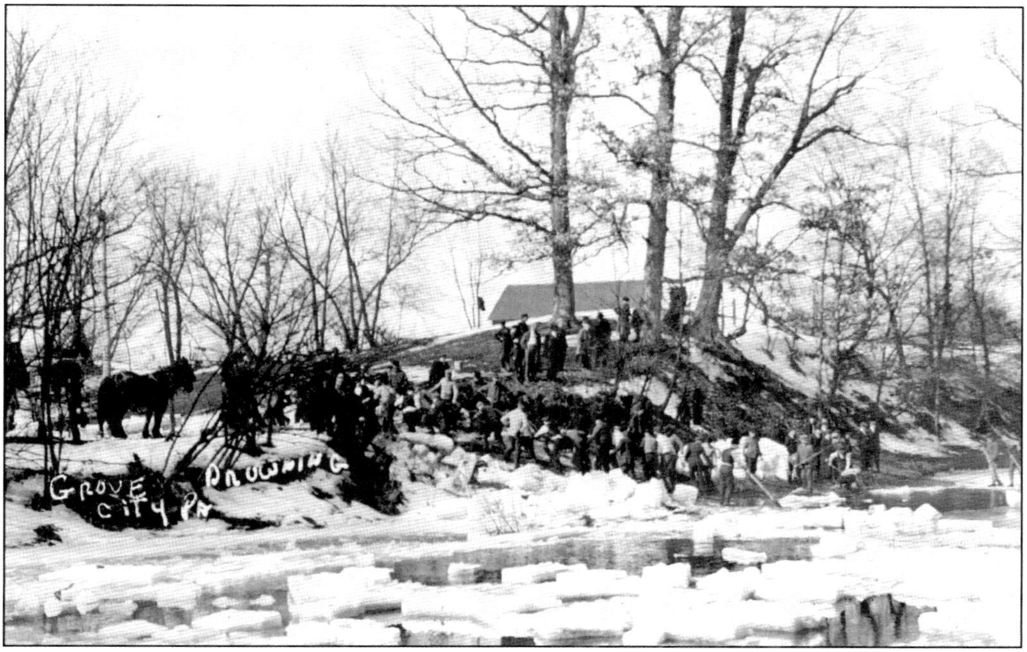

One of the explanations given for removing the 100-year-old dams on Wolf Creek is for the very reason shown in these pictures. While drowning accidents are relatively rare, the creek does create what insurance companies call an attractive nuisance, thus driving up the borough of Grove City's liability insurance premiums.

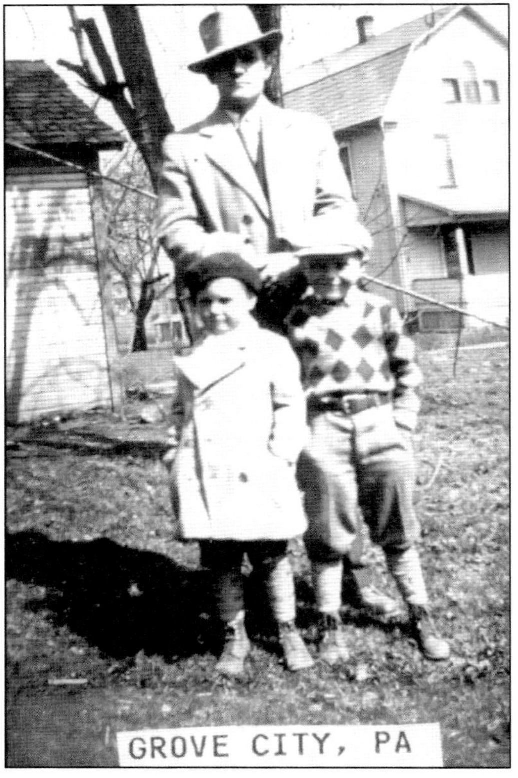

John H. Hummel Sr., one of Grove City's early policemen, stands behind his sons Don Hummel and John H. Hummel Jr. in the backyard of their home on North Broad Street. The boys' mother warned her sons not to play on the ice on Wolf Creek, but John Jr. did anyway. John Hummel Jr. said, "When I fell through the ice, I went completely under the water. After I got myself pulled out, I was soaking wet. To keep my mother from finding out, I rolled around in the snow a lot so she would think I was all wet from playing in the snow."

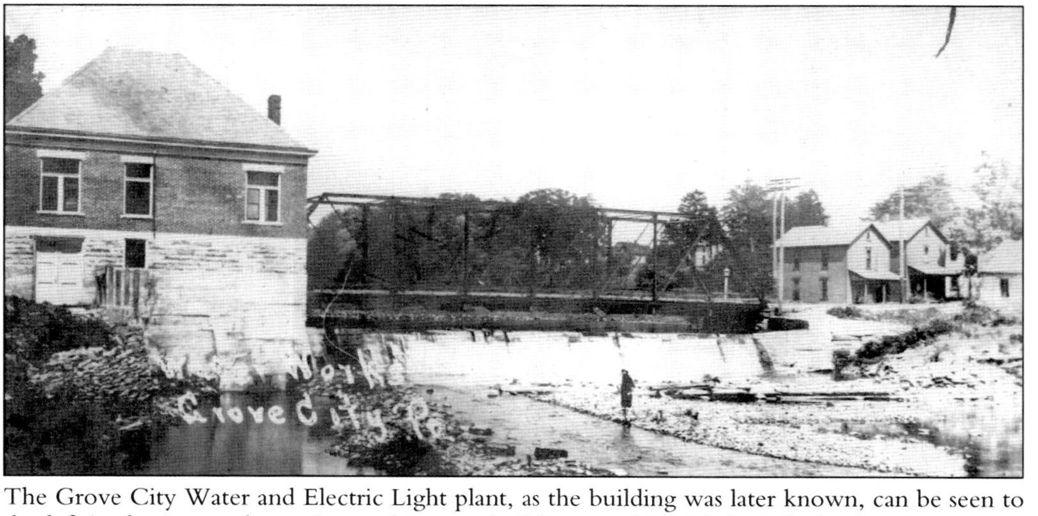

The Grove City Water and Electric Light plant, as the building was later known, can be seen to the left in the image above. Later, this same building would hold the jail, the fire department, borough offices, and the district justice's office all at the same time. The houses along East Main Street are situated where the Main Street entrance to Grove City College is now located.

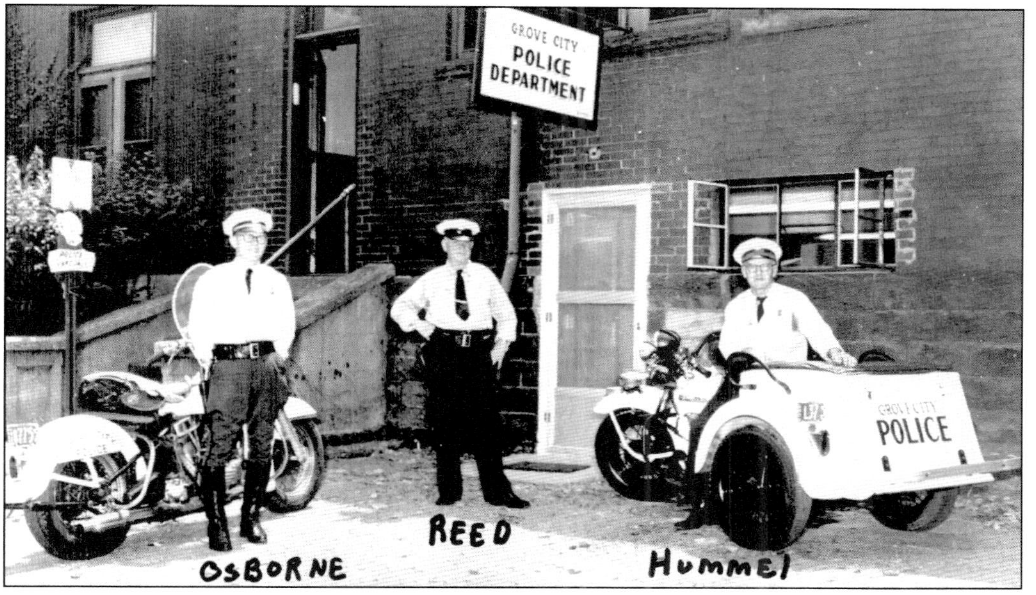

Officers Bill Osborne, Jim Reed, and John Hummel Sr. stand in front of the police station in 1954. In the early days of the police department, the officer used his own car to answer emergency calls and had no police radio or phone. Residents who needed assistance called the station in the Grove City Water and Electric Light plant, where someone was on duty around the clock. The person on duty at the plant would turn on a red light downtown. The officer would see the light and run to someone's home or business to find a phone. He would then call the station and get the details of where he was supposed to go to answer the call.

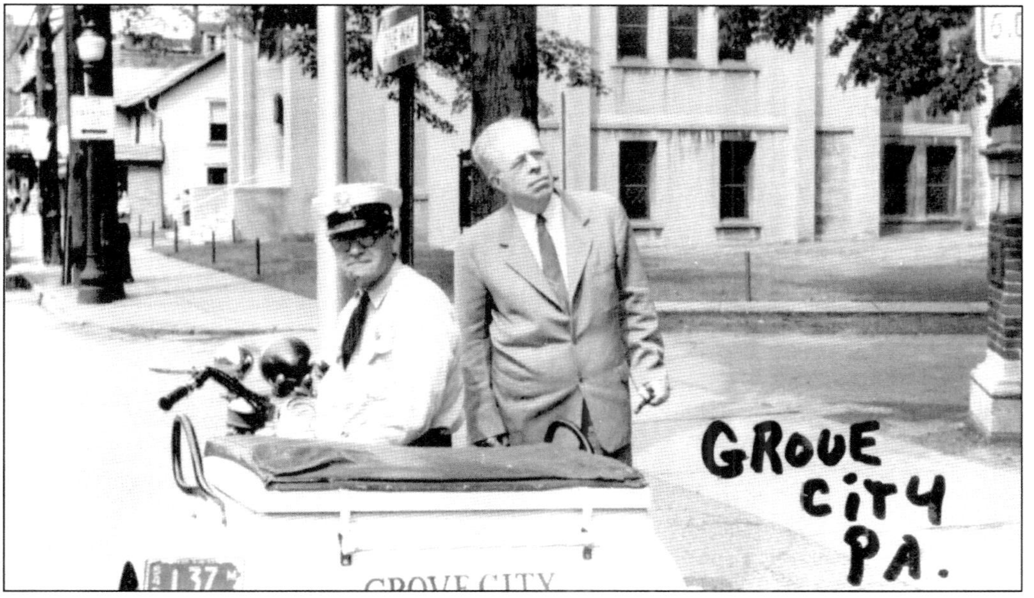

John Hummel Sr. and Dr. Carl Easter, a Grove City College English professor, are shown at the intersection of College Avenue and South Broad Street at the entrance to Grove City College's lower campus. Kids in town called the three-wheeled motorcycle that Hummel is riding, "the ice cream wagon."

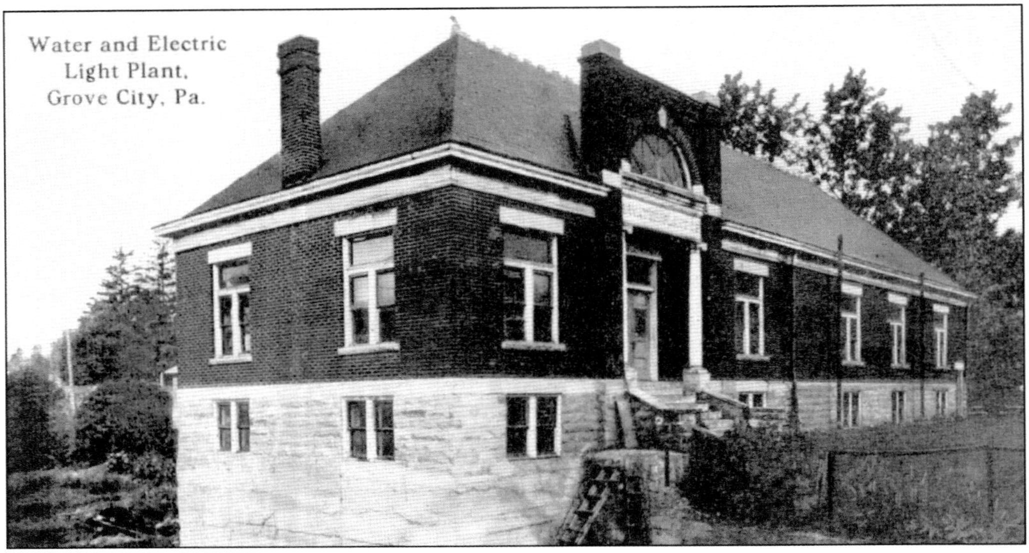

The borough of Grove City has turned the foundation of the Water and Electric Light plant into Cunningham Park. The turbine powered by Wolf Creek's flowing water can be seen through a grate placed over the foundation. The turbine once pumped the town's drinking water. The building and the Lower Dam were constructed *c.* 1915. Generating electricity from the creek's flow is not practical during the summer months when the current reduces to a trickle each year.

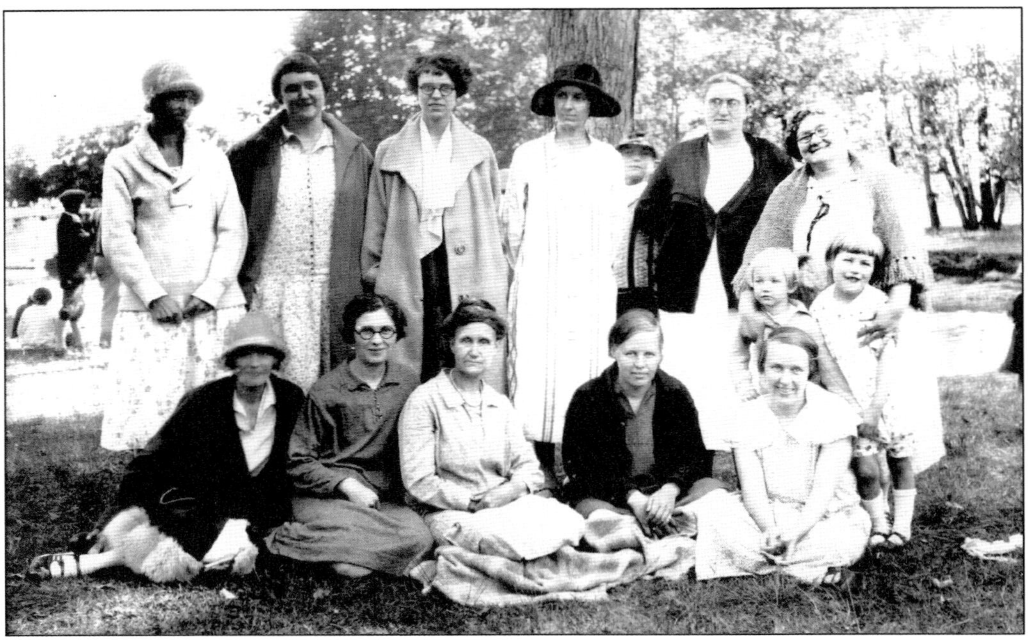

In this August photograph of members of the Nazareth Sunday School picnic, Jessie McRae can be seen in the back row, third from the left, wearing a heavy coat and glasses. Jessie was known for dressing warmly, even in summer. While working at the police station, a prisoner managed to get a gun and abduct her.The felon drove Jessie out of town before releasing her. She said the worst thing was that he would not let her take her coat or put on her scarf or galoshes.

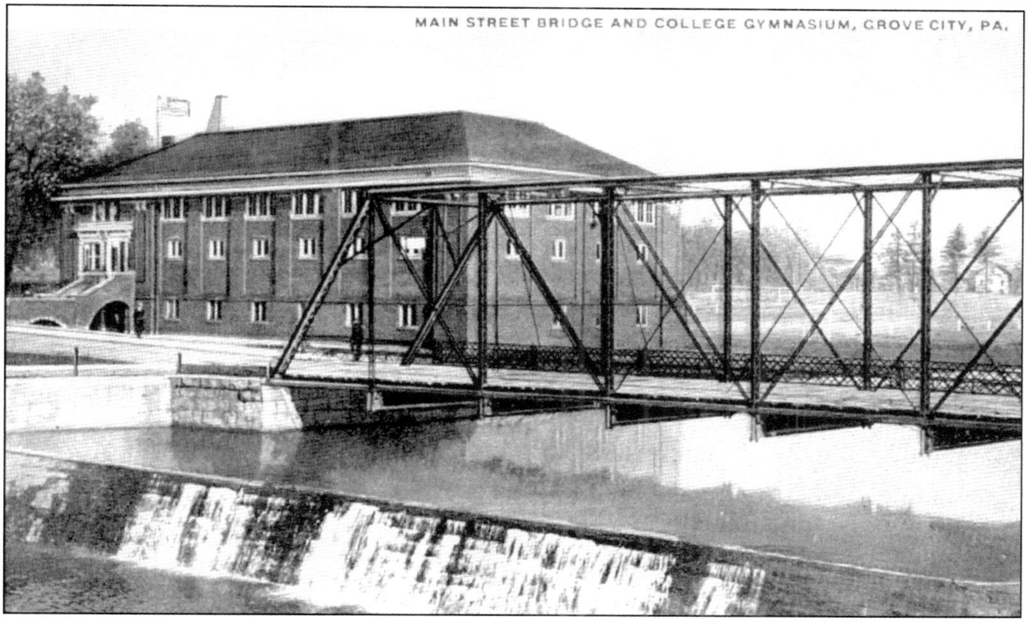

Across East Main Street from the police station and along Wolf Creek is the eastern portion of Grove City College's lower campus. The college's gymnasium can be seen behind the Main Street Bridge. Behind the gymnasium is the college's athletic field, where both baseball and football games were once played. Water spills over the hand-cut sandstone blocks from which the Lower Dam was constructed.

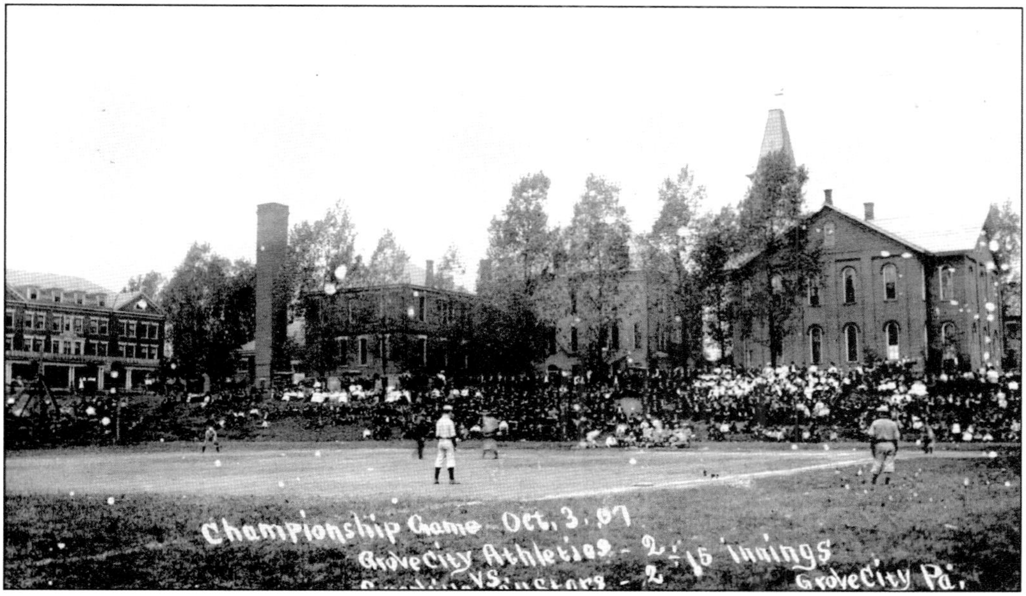

At one time, Grove City hosted a semi-pro baseball team called the Grove City Athletics. Here they are shown in a dead heat after 15 innings against the Greenville All Stars on October 3, 1907. The game is being played on Grove City College's athletic field. The buildings in the background are the Colonial Dormitory, Carnegie Library, the main administration building, and the Old Academy building.

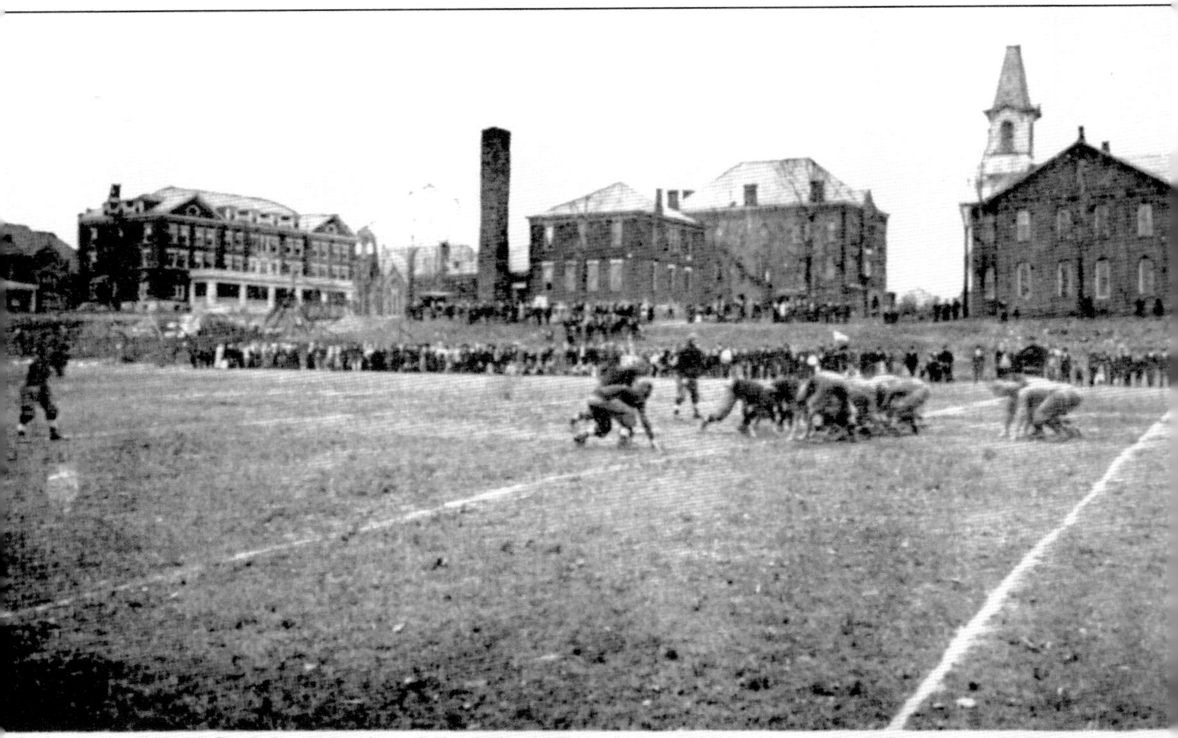

3002 FOOTBALL GAME, GROVE CITY VS. INDIANA STATE NORMAL, THANK GIVING DAY, GROVE CITY, PA.

Visible in the background are some lower campus buildings named in the previous photograph. The smoke stack is from the powerhouse that provided steam to heat the college buildings in the vicinity. Only the Carnegie building remains. Originally, football players did not wear any padding, but by the 1920s, when this picture was probably taken, players appear to be wearing padding and helmets. Notice the crowd is standing and there are no bleacher seats. This game was between Grove City College and Indiana State Normal School.

Two
Pine Street East and West

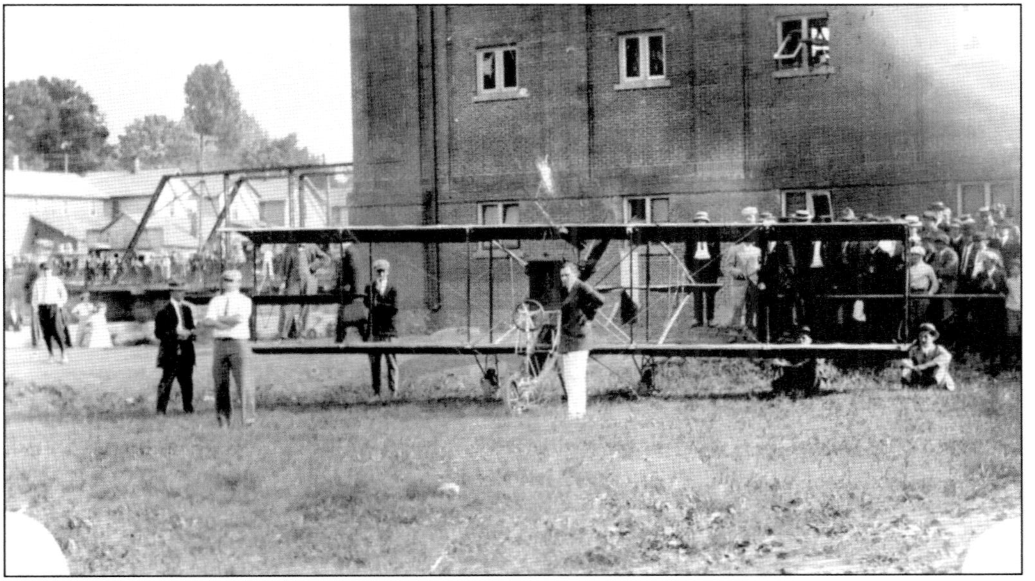

Aviation Pioneer Earl Sandt stands beside his canvas biplane on the college's athletic field behind the gymnasium on June 12, 1913. Sandt is credited with being the first person to fly over Pittsburgh and the first to make an international flight by flying over Lake Erie for the national weather service. A flight a few minutes after this photograph was taken was Sandt's last.

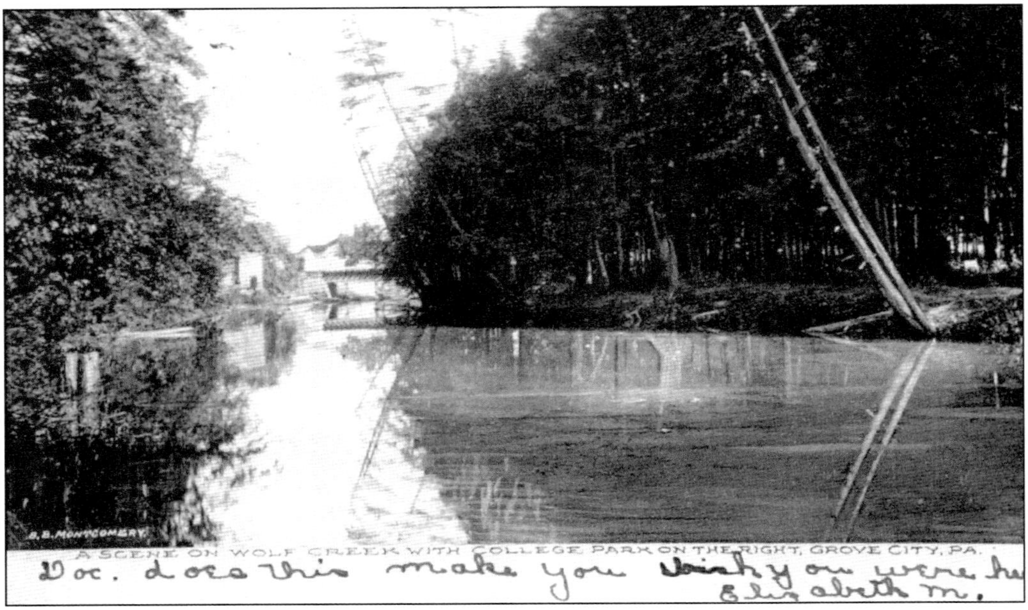

When taking off from the college's athletic field before a crowd of thousands, Sandt's airplane did not clear the tall pine trees growing along the banks of Wolf Creek. Perhaps if he had landed in the calm waters of the creek held back by the Lower Dam, his injuries might have been less severe.

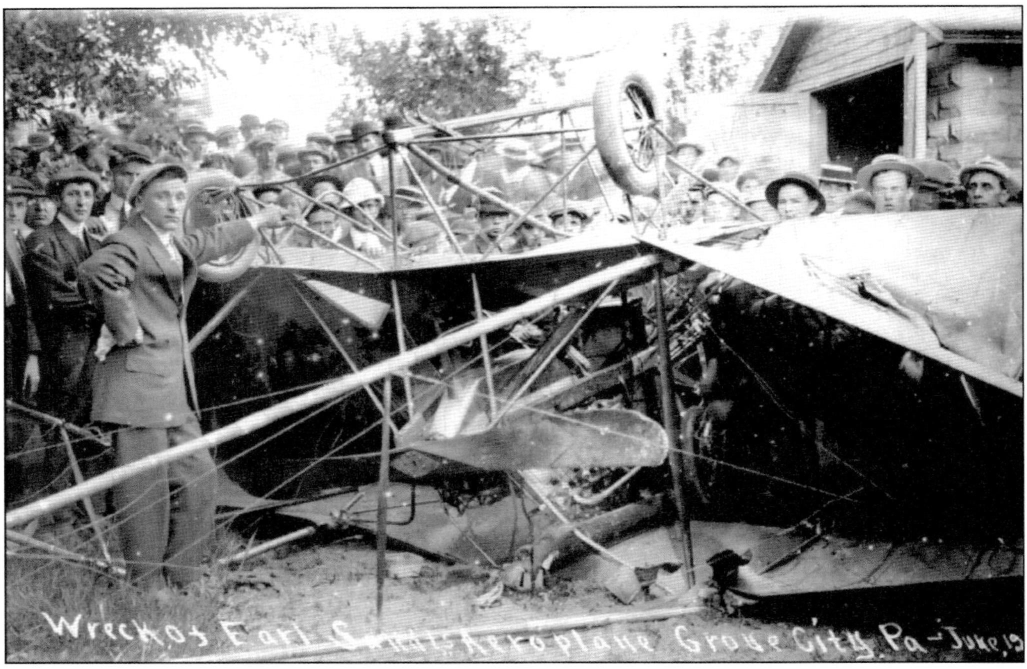

As bad luck would have it, Sandt cleared Wolf Creek and landed in a freshly manured rhubarb patch behind a home on East Pine Street. He had a badly broken leg with a compound fracture, possibly not a life-threatening injury now, 90 years later. The propeller of the upside-down flying machine is visible before the concerned crowd jostling to get a better view of the accident.

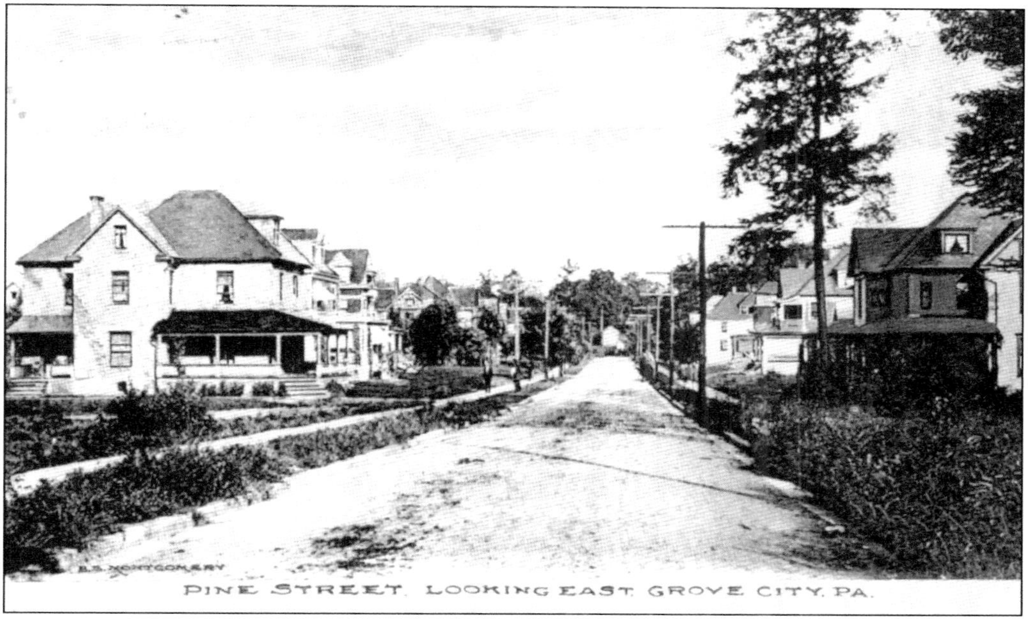

Reverend Hessop, a Presbyterian minister, watched the plane crash across the street from his home while he sat on his front porch. Townspeople who rushed to the scene loaded Sandt onto a truck to transport him to the Grove City Hospital. He crashed in the backyard of a house on the right side of Pine Street looking east. Sandt may have been taken to the hospital on West Main Street on a Bessemer truck that was manufactured in Grove City just a half-mile away from the accident scene.

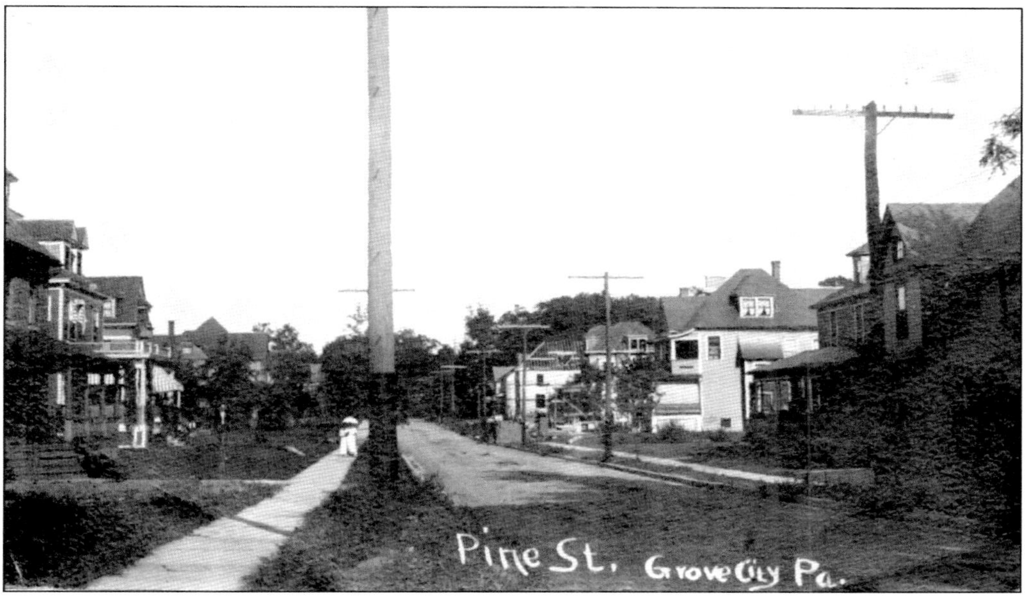

Across Pine Street from Sandt's crash site was the residence of local tycoon Edwin J. Fithian. In another 10 years, the Penn Grove Hotel was constructed beside where the photographer was standing when this picture was taken. Fithian completed training as a medical doctor but found his calling as an entrepreneur.

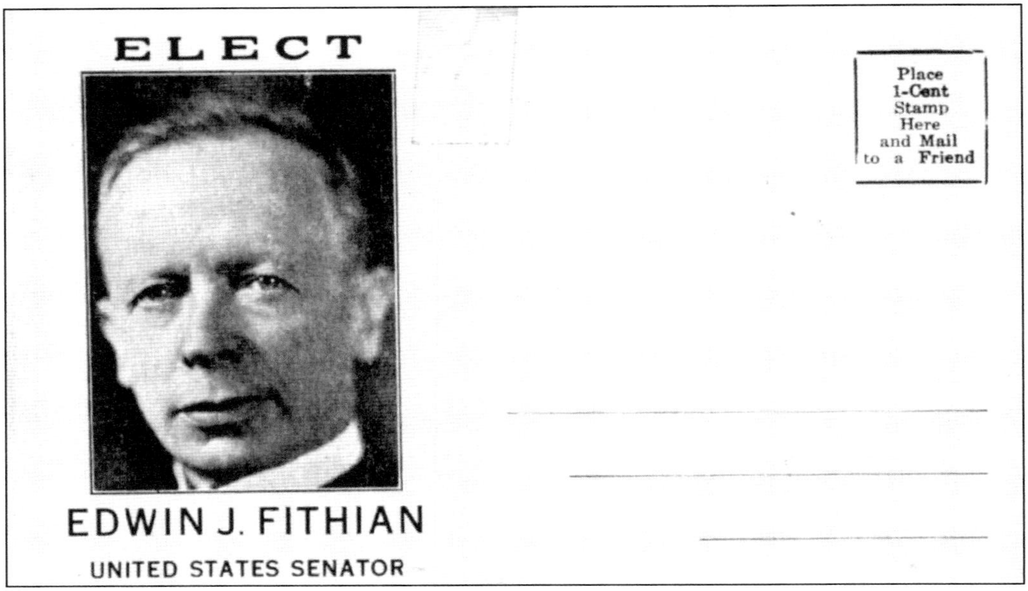

Edwin J. Fithian made his fortune after founding the Bessemer Gas Engine Company, which later became the Cooper-Bessemer Corporation. The plant was on Lincoln Avenue along the creek and just two blocks behind Fithian's home. He was also involved with founding Wendell August Forge, the Grove City Hospital, and the Grove City National Bank. In the 1920s he ran for the U. S. Senate on the Prohibition ticket.

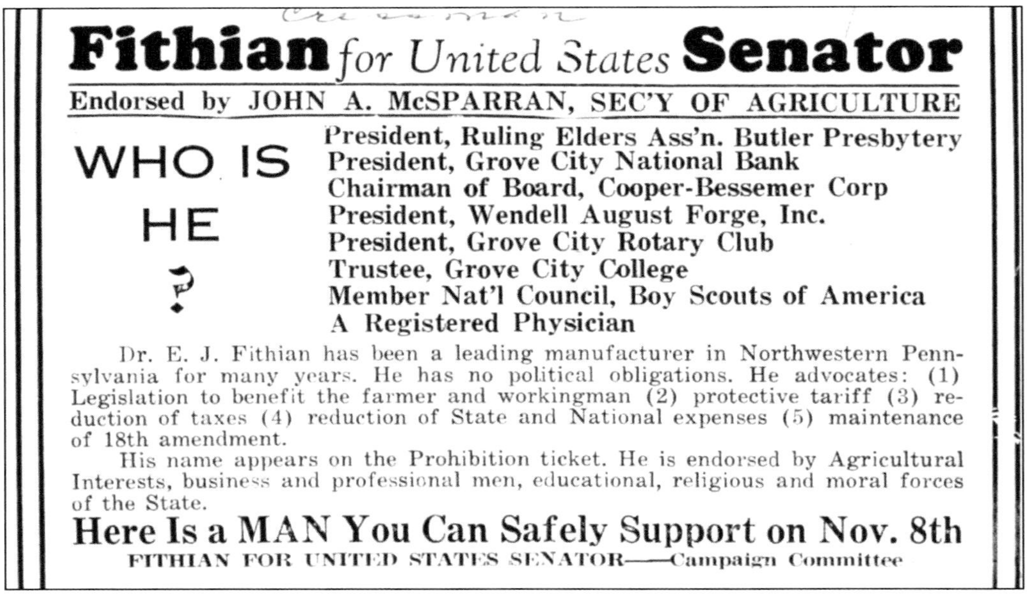

Fithian *for United States* **Senator**

Endorsed by JOHN A. McSPARRAN, SEC'Y OF AGRICULTURE

WHO IS HE ?

President, Ruling Elders Ass'n. Butler Presbytery
President, Grove City National Bank
Chairman of Board, Cooper-Bessemer Corp
President, Wendell August Forge, Inc.
President, Grove City Rotary Club
Trustee, Grove City College
Member Nat'l Council, Boy Scouts of America
A Registered Physician

Dr. E. J. Fithian has been a leading manufacturer in Northwestern Pennsylvania for many years. He has no political obligations. He advocates: (1) Legislation to benefit the farmer and workingman (2) protective tariff (3) reduction of taxes (4) reduction of State and National expenses (5) maintenance of 18th amendment.

His name appears on the Prohibition ticket. He is endorsed by Agricultural Interests, business and professional men, educational, religious and moral forces of the State.

Here Is a MAN You Can Safely Support on Nov. 8th

FITHIAN FOR UNITED STATES SENATOR——Campaign Committee

Grove City has always been a dry town, but that does not mean that alcohol has never been available here. Many private clubs serve alcohol to their members, and one can purchase alcohol for private consumption at beer distributors and state stores. In 2001, the Grove City Borough Planning Commission asked borough residents if alcohol should be sold by the glass. Fifty-five percent were opposed, but forty-five percent approved, indicating a closer division than many expected.

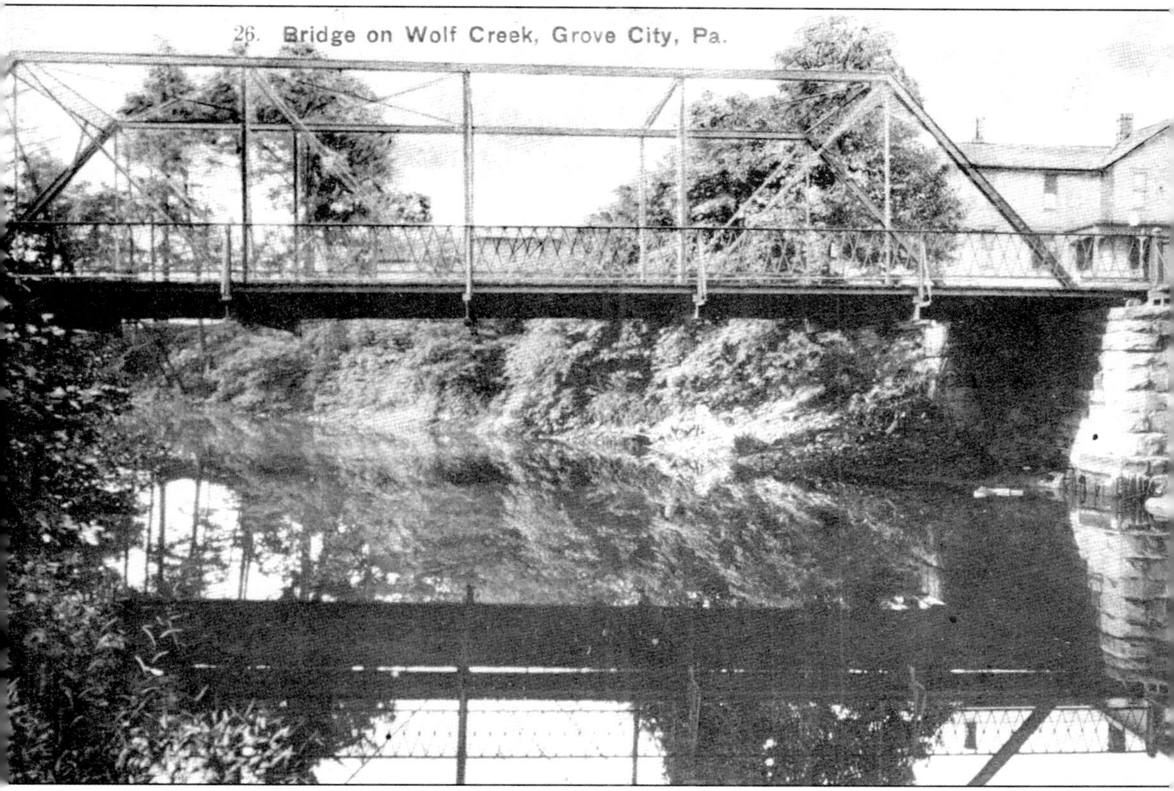

Following Sandt's route to the hospital, rescuers would have taken him back across Wolf Creek one last time over this bridge on Pine Street. Beginning in 2004, the dams are scheduled for removal. Opponents of the dam removal argue that the dams provide flood control.

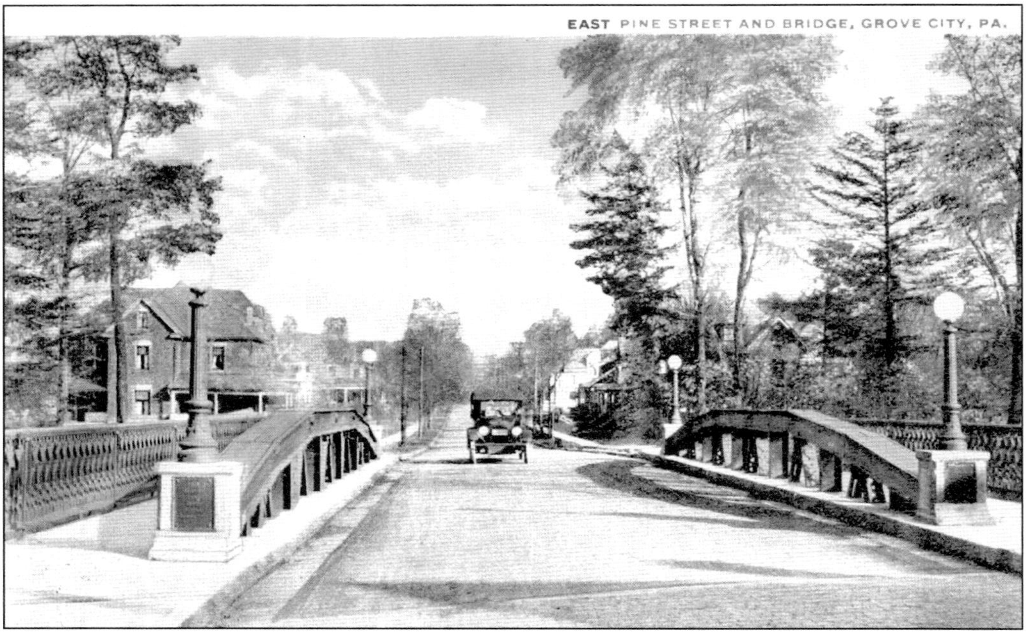

Looking east down Pine Street, a newer bridge spanning Wolf Creek is visible. The Penn Grove Hotel, which was constructed just across the bridge and to the left in 1929, is not yet visible. The hotel was one of many successful projects of the Commercial Club, a forerunner to the Grove City Area Chamber of Commerce. Realizing that customers visiting town on business did not have an option for high-end accommodations, the group sold shares and raised money to build the new hotel. Throughout the 1930s, it was known as the finest hotel on the Bessemer and Lake Erie Railroad between Pittsburgh and Erie.

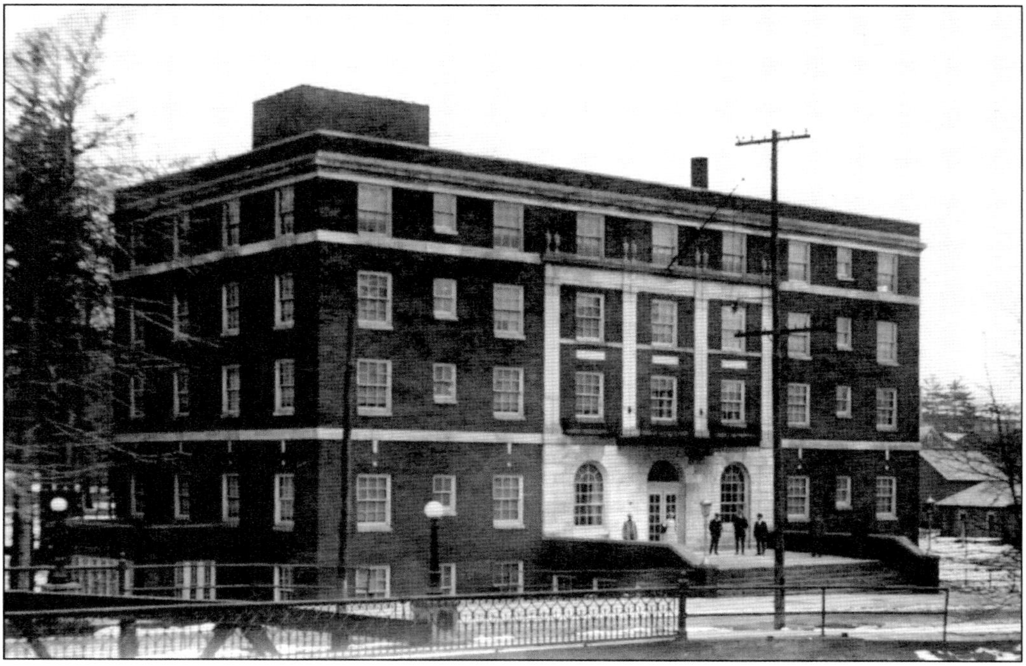

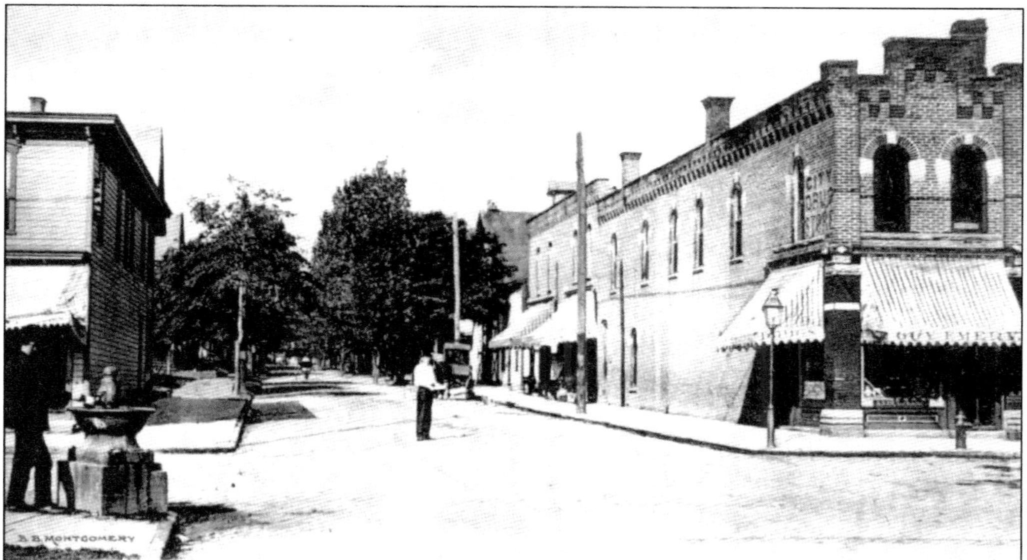

PINE STREET, LOOKING WEST FROM S. BROAD, GROVE CITY, PA.

Many consider the intersection of Broad and Pine Streets the center of Grove City. Behind the photographer is East Pine Street, ahead of him is West Pine Street. Beside the gentleman to the left is a watering trough for thirsty horses. Grove City's first gas streetlights can be seen in front of the store to the right. A fire hydrant can also be found in front of the store to the right.

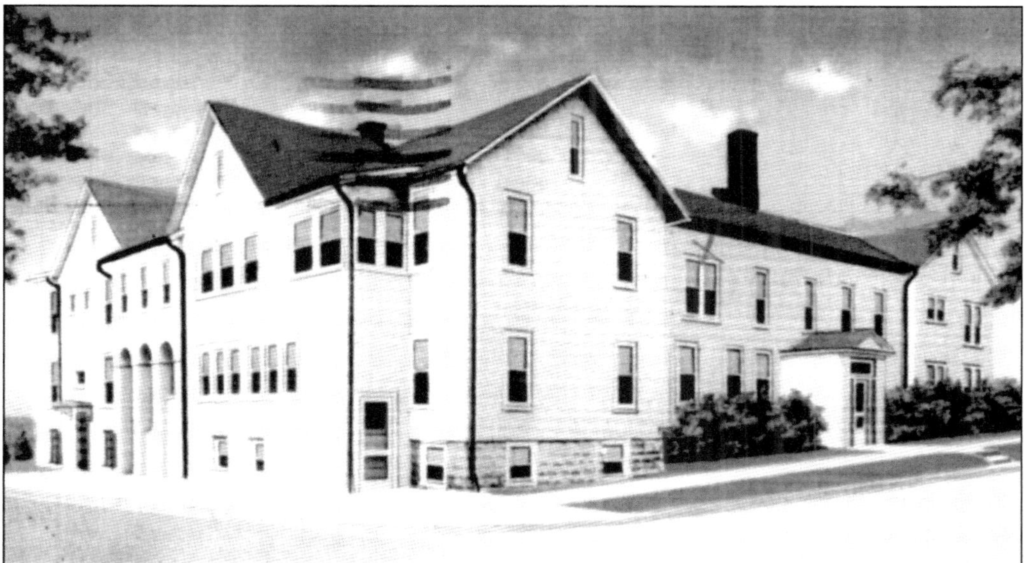

Bashline-Rossman Osteopathic Hospital and Clinic
Pine and Center Streets Grove City, Pa.

The Bashline-Rossman Osteopathic Hospital and Clinic at the corner of West Pine and South Center Street was built after a falling-out between the medical doctors and the osteopaths in town. Grove City's current mayor, Bruce Bennett, was born there, as was Mike Adams, one of this book's authors. Mike recalls climbing the steps behind the arches before entering a long dark waiting room in anxious anticipation of childhood immunization shots.

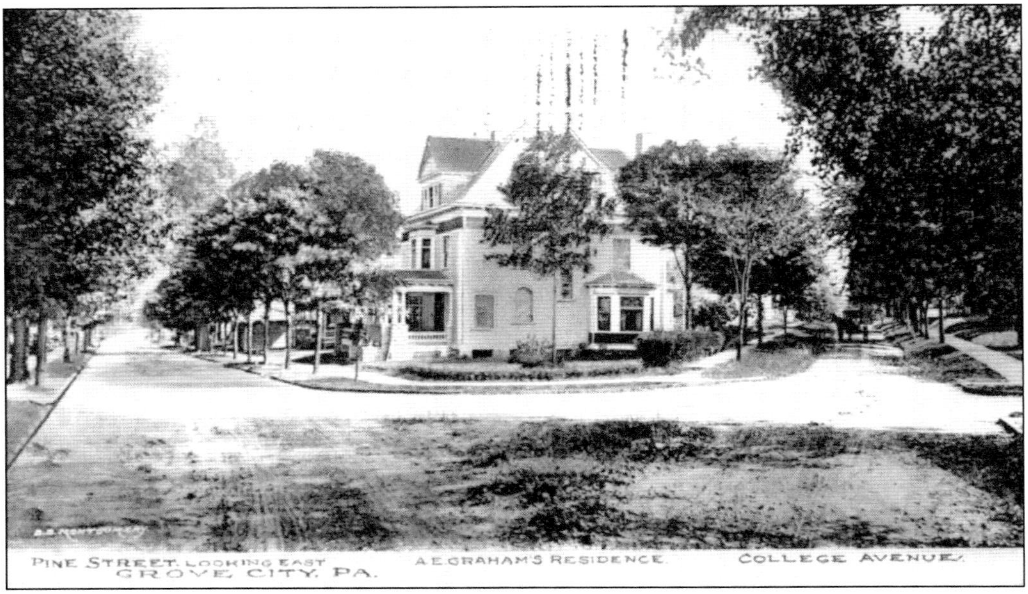

A. E. Graham, president of a Grove City bank, built his home at the intersection of Pine, College, and Elm Street. Graham's son Mark Graham, a member of the Commercial Club, was a corporate officer of the Cooper-Bessemer Corporation. Graham's daughter-in-law Ida Pearsall Graham grew up in the house later to become the town's first hospital. Another son married the daughter of movie star and Academy Award nominee Spring Byington.

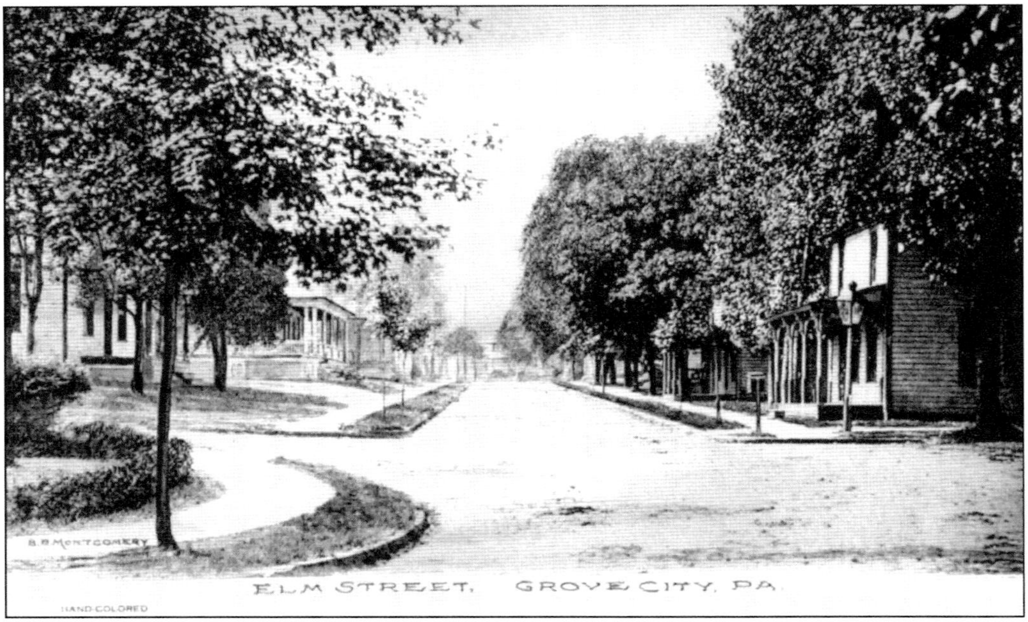

In the late 1800s, after Pennsylvania's oil boom ended, houses in boom towns were given away. The one at the end of Elm (at right in the image) was believed to come from the oil ghost town of Pithole. The home at the corner was actually two houses attached. Throughout the 1950s and 1960s it was used as gift shop called the Hobby House. Brenda Hillard later operated the Stock Exchange gift shop there.

Three
Stewart and West Main

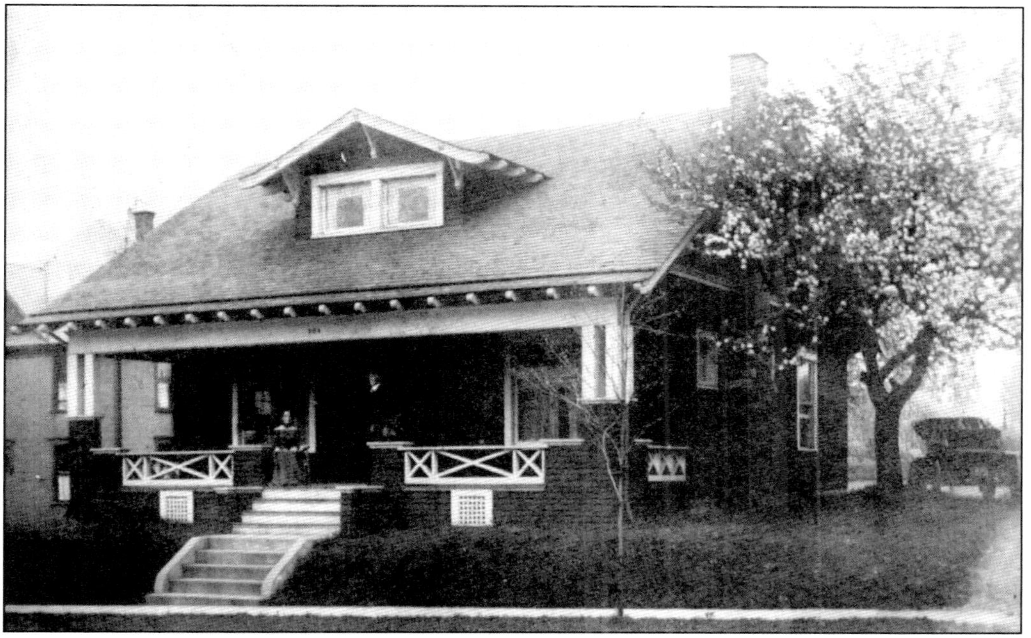

Turning the corner from College Avenue onto Stewart Avenue, one comes to the home of authors John and Marjorie Hummel. Built *c.* 1907, this house is a very early example of a bungalow style that has been popular for nearly 100 years. When constructed, this trend-setting home would have looked oddly out of place surrounded by the other large Victorian-style homes in the neighborhood. It was built by a doctor who worked at the first hospital in town, next-door.

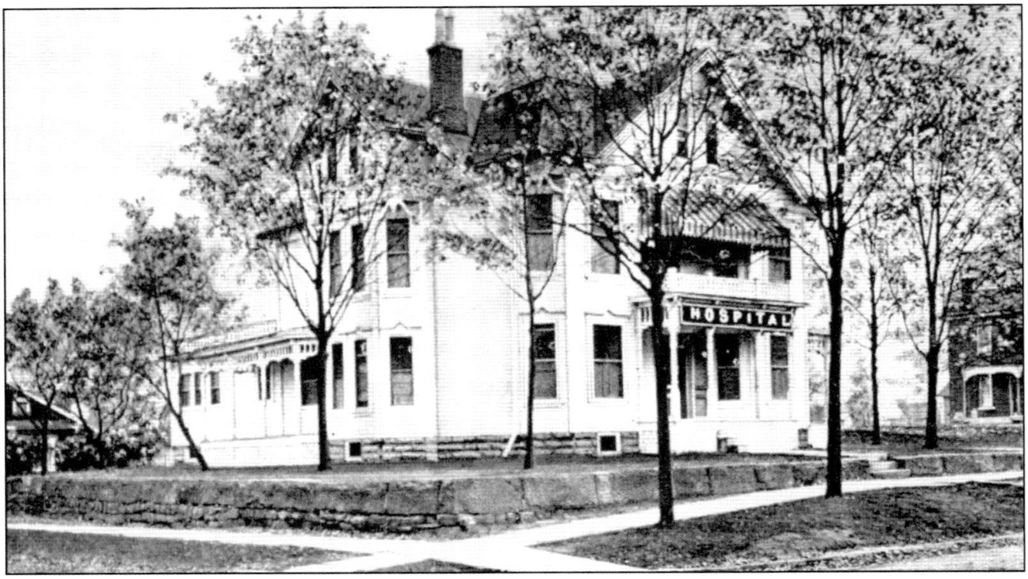

The James B. Pearsall house became the first hospital in Grove City. It operated from 1907 to 1921. Initially, both medical doctors and osteopaths shared this facility, but by 1911 a split occurred. For the next 70 years, the separate Bashline Osteopathic Hospital and Grove City Hospital existed in town. Not until the mid-1980s did the two systems combine to form United Community Hospital. Notice the bungalow to the left down Stewart Avenue from the hospital. Rumors of a tunnel connecting the two are unfounded.

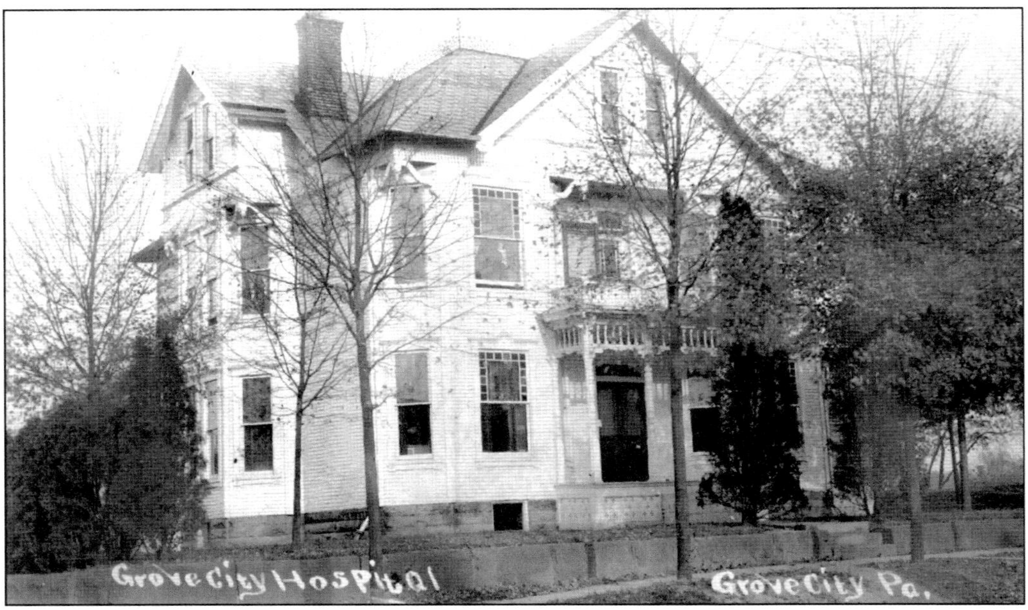

The town almost immediately outgrew this hospital. It was in service during a typhoid epidemic that swept the town in 1914, when water from Wolf Creek infiltrated the well-water supply. It was also Grove City's hospital during the 1918 Spanish flu pandemic. On a brighter note, many babies were born here, including Paula Kelly, who made famous the songs "Jeepers Creepers," "Stardust," and "Java Jive," while singing with the Modernaires and the Glenn Miller Orchestra.

Of course, not all broken legs were fatal. Presumably, Clyde Dickson recovered from his injury. Depending on the severity of the break, an injury like Clyde's may also have been dealt with in the doctor's office. Patients who needed to stay in the hospital were often in bad shape. With advances in medical imaging, exploratory surgery, in which doctors operate in order to learn the severity of a patient's condition by looking inside, is disappearing from use.

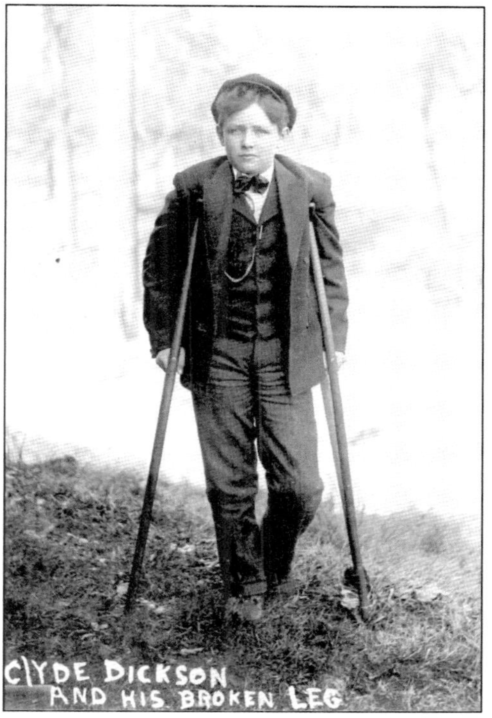

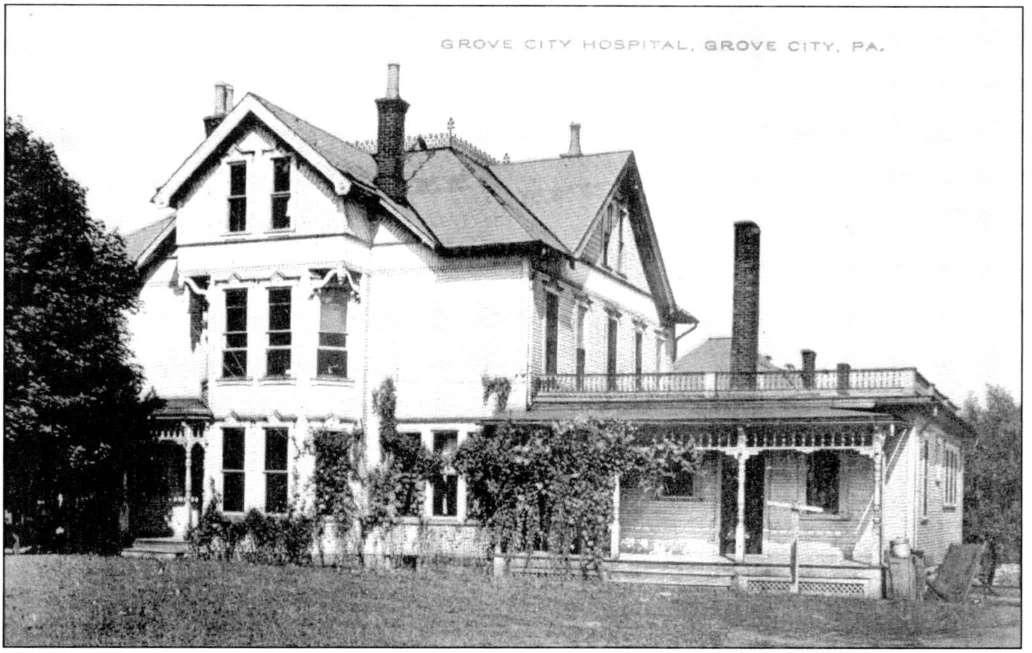

Before opening as a hospital, a one-story addition was added to the back of the J. B. Pearsall house. The addition contained the facility's operating room and kitchen. Aviation pioneer Earl Sandt died here from a tetanus infection after his gangrenous broken leg was amputated. In 1913, antibiotics, which may have saved his life, were not yet widely available.

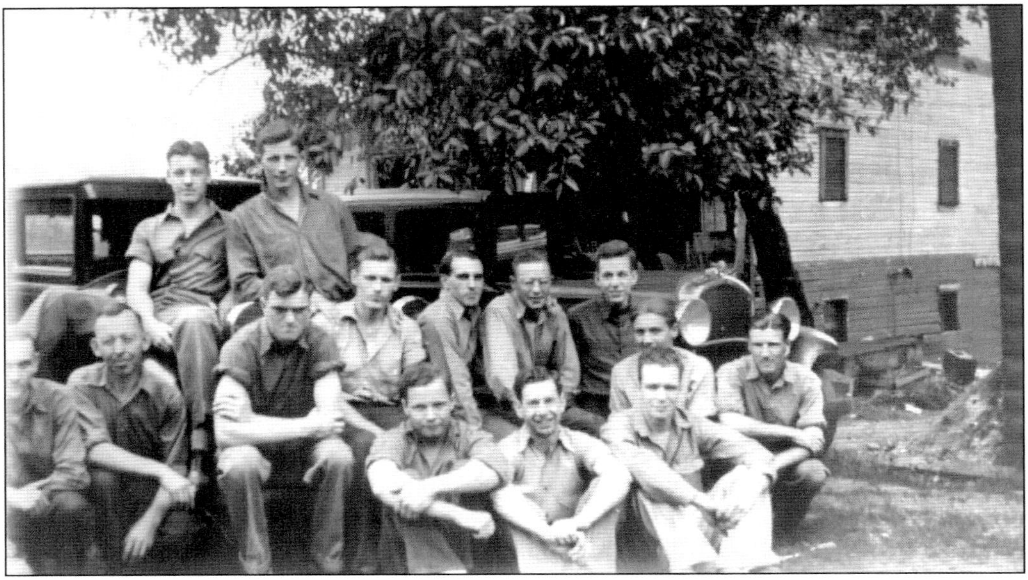

Artist Arthur Armour's workshop was next-door to the hospital. Aluminum craftsmen who worked for him are pictured here, from left to right, as follows: (first row) Edward Deniker, Ted Uber, and Wesley Findley; (second row) Max Neyman, Charlie Ray, John Deniker, Grant Atwell, James "Jimmy" DePonceau, Clayton Sheasley, George Pizor, Raymond Pizor, and Paul Rainey; (third row) Wendell McBride, and Robert Glessner. In the background is Armour's barn, which was used by his father as an icehouse. Ice from Barmore Lake, located outside of town, was cut and packed in sawdust here for use throughout the summer months.

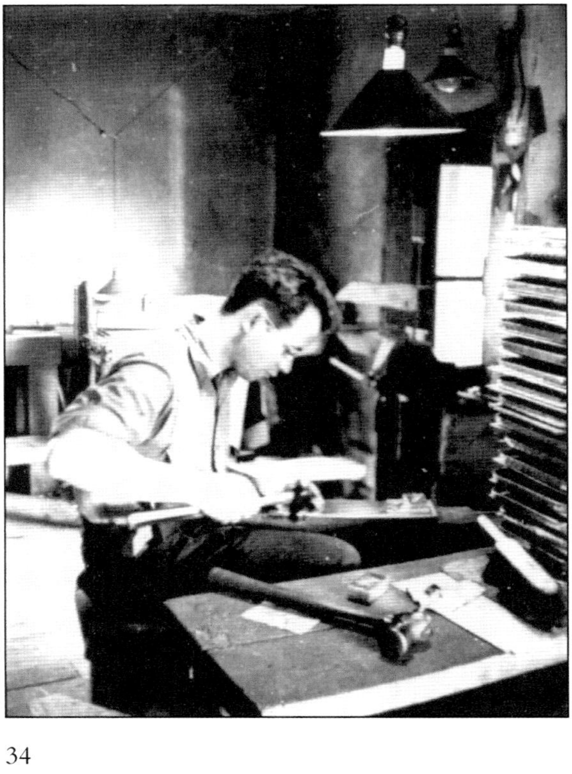

Wendell August pioneered the repousse' technique of hammering soft aluminum into hand-cut steel dies to form decorative aluminum ware such as jewelry, bowls, trays, and thousands of other household items popular throughout the 1930s and 1940s. Arthur Armour started his own workshop and cut his own dies in competition with August. Shown here is one of Armour's craftsmen, Edward Deniker, putting the finishing touches on a piece of aluminum artwork.

In this picture, taken behind Armour's workshop in the 1930s, Robert Glessner uses sign language to speak with fellow craftsman Max Neyman, who was deaf. Although pounding metals without any ear protection would have affected their hearing, this was not the source of Neyman's deafness. Communicating with Neyman was not a problem. He could read lips and many of the craftsmen learned enough sign language to get by.

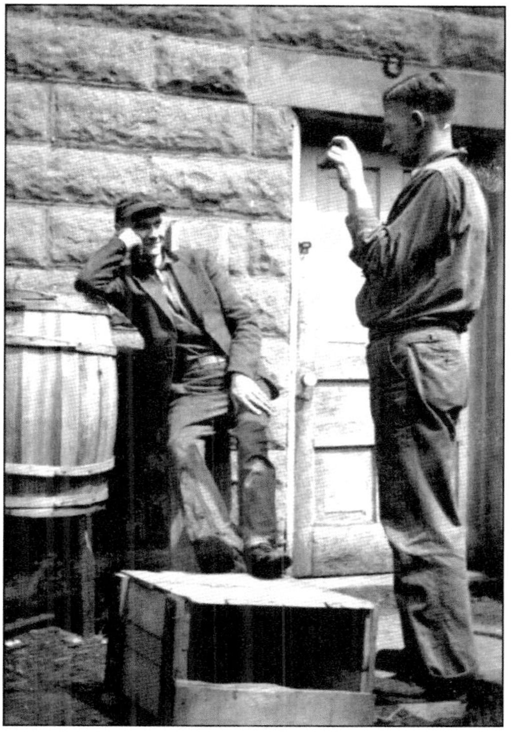

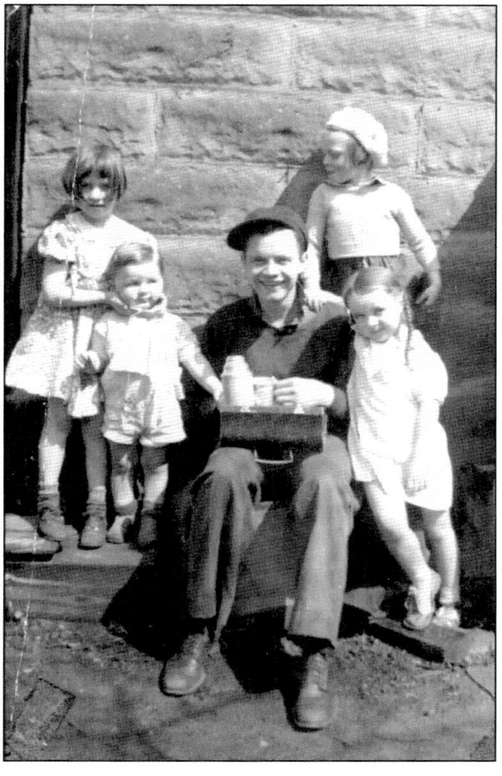

Shown in this picture is Edward Deniker sharing his lunch with Mary Jane Daugherty and other neighborhood children. Armour's building had previously been the Grove City Pop Works, which was the forerunner of the Nemo Bottling Company. Other lunchtime activities in the yard behind the workshop included wrestling and playing catch with a baseball.

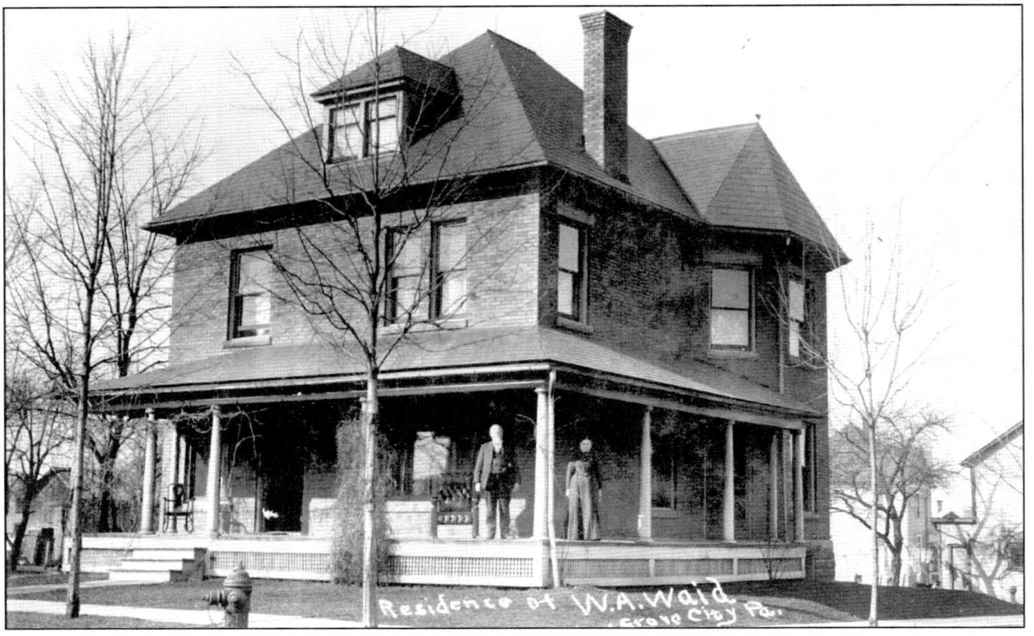

Across Stewart Avenue from the hospital was the home of W. A. Waid. It stands at the corner with West Main Street, known earlier as Mercer Street. The house remains, although the front porch has been removed. Like many large houses in Grove City, this one has been divided into apartments.

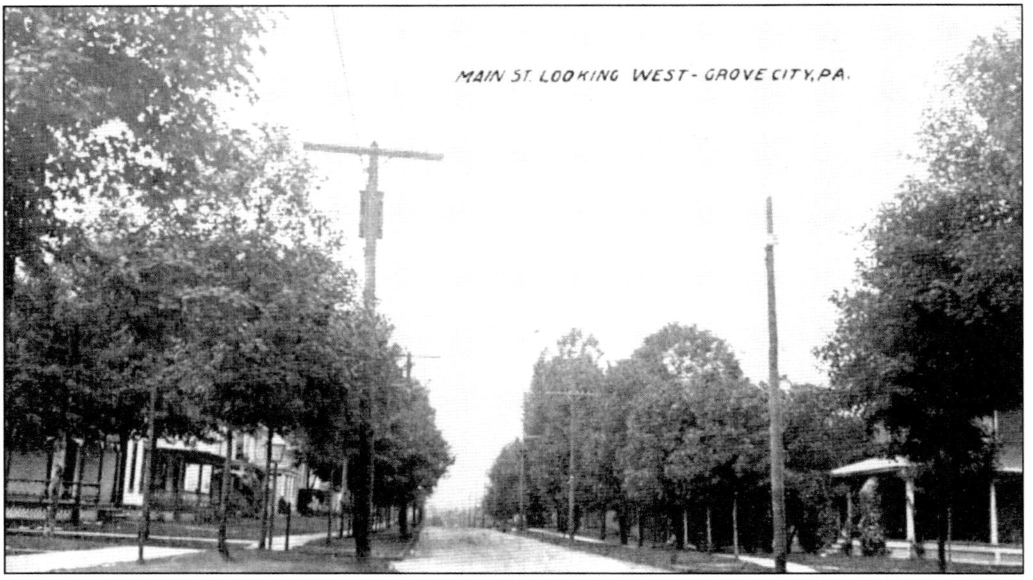

In this photograph of the intersection of Stewart Avenue and West Main Street looking west, W. A. Waid's front porch is visible to the right. Notice the telephone poles along the street. When homes in this area of town were being built most people relied on gas for heat and light. Electricity was somewhat unreliable. Homes often had both gas and electric light fixtures. By the 1890s, new homes also had central heating, telephone service, and the strangest of all modern conveniences for the day: indoor toilets.

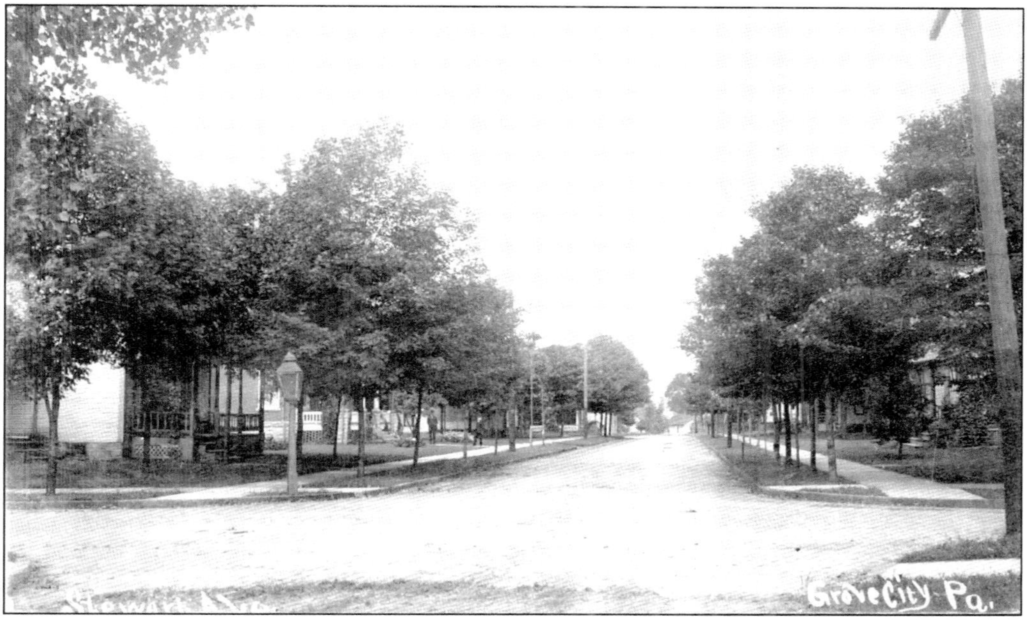

Although advertisements from this period boast many paved streets in town, at the time of this photograph the intersection of Stewart Avenue and West Main Street does not appear to be paved. A gas streetlight is visible on the corner. The hospital is to the photographer's right. West Main Street, designed for horse-and-buggy traffic, is somewhat narrow for the 10,000 vehicles that now use it daily.

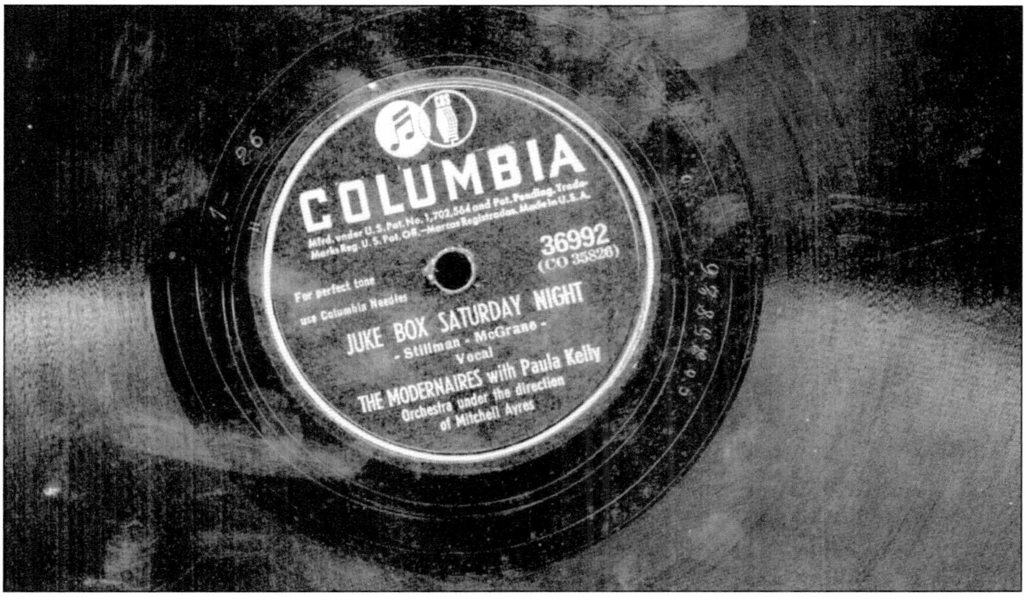

One block away on the corner of Stewart and Poplar was the home of dentist H. A. Kelly, father of the Big Band-era entertainers the Kelly Sisters: Paula, Martha, and Julie. The Kelly sisters got their big break *c.* 1935 performing on the national radio program Major Bowe's Original Amateur Hour. Paula Kelly, who later sang with the Modernaires and the Glenn Miller Orchestra, made famous the songs "Chattanooga Choo-Choo," and "Juke Box Saturday Night."

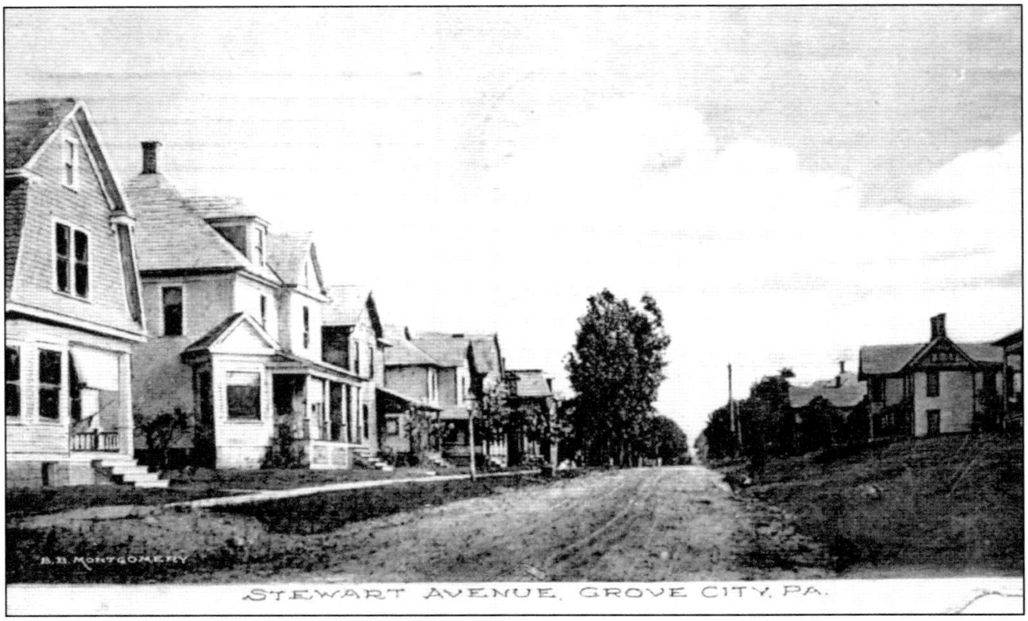

In this view of Stewart Avenue buggy tracks can be seen in the unpaved street. Singer Paula Kelly's family home is to the right, at the intersection of Poplar Street and Stewart Avenue. Martha Kelly, one of the Kelly sisters, died very young of tuberculosis *c.* 1937. Julie Kelly left show business and only Paula, the youngest Kelly sister, continued a career in music.

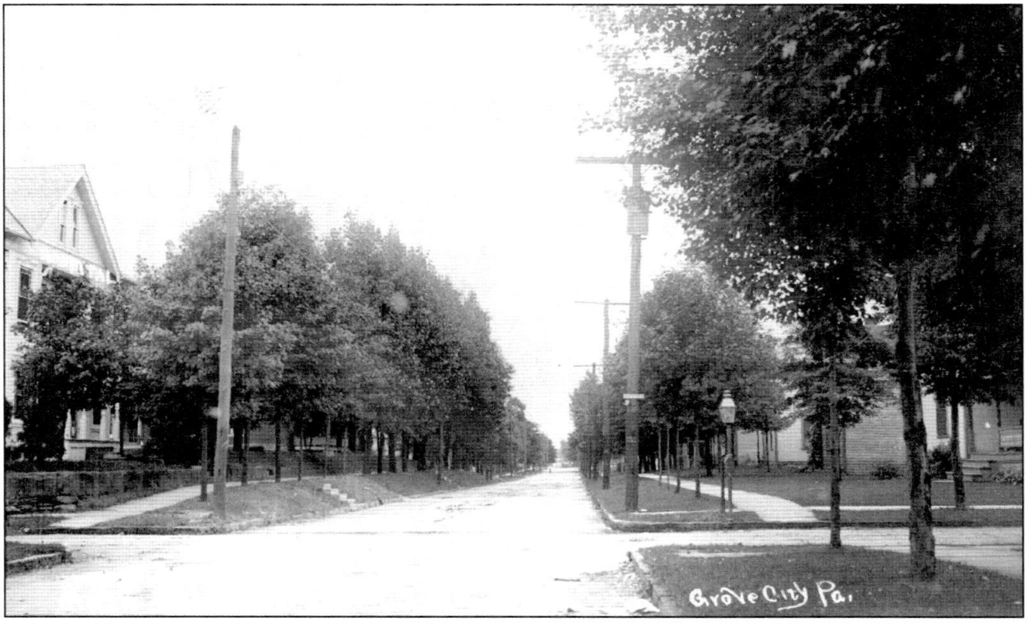

At the intersection of Stewart Avenue and Main Street looking east toward town, the hospital is on the left. Although no traffic is visible in this photograph, the Pennsylvania Department of Transportation reports nearly 10,000 cars now travel this section of West Main Street every day.

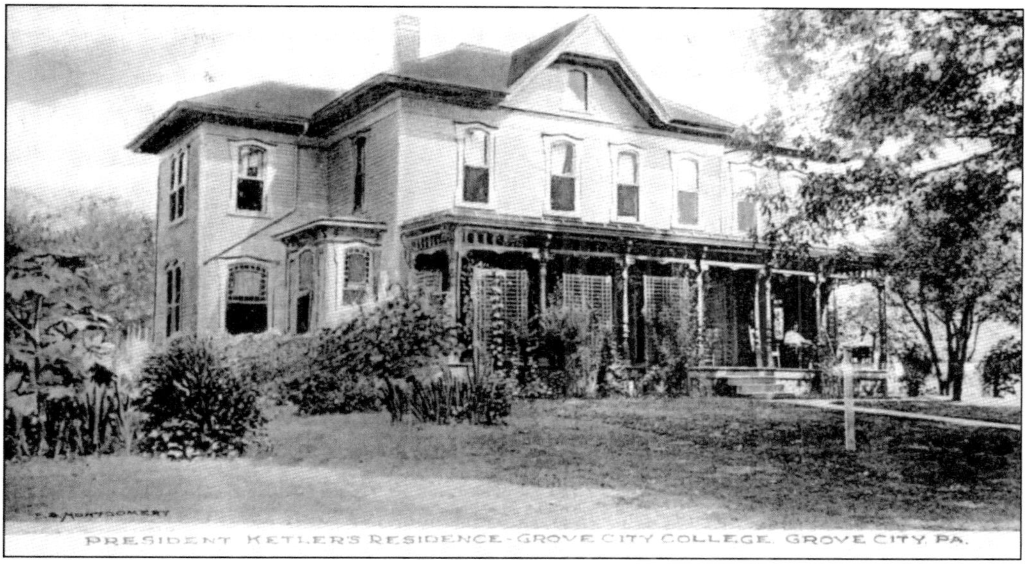

Rev. Dr. Isaac C. Ketler, founder of Grove City College, maintained this home on West Main Street near its intersection with South Center Street. In June 1913, Ketler fell ill from a ruptured appendix and was operated on in the hospital he helped found, just two blocks from his home. He lingered for three days before succumbing to the infection that ravaged his body. From his deathbed, Ketler wrote or dictated farewell notes to relatives and friends. Of Grove City College, he said it was a "labor of love."

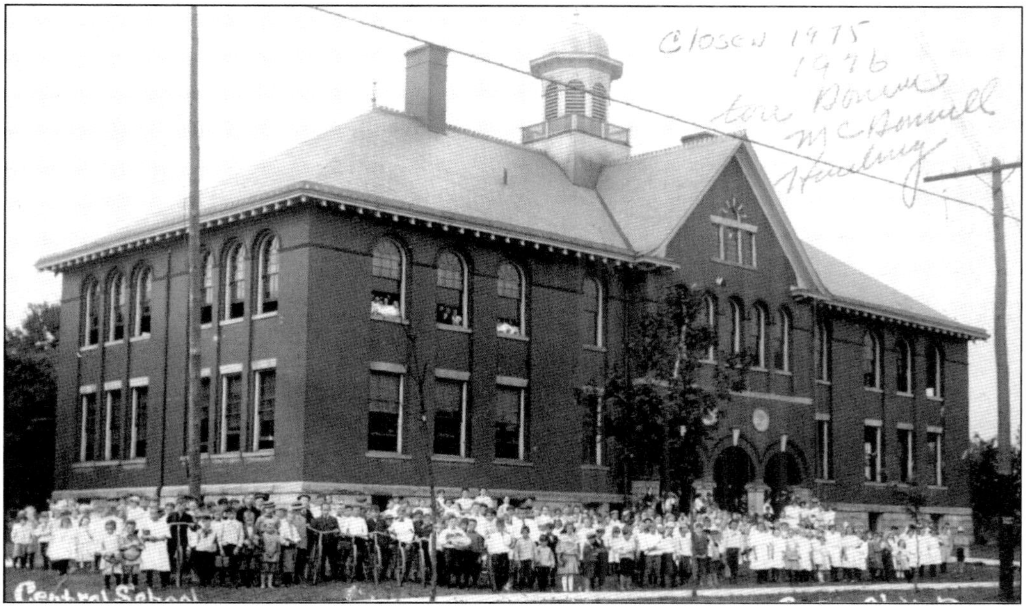

Across the street from Ketler's home was Central School at the corner of South Center and West Main Streets. Built in 1901, it was torn down in 1976. All that remains today are the two medallions from above the arches that have been incorporated into the landscaping of the McDonald's restaurant that replaced the school. The earliest maps of Pine Grove show a schoolhouse at this location possibly as early as 1804.

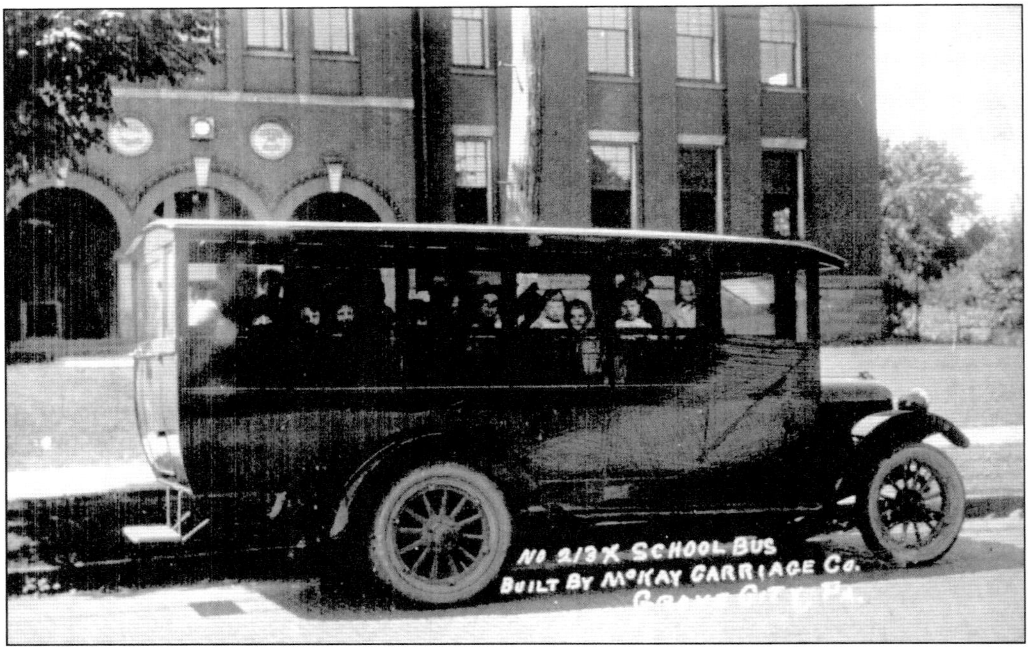

This card was likely used by the McKay Carriage Company as an advertisement for the school buses the company assembled in Grove City. Shown here is No. 2/3 X loaded with schoolchildren and parked in front of Central School. Edwin J. Fithian, candidate for the U.S. Senate, equipped a McKay bus with camping features; he used it while traveling around campaigning before the election. Dr. Fithian's early RV is now part of an antique car collection of the Imperial Palace in Las Vegas.

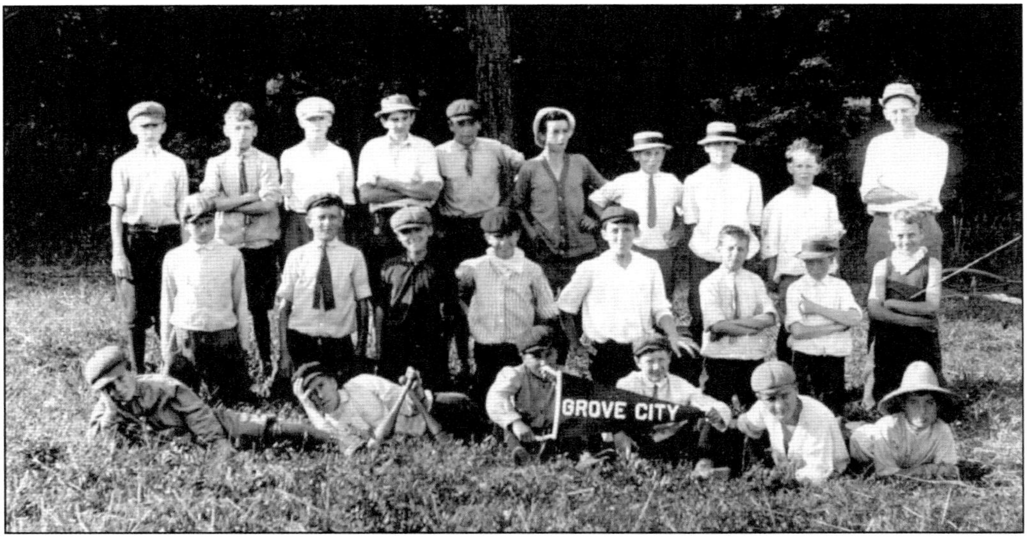

School field trips at the turn of the 19th century involved outings to actual fields. This does not appear to be a class trip, however, as only boys and young men appear in the picture. It is possibly an athletic-club outing. One boy is holding Indian clubs, another appears to have a fishing pole, and a bicycle lies in the background. The fishing pole suggests that the group is probably being photographed at a location either along Wolf Creek or Barmore Lake.

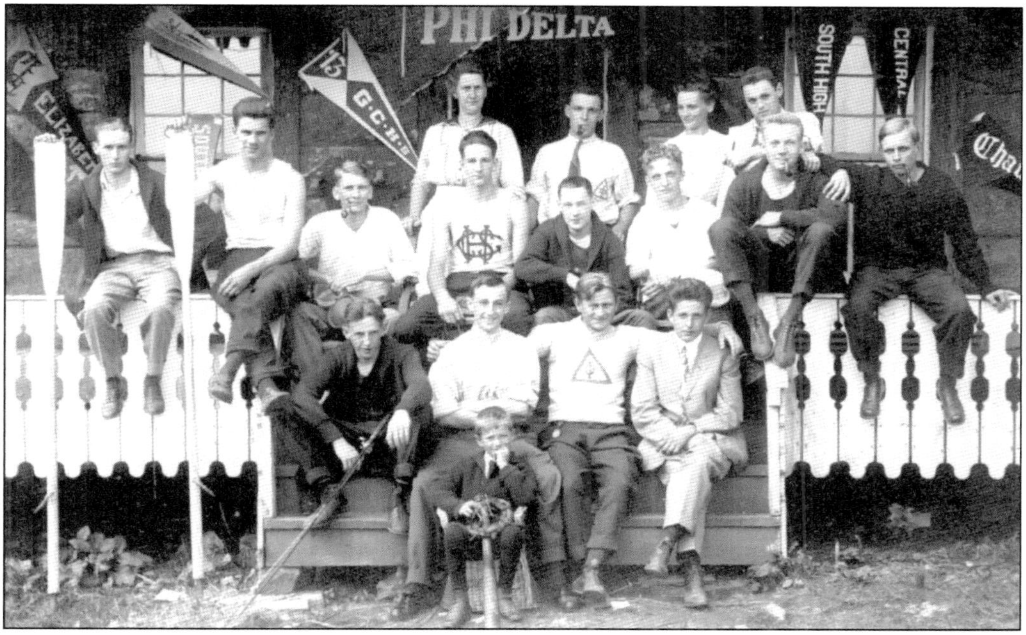

For a very short period of time in history, Grove City High School had fraternities. They were later banned. Rev. Dr. Isaac C. Ketler, founder of Grove City College, referred to fraternities as "secret societies" and kept them out of the college while he was alive. This photograph shows the Phi Delta chapter of Grove City High School. A pennant in the background includes the date '13. The porch is decorated with pennants from other schools as well.

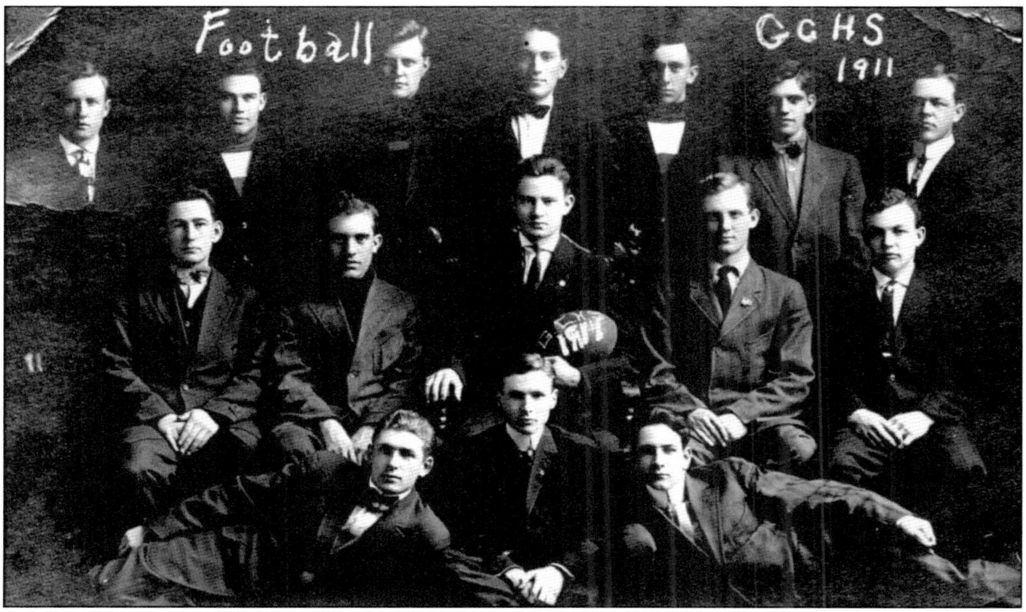

High school football games have changed a lot in the 90 years since these fellows posed for this team photograph. If a player went out of the game, he was not allowed back in for the rest of the the game. Home games were played on the Grove City College field. The team traveled to away games by train on the Bessemer and Lake Erie Railroad since there were no cars.

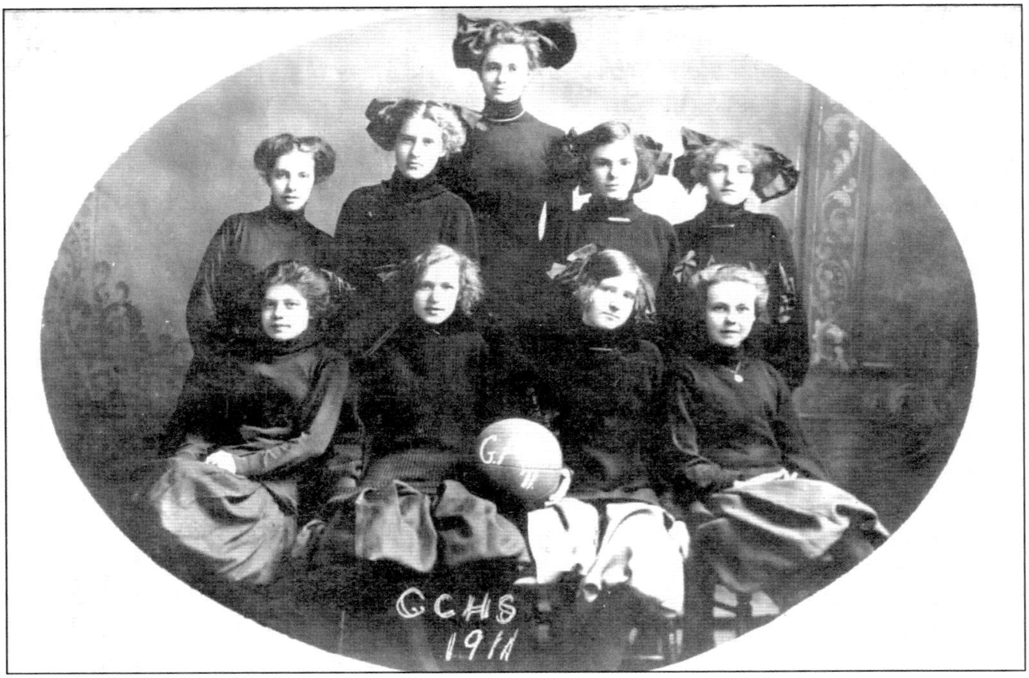

Young women have been playing basketball in Grove City for more than 100 years. The Grove City High School girls' basketball squad is shown here in a 1911 team photograph wearing bloomers and bows. Bloomers permitted increased mobility for players, which was not found while wearing corsets and long dresses to play as earlier teams did. Although covered from head to toe by today's standards of dress, to old timers of the day it would have appeared as if they were playing in their underwear.

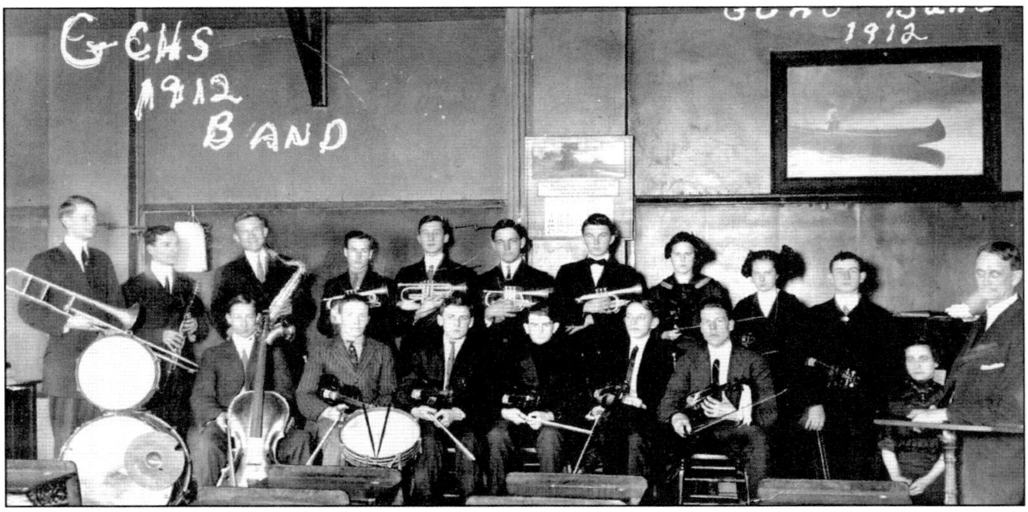

Likely taken in a Central School classroom, the Grove City High School Band shown in this 1912 photograph was much smaller than it is today. It has also been quite a while since the Grove City High School band was composed mostly of string instruments. One student appears to play both a violin and a drum.

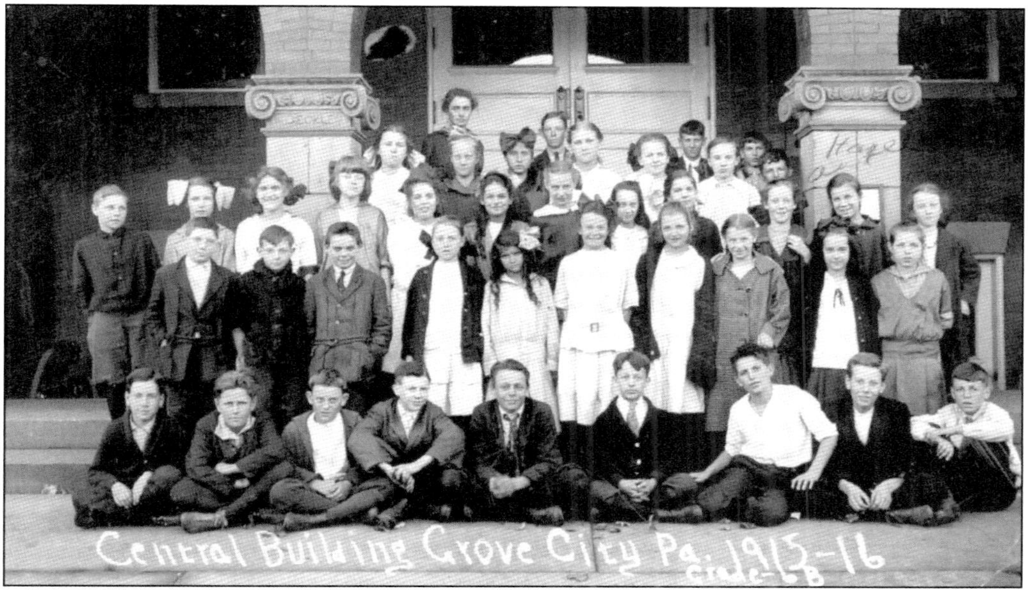

Central School was also home to some of the town's elementary-school classes. This group of more than 40 students is one of the sixth grade classes from the academic year of 1915–1916. Teachers routinely employed corporal punishment and parents were behind them 100 percent. If a child "got a lickin'" at school, he or she would get another one at home when their parents found out.

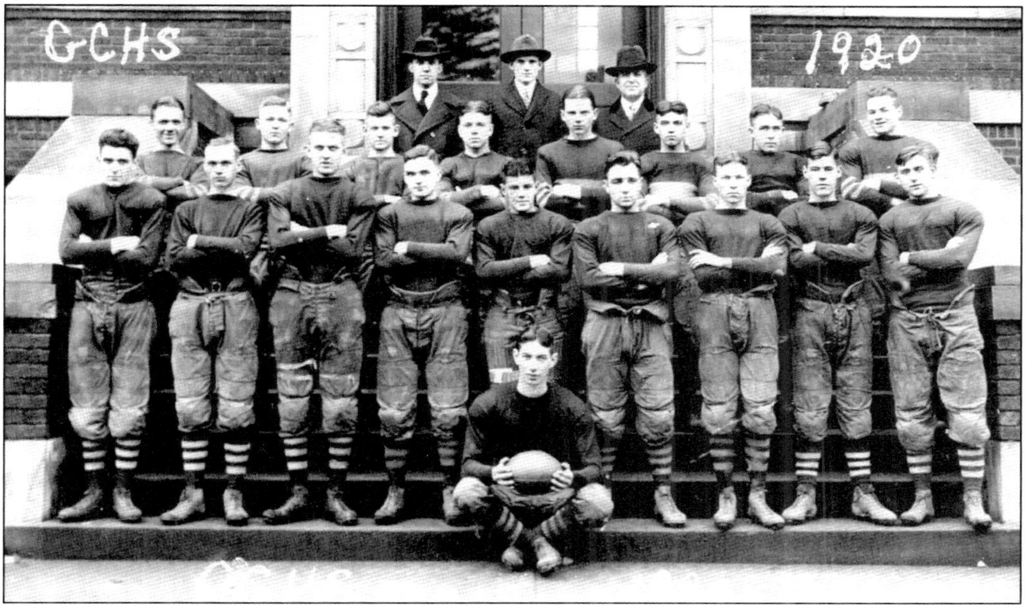

By 1920, football players wore more padding, but still played without helmets of any kind. The three men in the back are coach Rollin Filer, George Gould, and principal Homer Lehn. John Hummel recalls principal Lehn visiting one of his classes to observe his teacher, Aletha Philpott: "One time he stopped in to watch Miss Philpott teach and he put his hand on my back. I was scared to death of him. I was shaking."

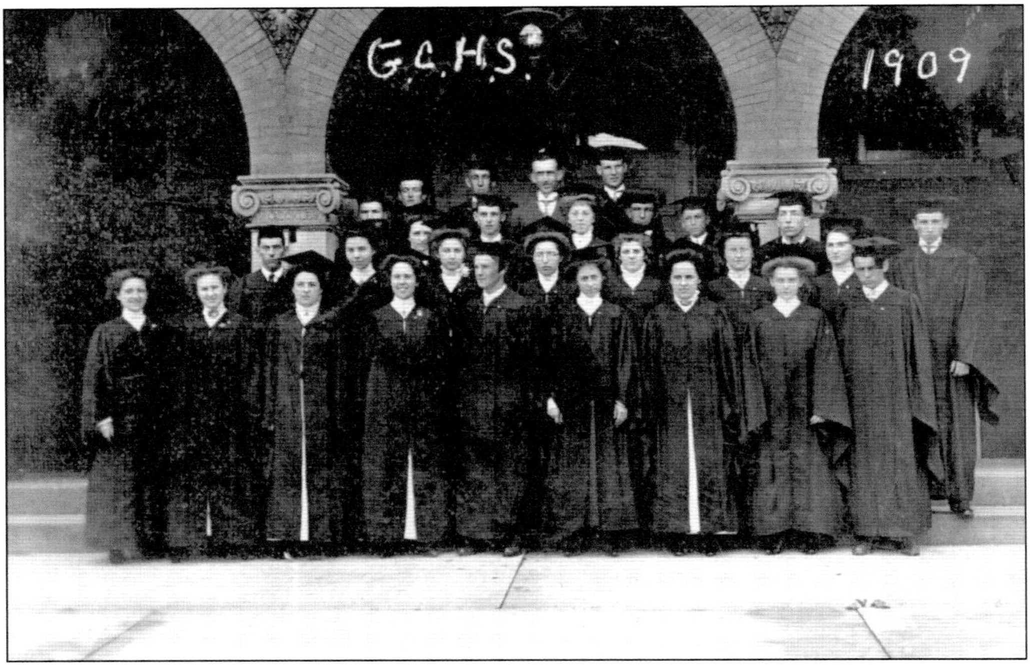

Shown here is graduation day, 1909. Only a few students who began school in 1st grade made it all the way through 12th grade; they usually were students wishing to continue on to college. For the rest, there was work to be done on the farm or in the coal mines.

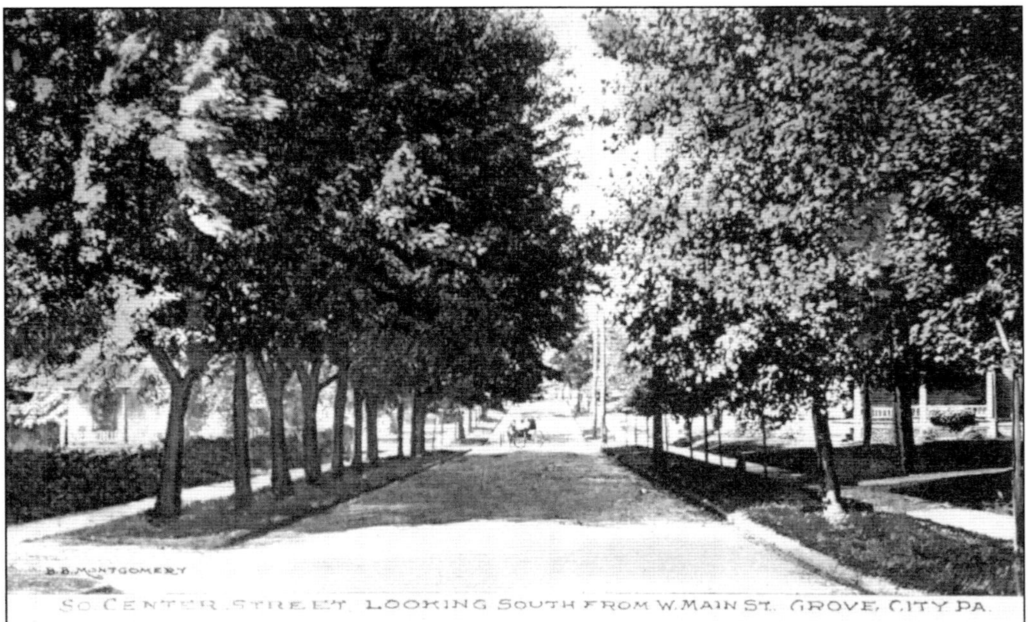

This was once the view from Main Street looking south on South Center Street. The horse and buggy in the distance is at the intersection of Poplar and South Center Streets. That intersection now has a blinker-light traffic signal. The trees lining the street have all been removed.

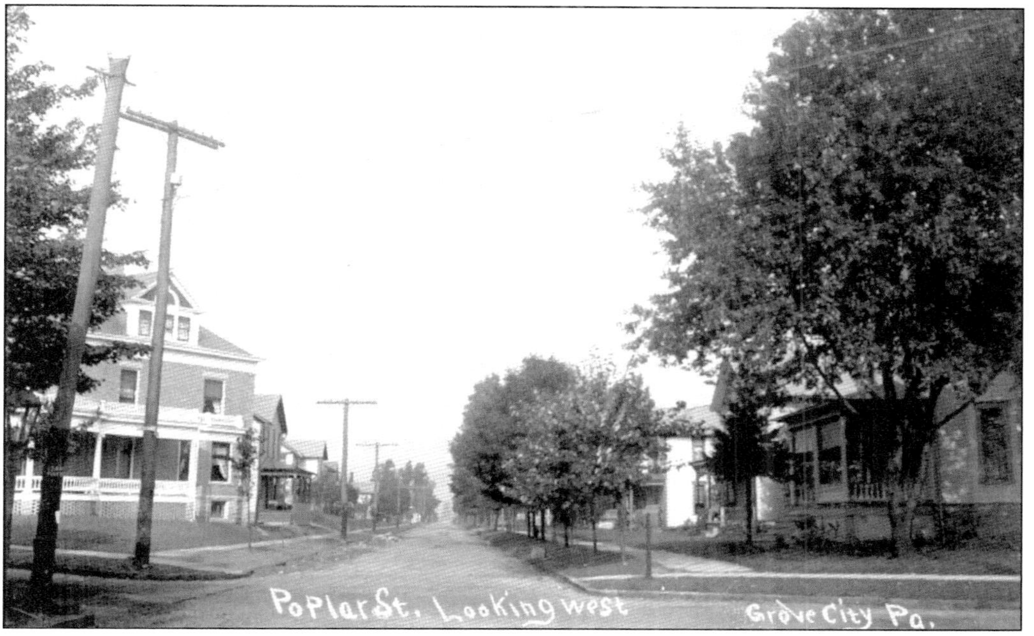

The yellow brick house with the large front porch at the intersection of Poplar and South Center Streets was the John Guthrie house. He built the Guthrie Theater and operated the Guthrie's Shoe Store. Both were on South Broad Street. The Guthrie Theater had a huge organ that Carlie Hulbert played during intermission and before the movie started while people entered the theater. Later on, the organ was used by East Main Church.

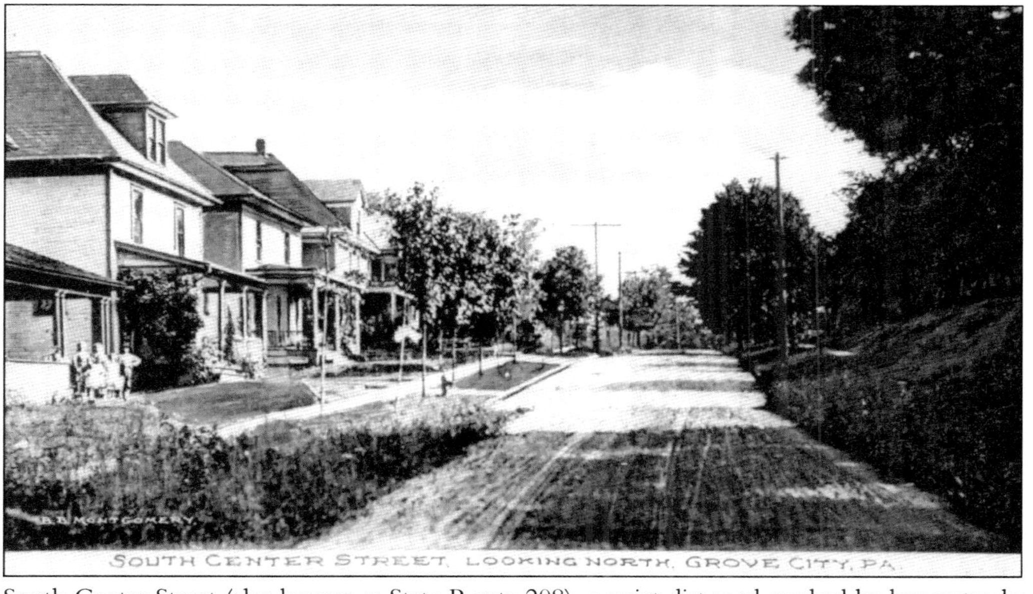

South Center Street (also known as State Route 208), a quiet dirt road marked by buggy tracks in this picture, now carries thousands of vehicles per day. All of the homes in the picture remain with the exception of the one where the children are standing on the front-porch steps. That home was torn down in 2003 after being badly damaged by a fire. While the rest of the homes remain, their front porches have been altered significantly or removed altogether.

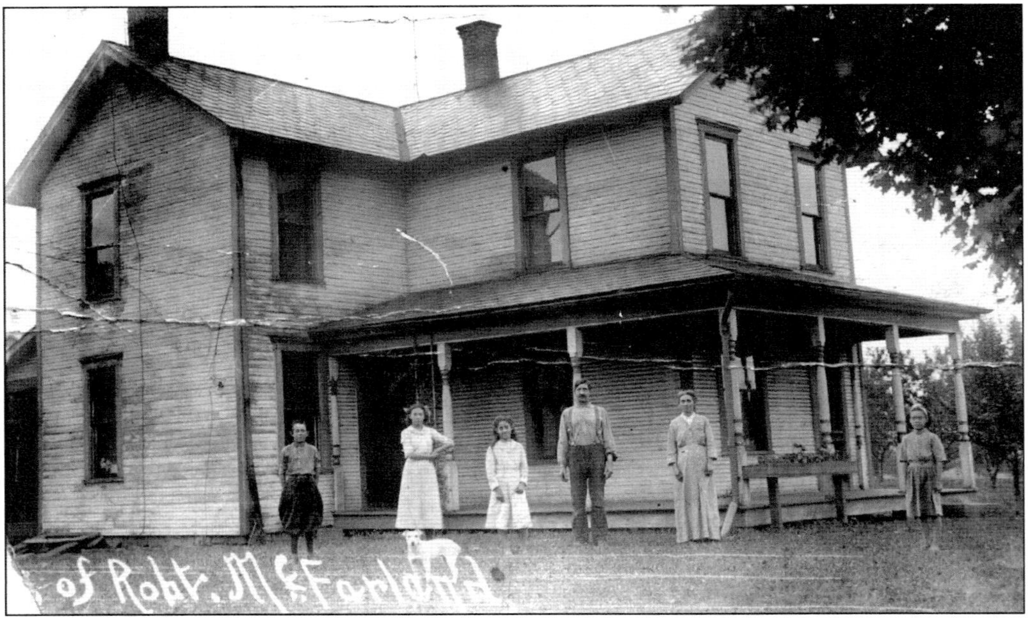

Following South Center Street out of town, a traveler would encounter two-story frame farmhouses like this one Robert McFarland built. McFarland was a cabinet maker near London and also built the house where Lucas Photography operates outside of London today. McFarland's workshop and pump house were built onto the back of his home. In 1940, he traded his house and farm for Kathryn Urey's house on Stewart Avenue in Grove City "with boot," meaning payment beyond the trade.

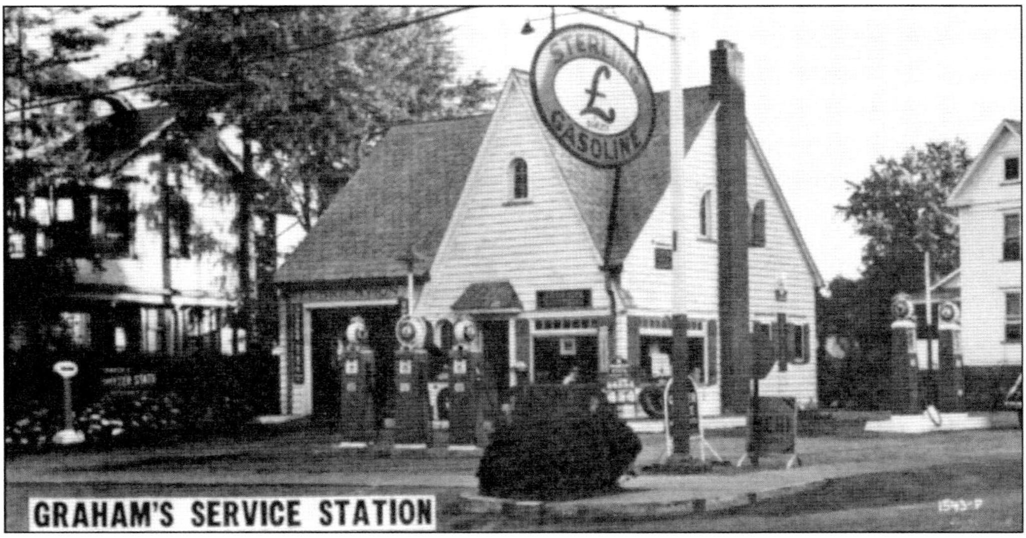

At the intersection of West Main and South Center Streets, this Sterling Gasoline station, operated by Joe Graham, was across South Center Street from Central School. The house in the trees to the left was the first nursing home in Grove City. It was named Webster's Convalescent Home and was operated by Marie H. Webster and Ellen M. Truran. Just visible through the trees is the second-floor sleeping porch, popularized by osteopath Dr. O. O. Bashline, who believed sleeping outside in fresh air had restorative properties.

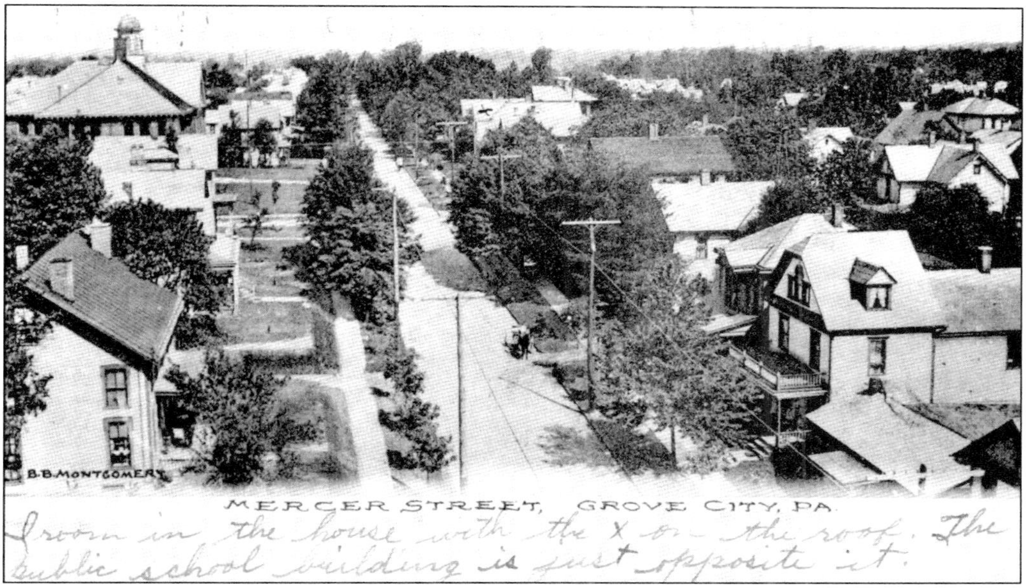

While some streetscapes in town have not changed in the past century, the houses shown in the distance are all that remain in this area of town. The photographer was standing in the tower of the Presbyterian church on West Main Street looking up Mercer Street, as it was also known. At the summit of the hill, the cupola atop Central School is visible above the horizon. The houses to the right in the photograph between Broad and Center Streets were razed to make room for a new Grove City Borough building, College View Towers, and a municipal parking lot.

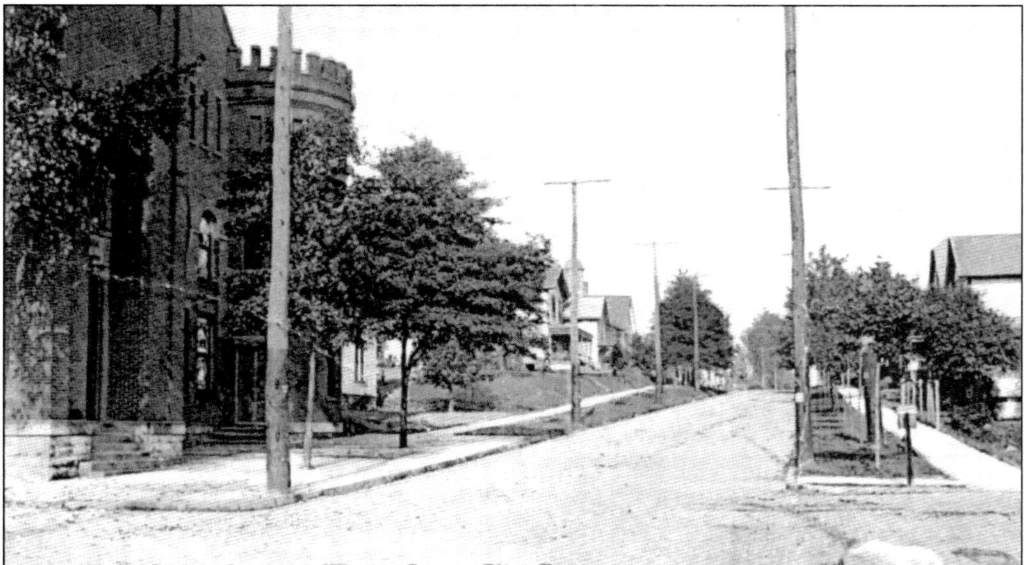

A view from street level of the same area shows the church where the previous photograph was taken, as well as utility poles lining both sides of West Main Street. For a time, the town had two competing telephone companies. Grove City College's new Carnegie building is out of the picture to the right. Notice the large stone placed at the corner to deter drivers from cutting the corner.

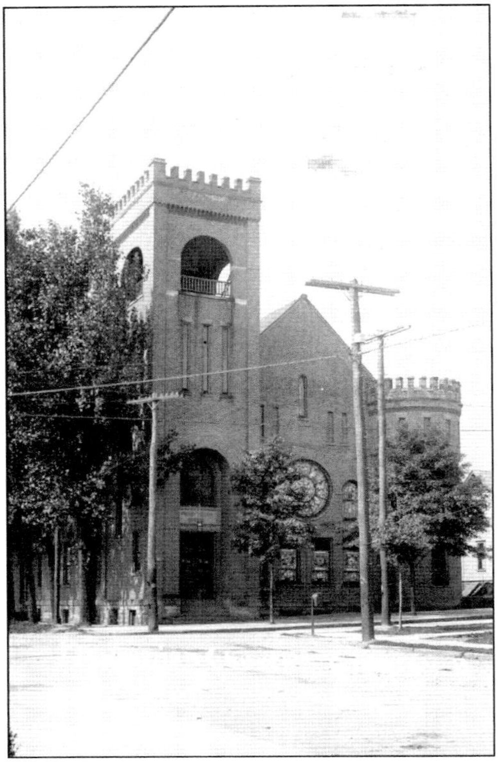

Presbyterian missionaries Frank Simcox and his wife, May Gilson Simcox, worked in China throughout the 1890s. In 1900, the Simcox family, including their three children and the other members of the China Inland Mission, were murdered by an angry mob during the Boxer Rebellion in Paotingfu (now Baoding), China. May Gilson Simcox was the niece of Isaac Ketler, founder of Grove City College. Using letters May wrote home, family photographs, and official reports after the rebellion, Ketler reconstructed the events leading up to their deaths in his book *The Tragedy of Paotingfu.*

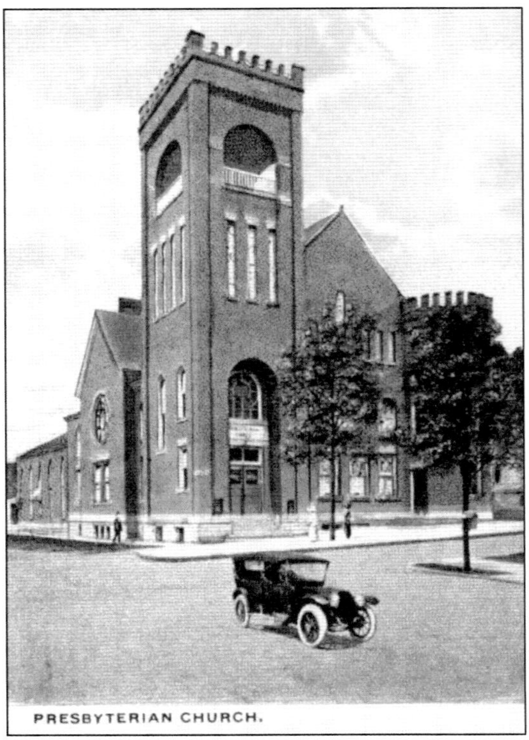

Postcards are not always what they seem. Probably drawn from a projection of a real photograph, this rendering improved somewhat on reality. Note that the forest of utility poles surrounding the church has vanished. The artist has also rearranged the location of trees and sidewalks. Look closely at the tree growing in front of the church in the actual photograph. In the drawing, the trunk grows on the other side of the street. Notice too, that the artistically placed automobile is not drawn to scale.

Four
East Main and Pinchalong

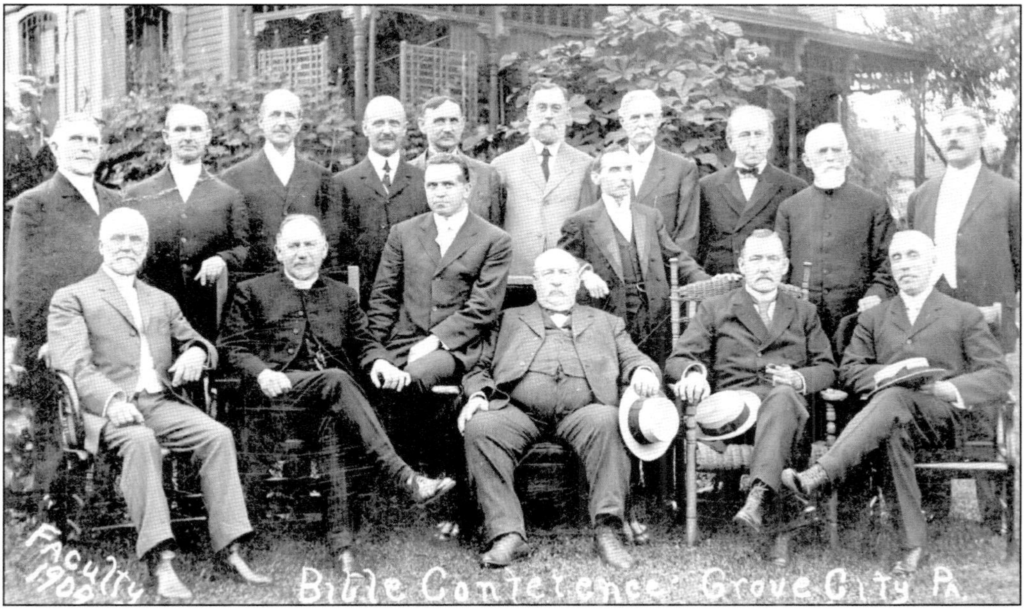

An August assemblage of doctors of divinity had their photograph taken on the front lawn of Ketler's home on West Main Street. Among them are Rev. Dr. Isaac Conrad Ketler, founder and president of Grove City College and Dr. Dean Ormond, who succeeded Ketler after his death.

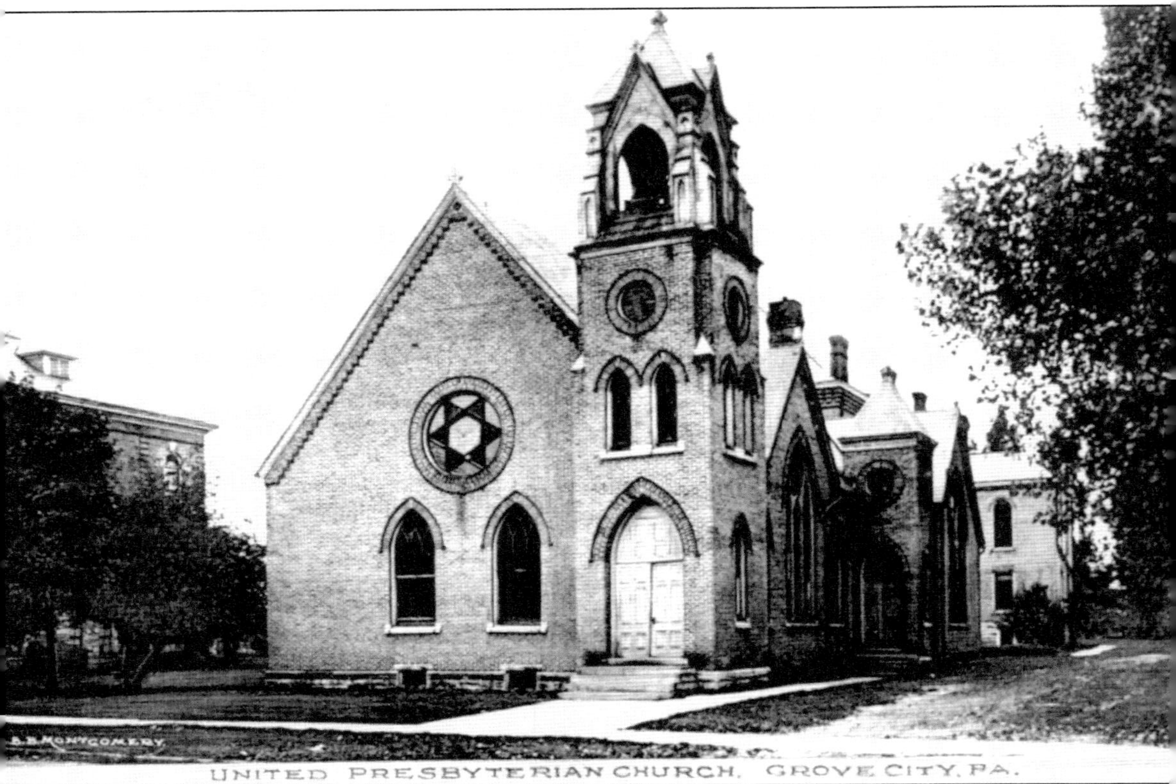

When crossing Broad Street, West Main Street becomes East Main Street. A few yards from the intersection on East Main between the Carnegie building and the Colonial Dormitory was another United Presbyterian church, later known as Ivy Chapel. On the lower campus of Grove City College, Ivy Chapel was also used as a lecture hall. Grove City College students were then, as now, required to attend a certain number of chapel services each semester. Ivy Chapel was also used for summer Bible conferences, which Isaac Ketler organized.

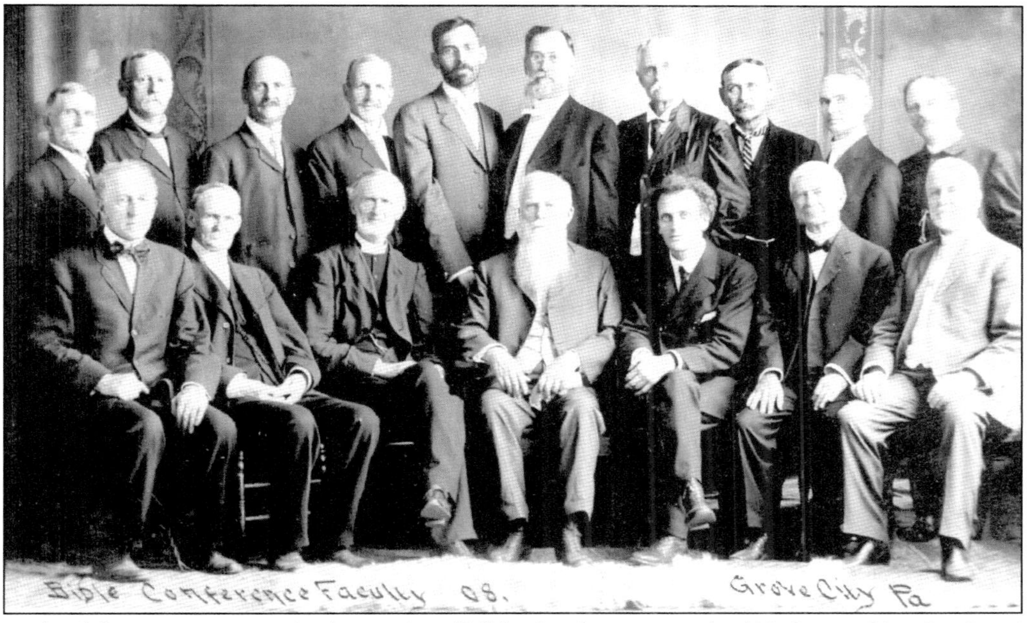

Both of these images contain the caption "Bible Conference Faculty '08 Grove City, Pa.," and appear to be taken in the same photography studio. However, the two photographs contain different gentlemen. Bible conference lecturers came from all over the United States and as far away as Great Britain. Ketler intended the summer sessions to be a resource for public school teachers who wished to continue their educations while their own students were on vacation. One consequence of this, however, was that Grove City College professors had little vacation time. When Ketler required faculty members to sign a contract promising to teach four terms per year, several prominent teachers who had been with the college for years resigned. To this day, Grove City College does not offer faculty members tenure.

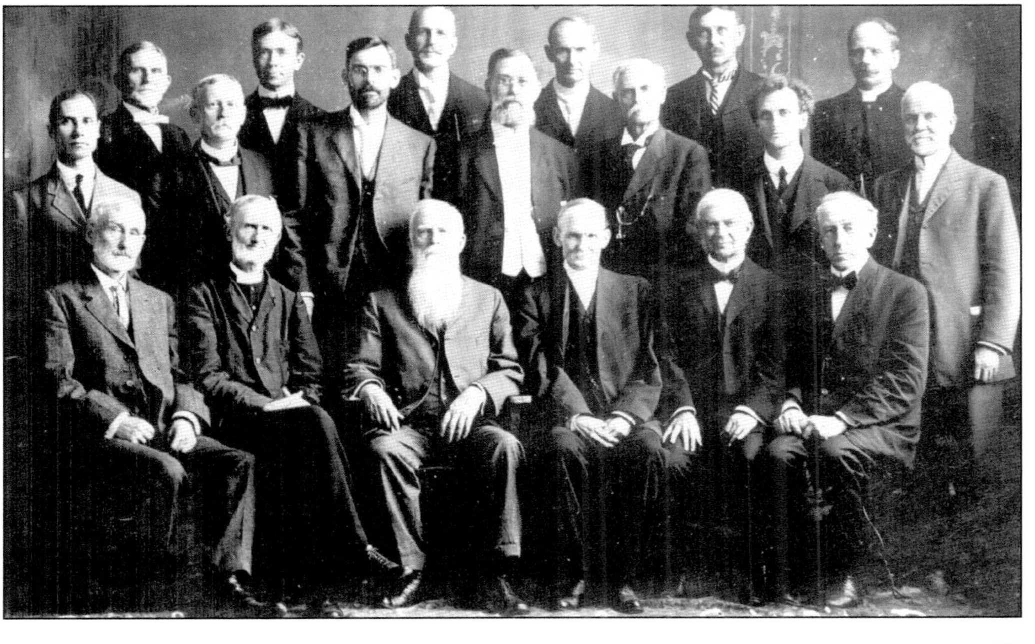

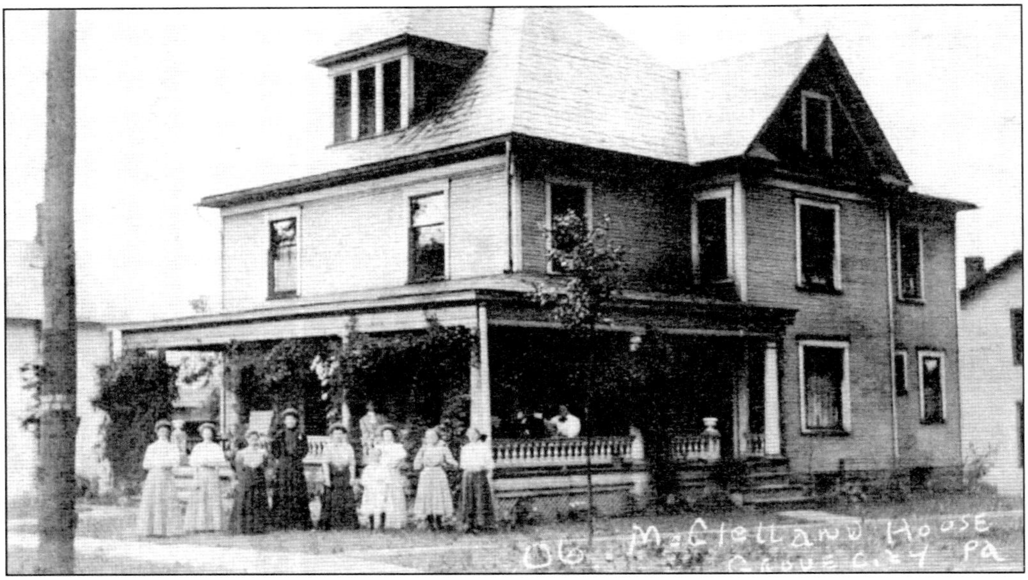

Across the street from the Ivy Chapel is the James B. McClelland House, which once sat at the corner of Main and Broad Streets, where the Grove City Diner is now located. J. Howard Pew, chairman of the board of the Sun Oil Company and alumnus of Grove City College, had the house moved from the corner to make room for an early Sunoco station. McClelland was the college's vice president. The home is now in operation as the Snow Goose Inn Bed and Breakfast.

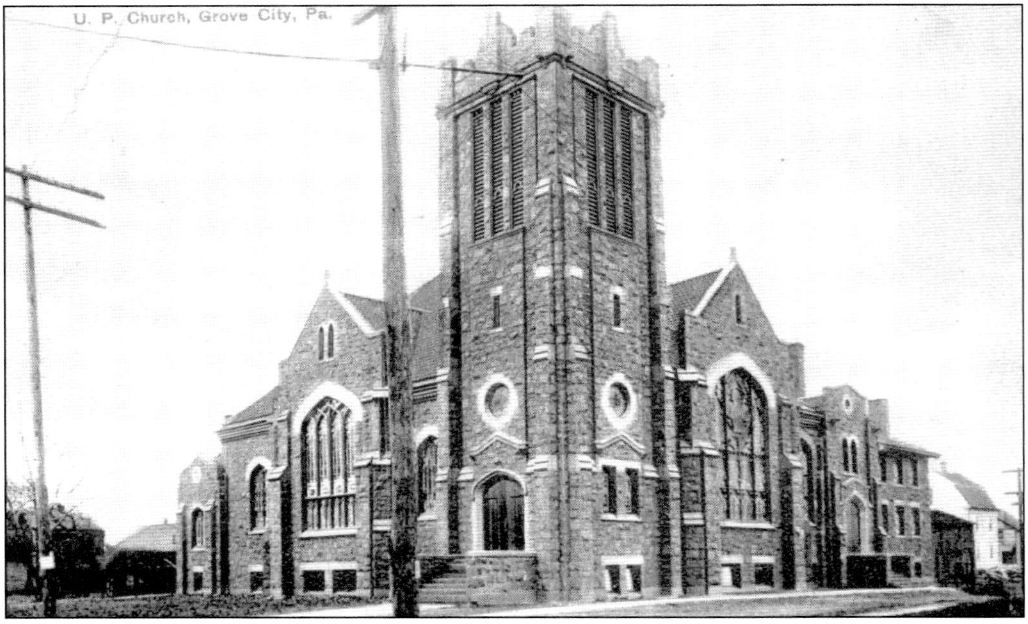

The East Main United Presbyterian congregation celebrates its 125th anniversary in 2004 and traces its origin back to 1879. The congregation met in various locations before settling into this church building, built in 1909, just 30 years after the formation of the congregation. The impressive stone structure has a seating capacity of more than 1,000 people.

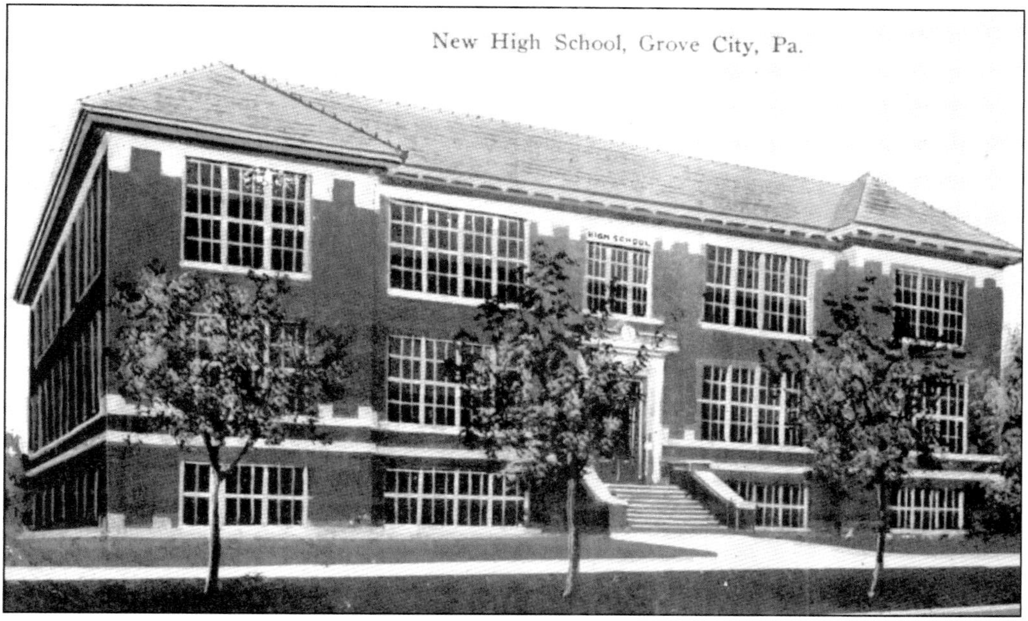

In just 15 years, the town outgrew the Central High School building and built the "new high school" between 1914 and 1915. It is currently used as the Grove City Area School District's middle school. During the last major renovations to the building, the front entrance toward Main Street was closed and the steps removed. Students now enter and exit the building from the rear, which faces quieter streets.

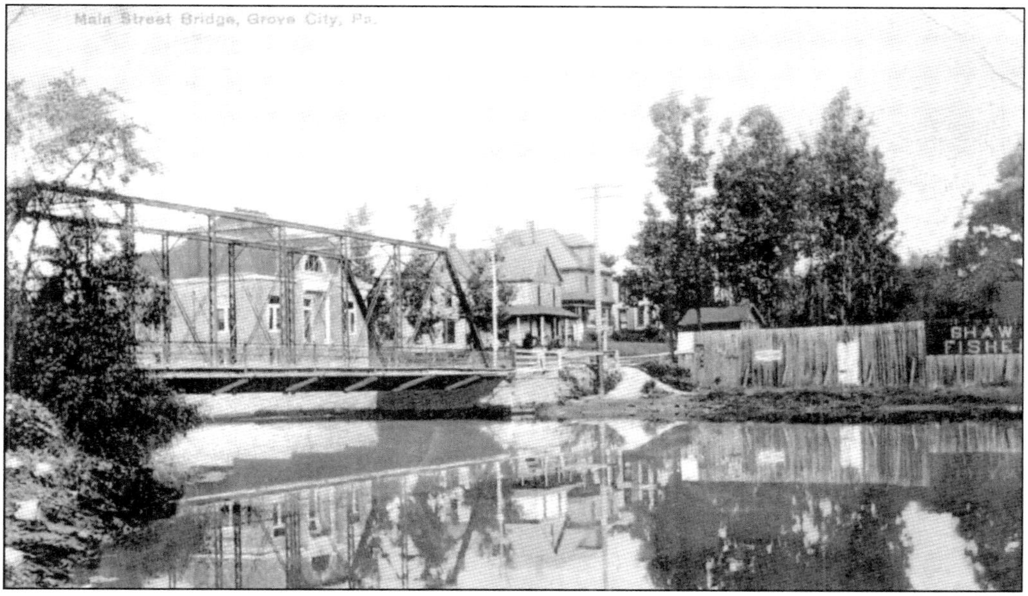

The Main Street Bridge is about half a block from the school when traveling east on East Main Street. This portion of Wolf Creek has been dammed for more than two centuries. When the dam is removed, the lake shown in this picture will drain and the creek will be restored to its natural flow. In the background, the fence surrounds the Shaw and Fisher Lumber Company on the grounds of what is now Grove City College's athletic field.

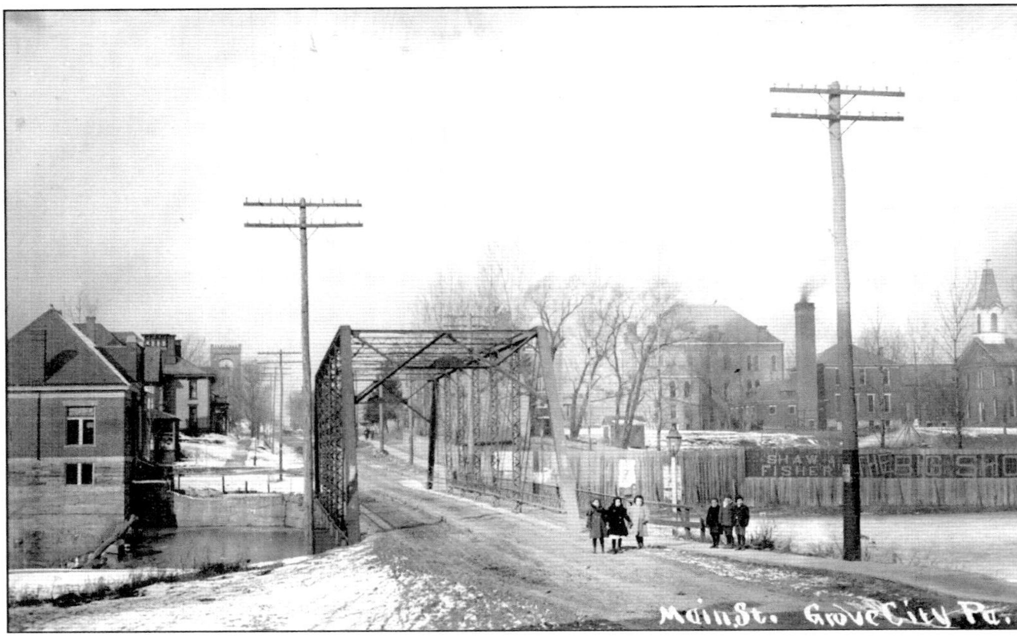

In the days before environmental regulations, the Cooper-Bessemer plant dumped used oil and turpentine into Wolf Creek. Prankster and Grove City College student John Calderwood wondered if this volatile smelly mixture would burn. The resulting blaze was hot enough to damage the Main Street Bridge spanning the creek. That is not exactly what was intended by the chamber of commerce's slogan: "Grove City–Where Industry and Education Unite."

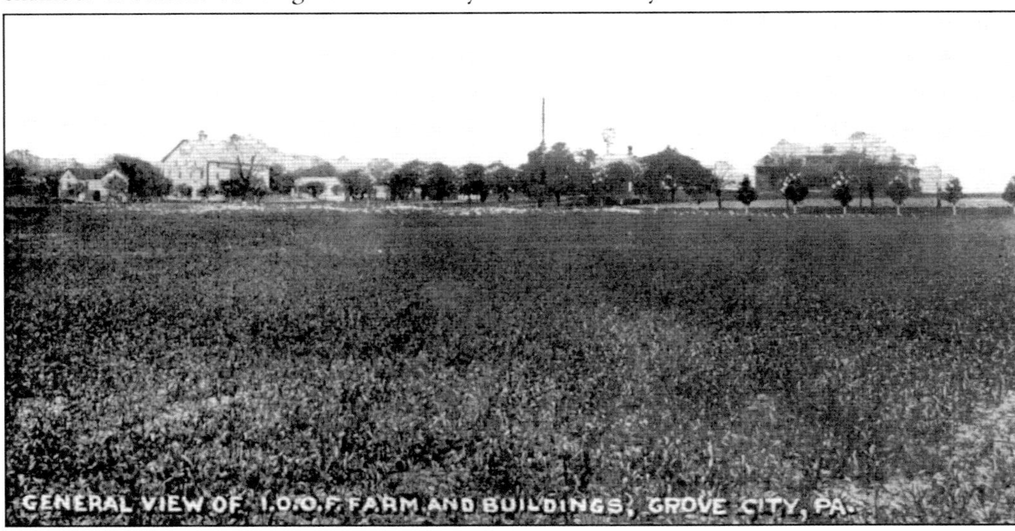

In this photograph of the Independent Order of Odd Fellows (IOOF) grounds, the photographer is standing along Madison Avenue at what was once the edge of town and near what is now the Grove City College student parking lots, affectionately referred to as "Siberia." Shown across Pinchalong Road are the caretaker's house, the barn, and the rear of the asylum. These buildings have since been razed to accommodate the modern treatment facilities of Orchard Manor and Fellowship Manor. Hints of these earlier structures remain in the fragments of foundations and the position of trees and shrubs that once surrounded them.

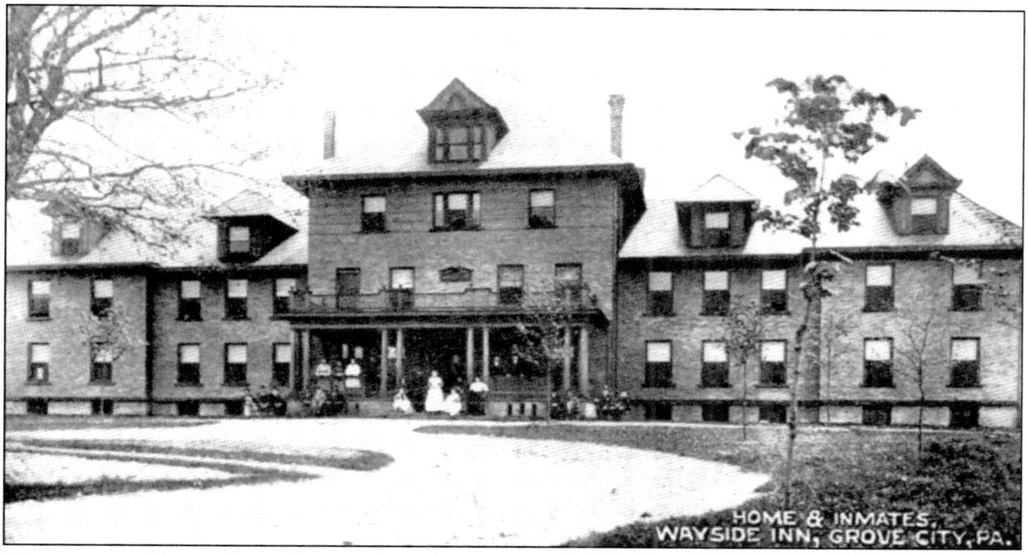

The motto of the Independent Order of Odd Fellows, "To visit the sick, relieve the distressed, bury the dead, and educate the orphan," in practice meant to initiate the establishment of homes for the aged, indigents, widows, and orphans. The motto continues, "The strong support the weak, the well nurse the sick, the learned instruct the unlearned and the rich help the poor." Members built this new home *c.* 1902 at the top of the hill overlooking town.

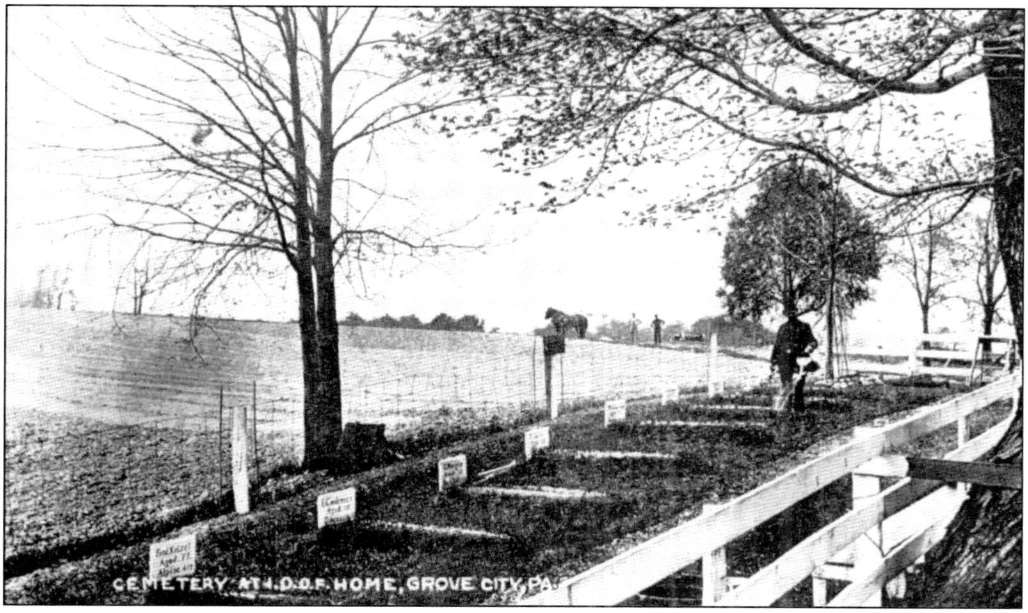

Burying the dead was an important function of the IOOF, as it was known, especially for those with no family members to handle the arrangements. The IOOF once provided all the funeral and memorial services that are now usually provided by a funeral director or undertaker. This quiet cemetery at the top of a hill provided a final resting place for "inmates," as residents and patients of the Wayside Inn were once called. The man in the cemetery appears to be holding a watering can. Farmers stand behind a draft horse on the horizon.

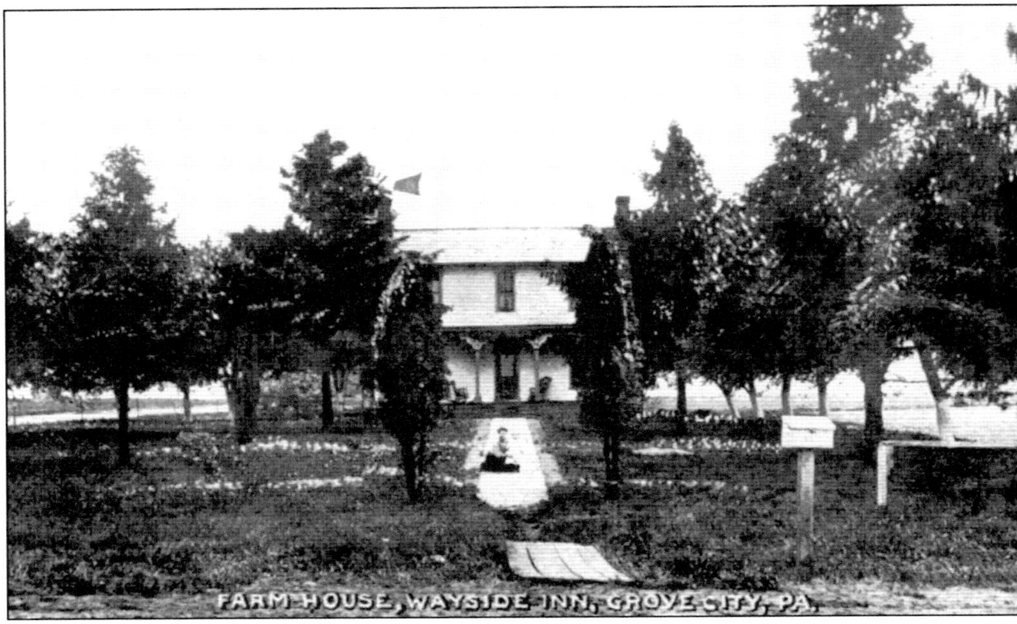

The IOOF. was a self-sufficient organization that produced its own food for patients and residents of the Wayside Inn at the turn of the 19th century. The caretaker's house was located on Pinchalong Road. The IOOF grounds spread between East Main Street and Pinchalong Road near Madison Avenue. Around the present site of the Orchard Manor nursing home, the organization's current facility, some of the foundations of the buildings seen in these cards are still visible.

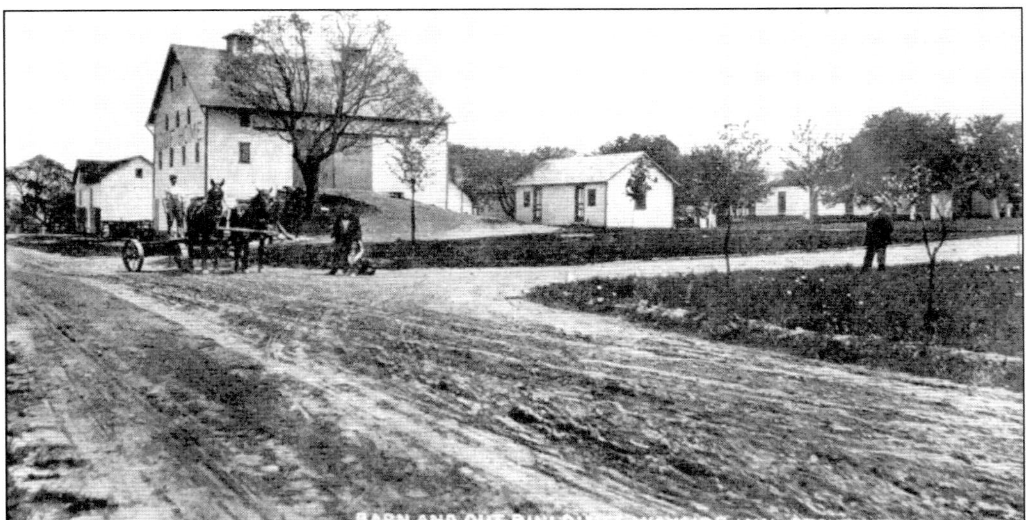

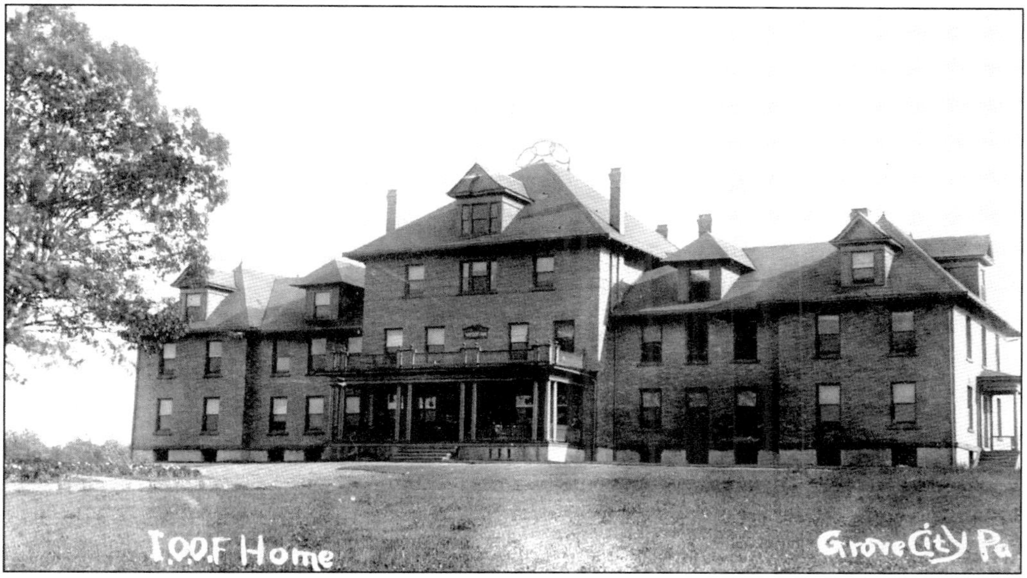

The three-ring logo of the IOOF visible on the top of the building represents the joining of friendship, love, and truth. However, to mischievous local residents, it looked like a pretzel and some referred to the stately structure with the Odd Fellow's logo on top as the pretzel factory. "When I first came to Grove City, John told me that was a pretzel factory, and I believed him," said Marjorie Hummel.

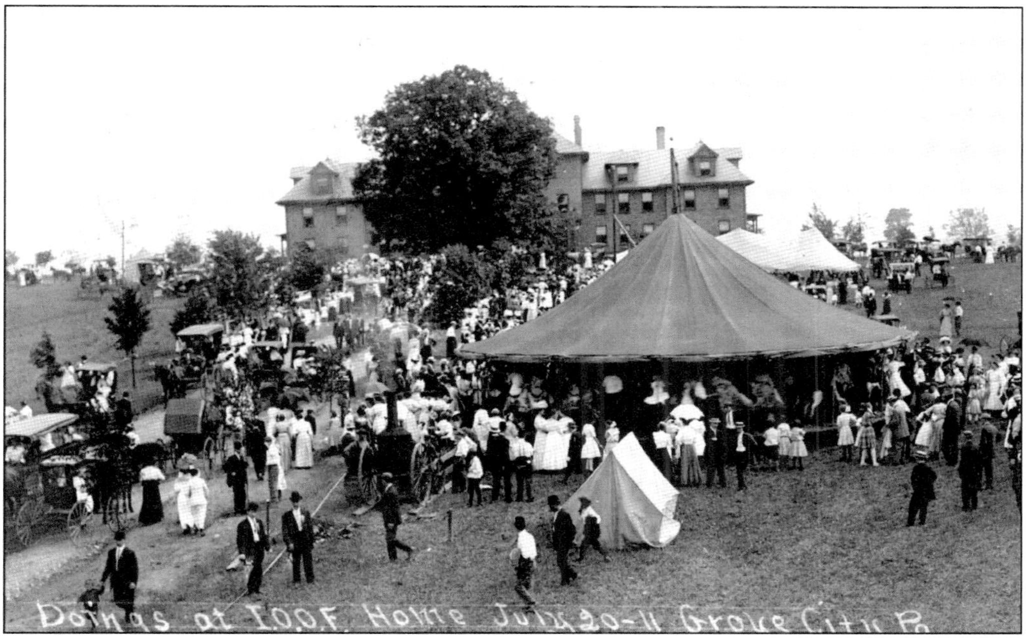

The building shown here was sometimes referred to as "the IOOF Home" and sometimes the Wayside Inn. The organization held a carnival in the summer that was likely used as a charity fund-raising event. Notice the steam engine powering the carousel set-up on the home's front lawn. The driveway leading to the home is the same road that leads to the Orchard Manor and Fellowship Manor facilities today.

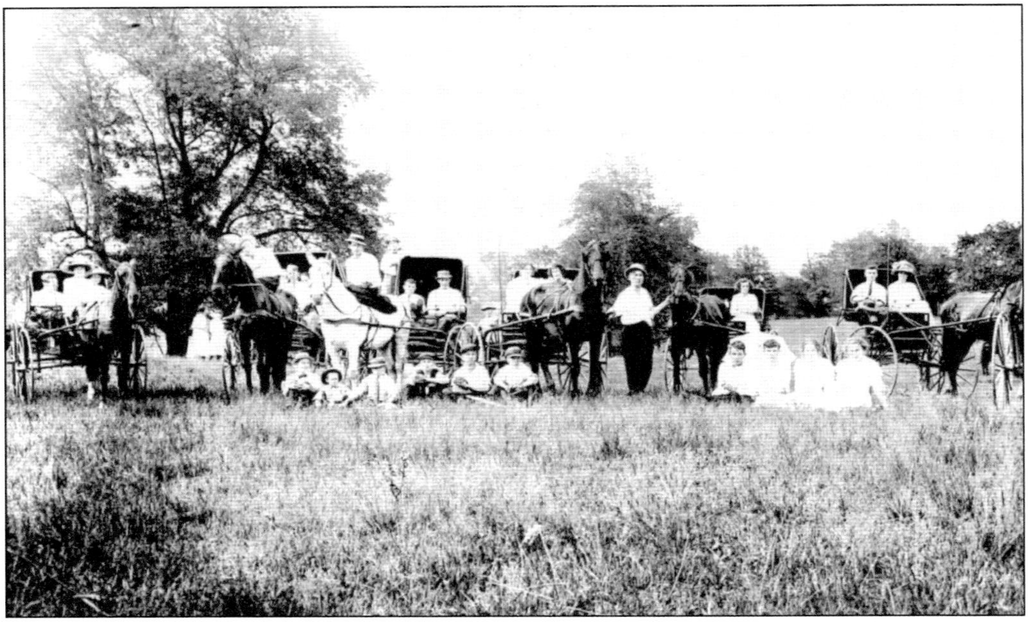

Horse and buggy was the main form of transportation in 1908. In the winter, if there was good snow, sleighing was also an option. Because of the age of the drivers in this picture, it is likely this was an outing of Grove City College students. Revelers at the IOOF fair could have walked or arrived by buggy. There was also a special train which brought fair goers to the fun.

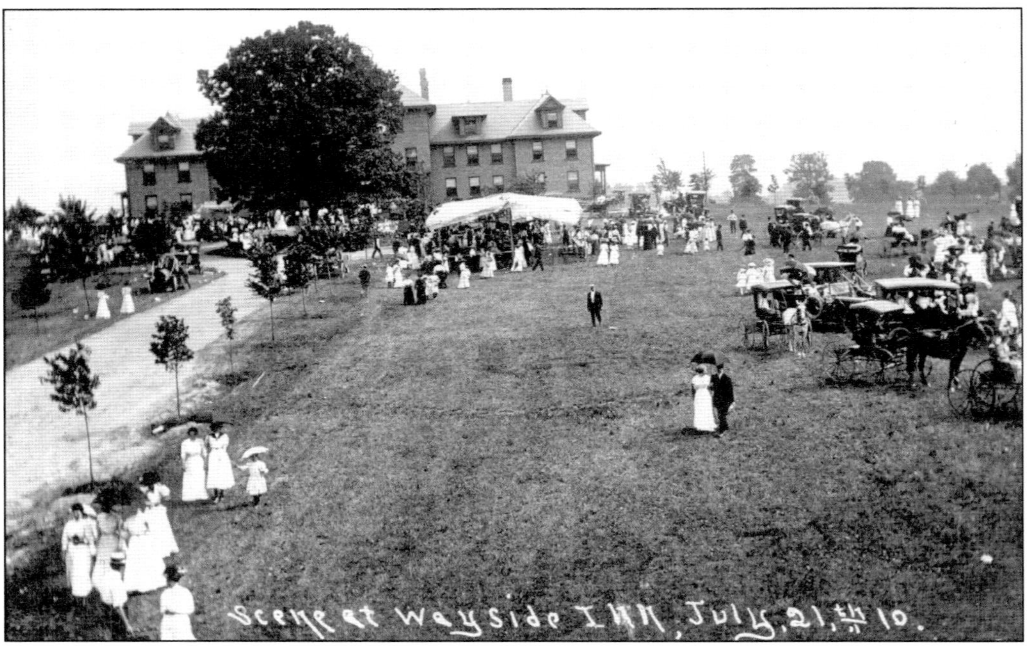

Many townspeople walked the mile to the IOOF fair or arrived by horse and buggy. Train service was also available using the tracks servicing the nearby Pinchalong Mine. The trains stopped near Madison Avenue and made it possible for visitors from other towns to enjoy "the doings" at the Odd Fellows home.

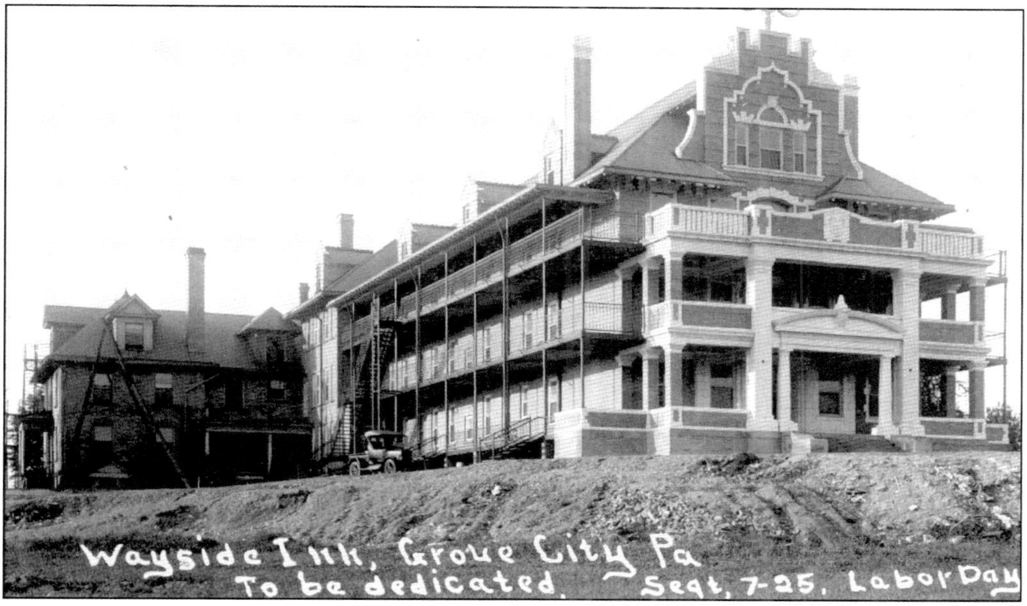

By 1925, the Odd Fellows home expanded again. This handsome new edifice was attached to the front of the existing IOOF building and remained in service for about 50 years until the 1970s. By the end of the 20th century, standards for patient care had changed, favoring facilities that did not require stairs, ramps, or elevators. All of the structures in this photograph were razed, and a nursing-home facility, Orchard Manor, was erected to further the aims of the Independent Order of Odd Fellows.

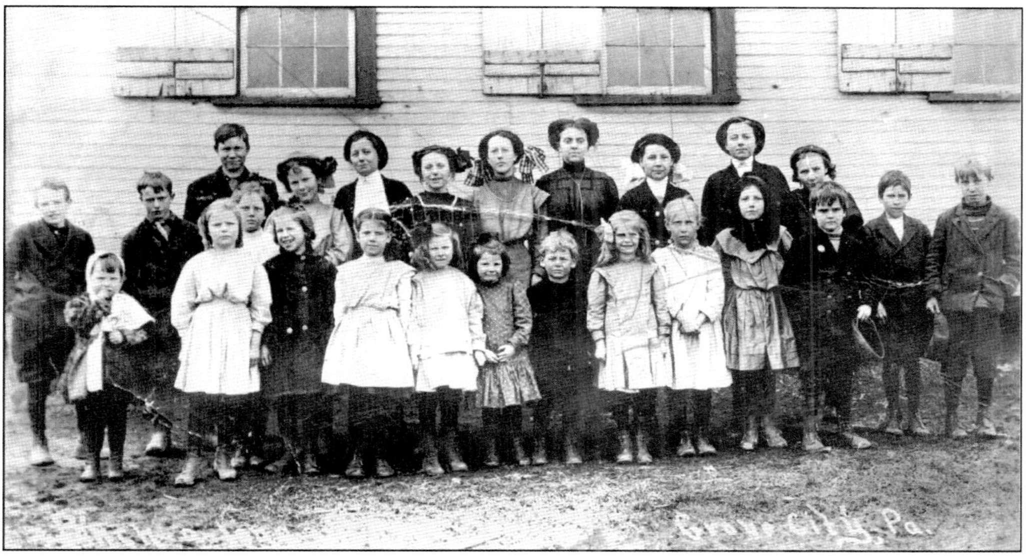

Pinchalong School served the children of miners near Pinchalong Mine. The name Pinchalong comes from miners asking for advances and the boss telling them to "pinch along" until payday. "Pinch," as it was also known, was only a half-mile east of Madison Avenue on Pinchalong Road. What is striking about this school picture of 25 students is that only 7 were boys, and only one boy appears to be over the age of 10. Every boy able to dig was underground bringing coal up out of the mine.

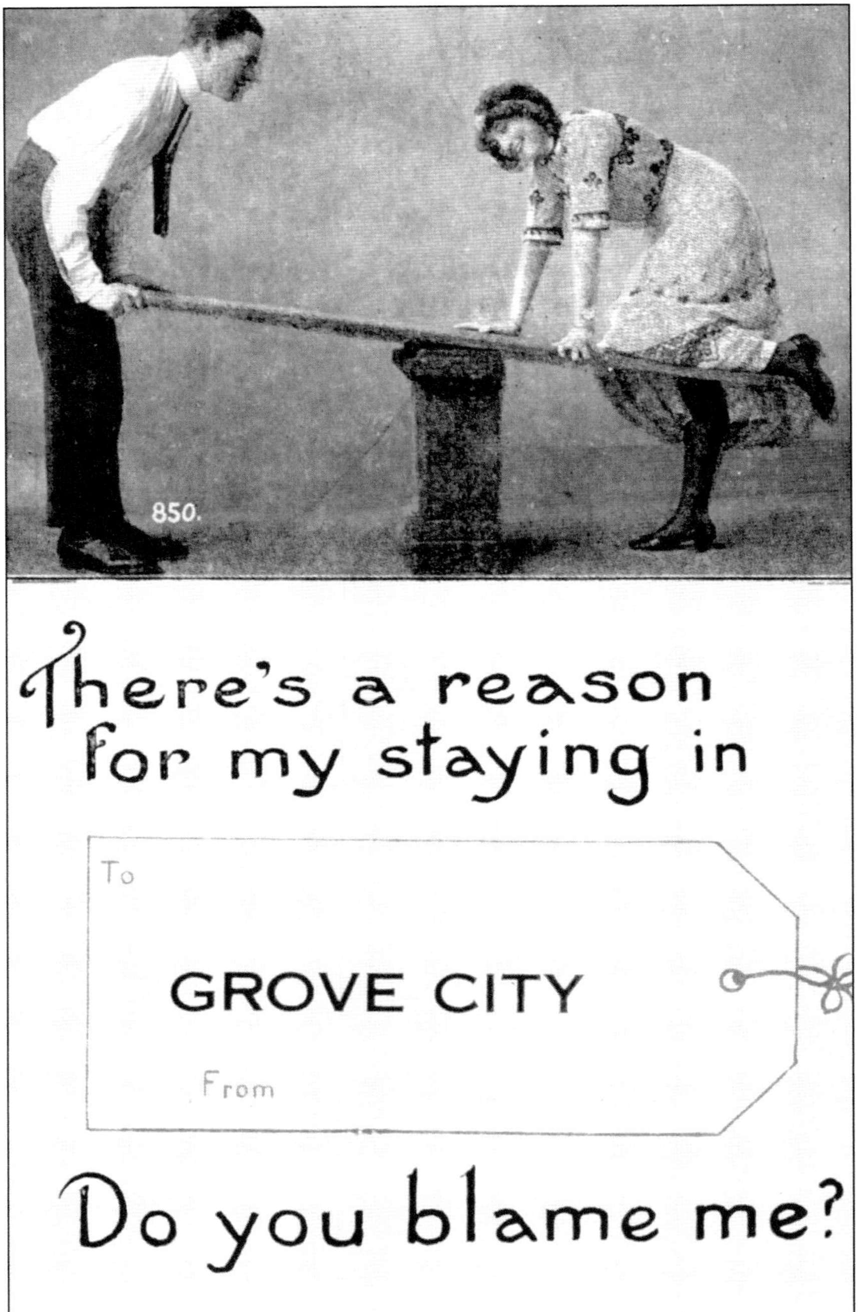

Long before the popularity of blue jeans and T-shirts, a respectable young man wore dress pants, polished shoes, and a shirt with a tie when accompanying a young woman on a date. In contrast, respectable young women's fashion was changing rapidly at this time. They no longer wore floor-length skirts and corsets by the 1920s. It was probably a little risqué for a woman to have short sleeves with her arms bared, as in the novelty postcard above, and to allow her dress to reveal her ankles.

Five

The Good Old Days

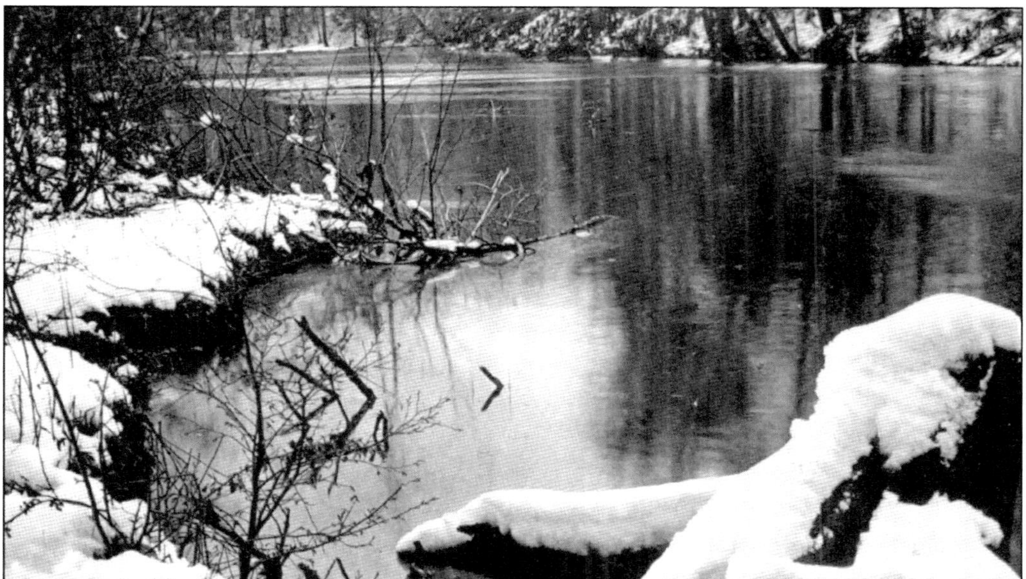

Scene on Wolf Creek, May 1st, 1908, Grove City, Pa.

Arguably, the years between 1907 and 1909 were the good old days in Grove City's history. People and investment capital poured into the town, churches were built, businesses thrived, and Grove City College was successful and expanding. The town grew quickly as homes and industries were built at a rapid pace. Oblivious to the toils of men, Mother Nature dumped a late-season snowstorm on the town on May 1, 1908. At least two postcard photographers recorded this unusual event for posterity.

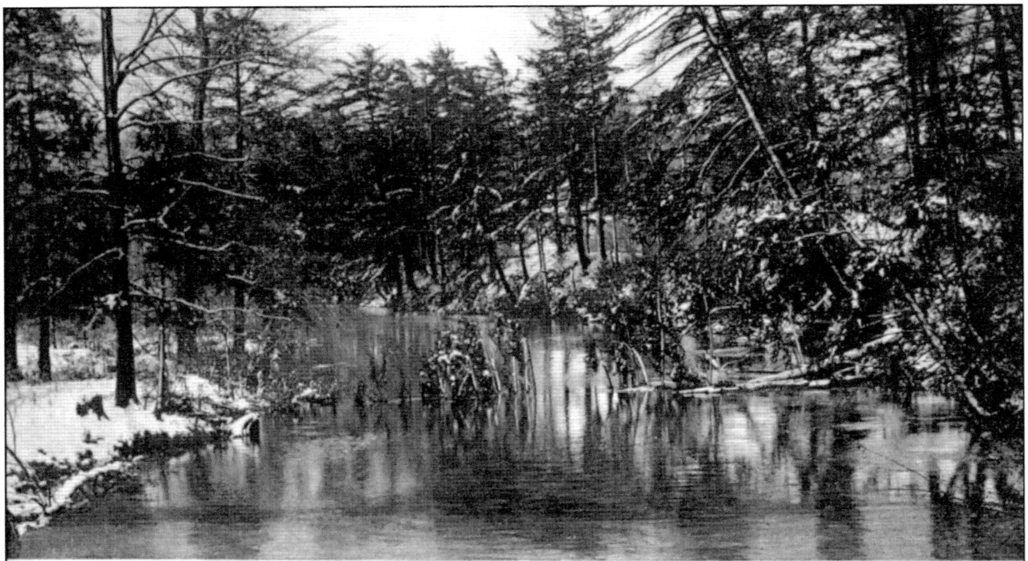

Scene on Wolf Creek, May 1st, 1908. Grove City, Pa.

This image was probably taken from the aptly named Pine Street Bridge, looking downstream. Through the trees across Wolf Creek in the background was the Grove City College athletic field. The slow-moving waters in this photograph will be gone forever with the impending removal of the Lower Dam. Those in favor of removing the Lower Dam say Wolf Creek can once again support native trout. Those opposed say the dams provide flood control by slowing the creek's flow as it moves through town.

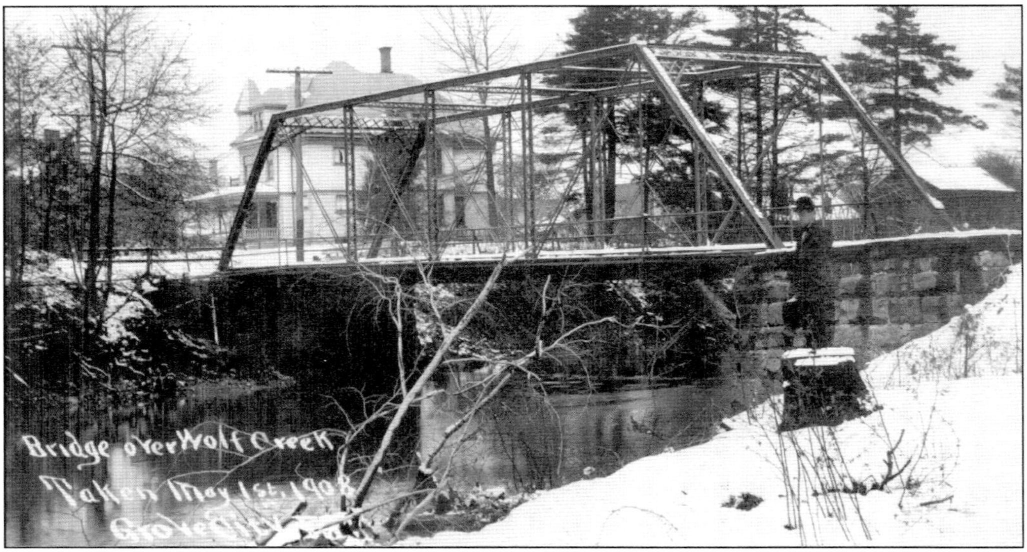

The house visible through the Pine Street Bridge girders was erected where the Grove City post office now stands. By the early 1930s, a new bridge with a lower profile spanned the creek, making it possible to move the house to a new location across and just at the end of the bridge near where the photographer of this shot was standing. The home still stands across the street from the Penn Grove Hotel. Notice the man in a bowler hat standing on a manhole cover regarding the creek and the unusual May snowfall.

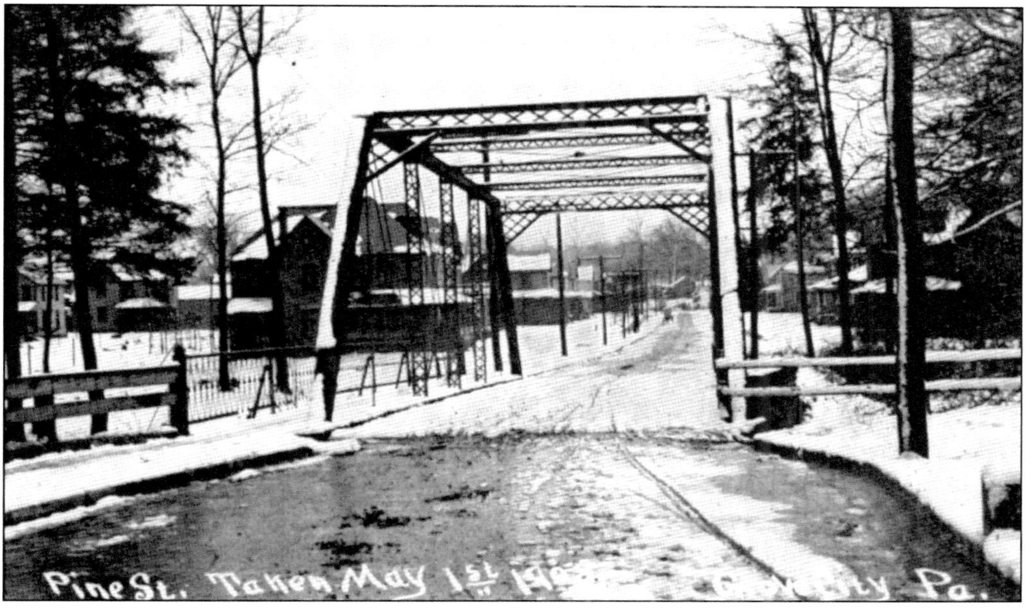

To the left where the trees stand in this photograph is the present site of the Penn Grove Hotel. Before the Penn Grove Hotel was erected, the site was a park with a swimming pool, picnic tables, and a place to launch boats. Directly across the street, to the right in this photograph, is the current site of the house that moved across the creek.

GROVE CITY is not only the most beautiful, but one of the most prosperous towns in the Keystone State. Fifty new dwellings were built here last summer and more than $180,000.00 will be expended this year in improvements. Among the new buildings in course of construction are the United Presbyterian Church costing $40,000.00, Pennsylvania State Armory, $20,000.00, Methodist Episcopal Church, $30,000.00, Montgomery Broom Manufacturing Co.'s Plant, $15,000.00, Hercules Novelty Works, $15,000.00, Filer's Livery Barn, $7,000.00, Craig's Business Block, $7,000.00, and more than $50,000.00 will be expended in dwellings. Grove City has doubled in population in the past five years; our factories are all running full force, and from present outlook the year 1908 will be the most prosperous of its history.

As with any small town, Grove City was not exempt from local rivalries. In the case of this card boasting of the town's many recent accomplishments, curiously absent is any mention of Grove City College, which was also growing and expanding. Nevertheless, the claims are genuine; the town was prospering.

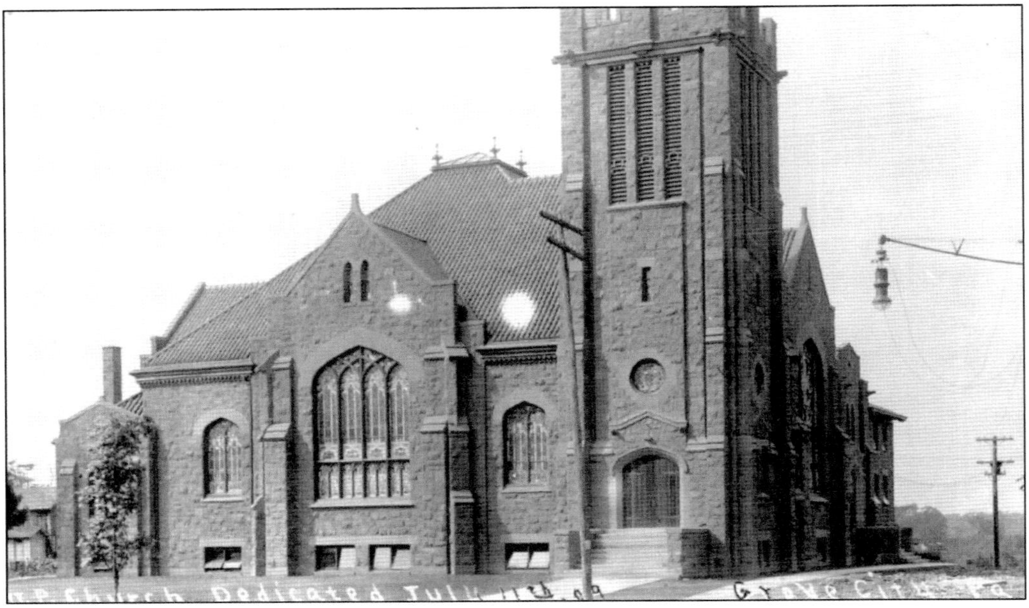

The construction of East Main United Presbyterian Church began in 1908, and the building was dedicated in 1909. Currently with a congregation of around 800 members (in a town of 8,000 people), the East Main congregation is one of the largest churches in town. As the needs of the congregation have increased and expanded, so has the East Main church building, which now extends from East Main Street to Poplar Street in the rear.

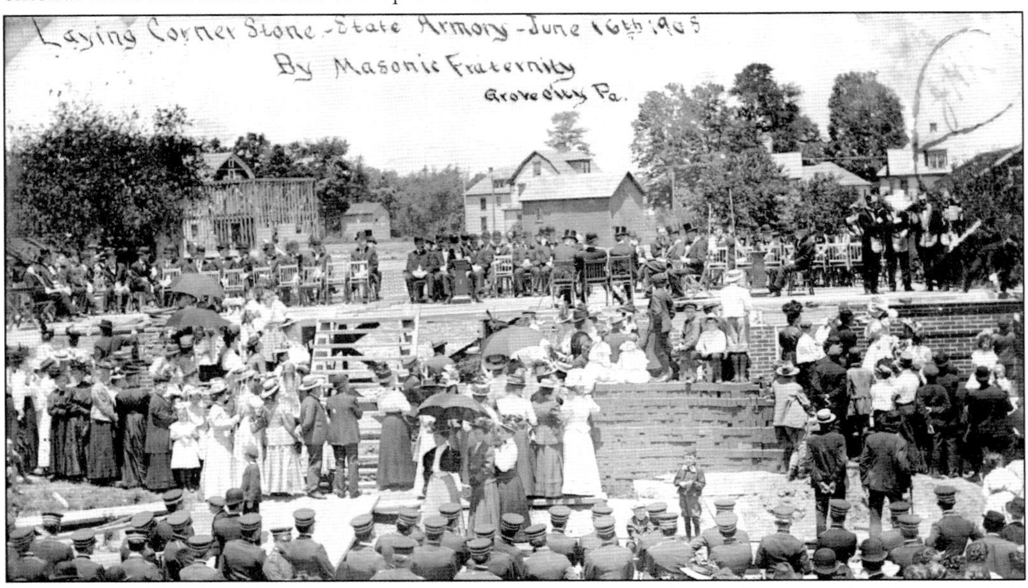

The cornerstone of Grove City's second Pennsylvania National Guard Armory building was laid on June 16, 1908. Now owned privately, the structure stands on Erie Street. Houses in the background are along Edgewood Avenue, which was then called Second Street. To the extreme right of the photograph is a man bending down who appears to be actually laying the building's corner stone. Ladies carried umbrellas to protect themselves from the sun. Most of the gentlemen on the stage are wearing black top hats for the occasion.

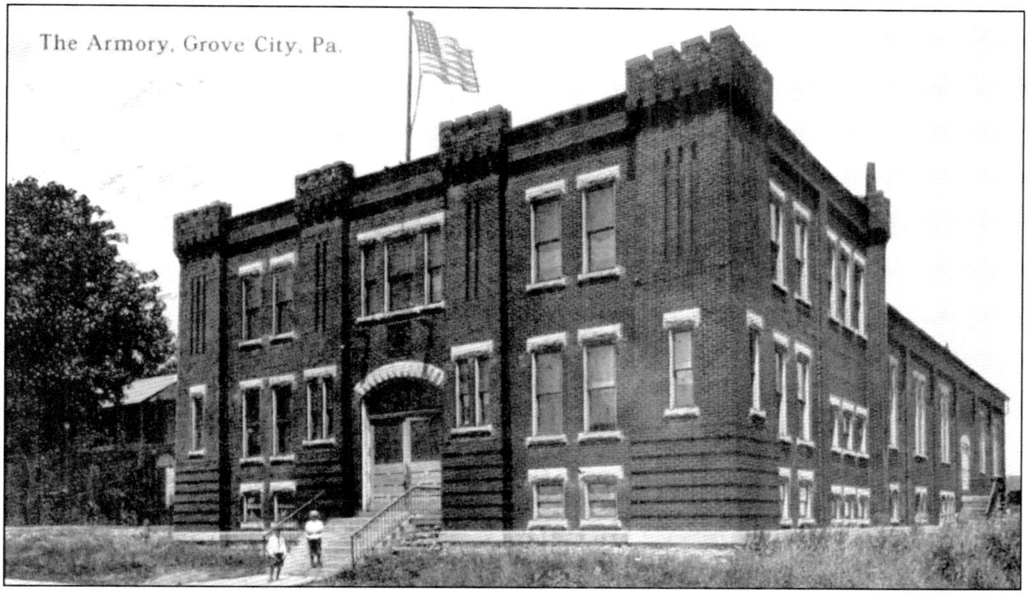

The first armory building in Grove City was on Broad Street and burned *c.* 1900. This second armory building was home to the Pennsylvania National Guard for nearly 70 years until a new facility was constructed in the early 1980s at the edge of town. That time period included both World Wars and the Korean and Vietnam wars. The building was later used as a youth recreation center and as an incubator for Grove City's popular YMCA.

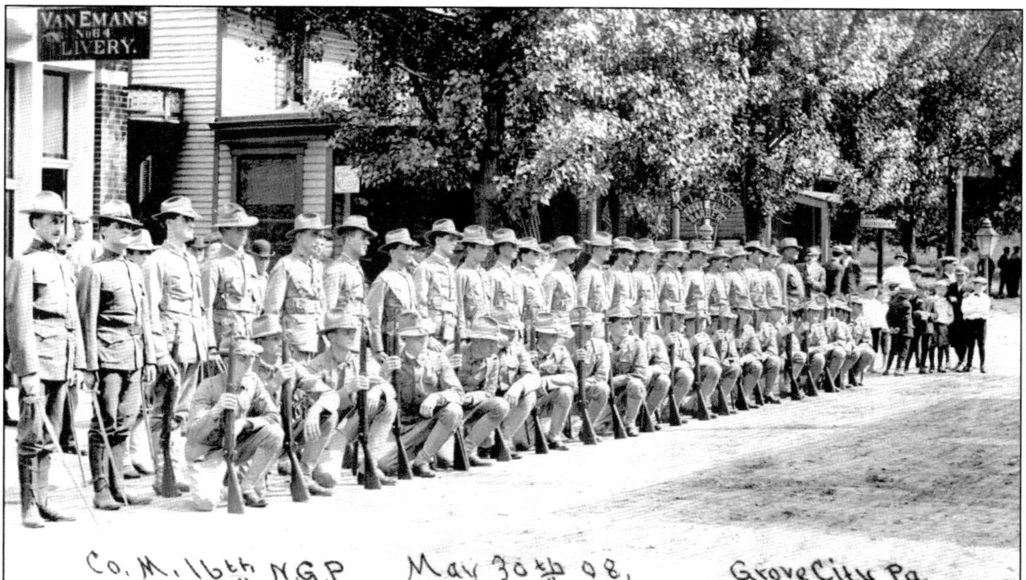

At the beginning of May 1908, there was a heavy snowfall. By the end of May, Company M, 16th Regiment of the Pennsylvania National Guard, drilled on Broad Street. This was a relatively peaceful time in American history; the Spanish American War was 10 years in the past and World War I still a decade away. Notice Van Eman's Livery stable in the background. Cars were not yet widely available; however, if one wanted to travel out of town and did not own a horse and buggy, they could be hired at the nearest livery stable.

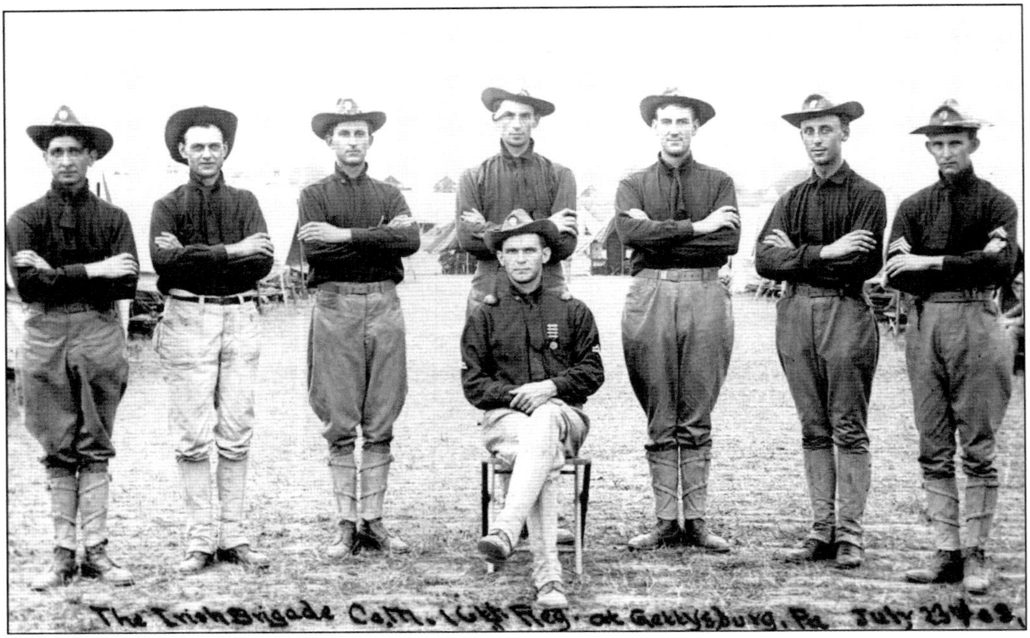

By July 1908, the soldiers of Company M, 16th Regiment, were participating at an encampment in Gettysburg, Pennsylvania. Notice the tents in the background. At one time, five Faull brothers were in the same company, and during World War I, four Drennen brothers were in the same company. The new armory building, under construction while the soldiers were in Gettysburg, cost $19,875.73. It was completed in the fall of 1908, and the governor of Pennsylvania attended the dedication ceremony. The state gave the 92-year-old structure to the borough of Grove City *c.* 2000, which in turn sold the historic building to a private owner.

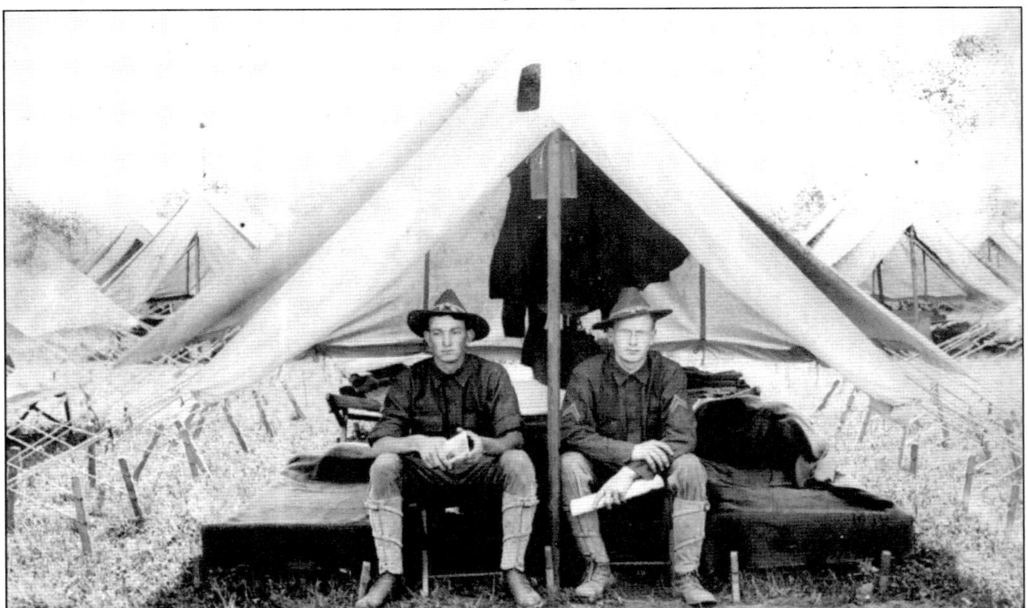

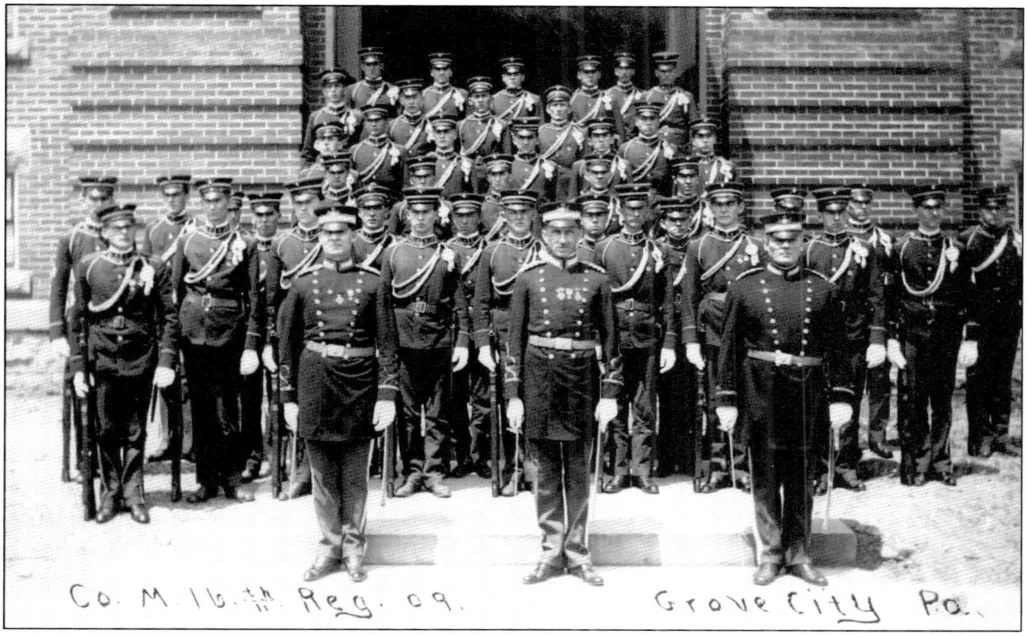

Members of Company M, 16th Regiment, pose in full dress uniform in front of the new armory building on Erie Street. The first National Guard company was organized in 1884 in Grove City by Brig. Gen. Normal J. Maxwell, a veteran of the Civil War. In the late 1890s, members of the National Guard stationed in Grove City were called to Pittsburgh to suppress rioting steel workers during the Homestead steel mill strikes.

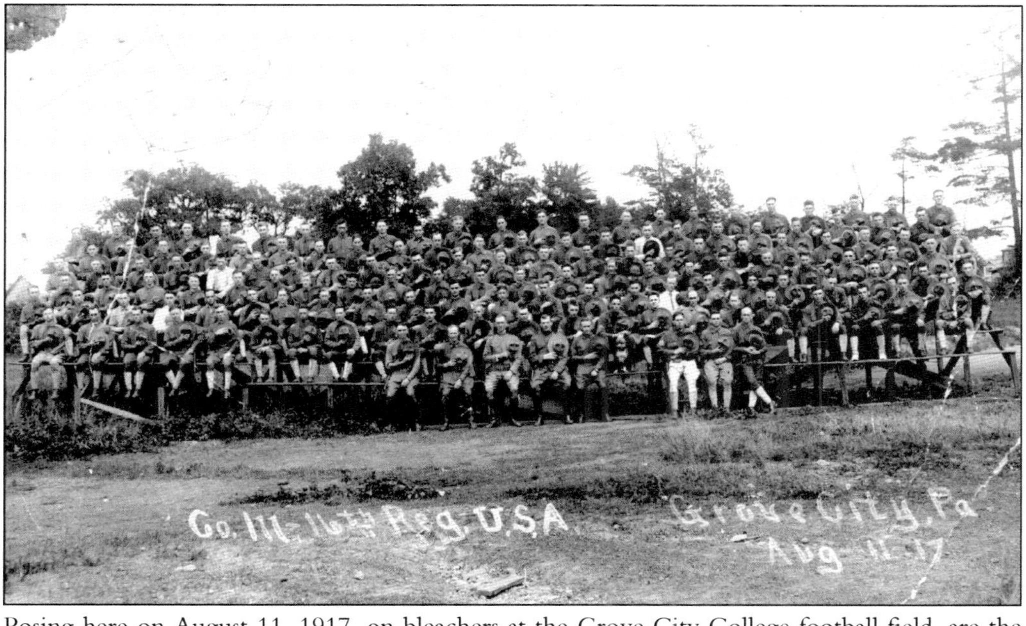

Posing here on August 11, 1917, on bleachers at the Grove City College football field, are the members of Company M, 16th Regiment. Company M saw action in the battle for Argonne Forest in France during World War I a year later. Notice the construction of the bleachers; the first step is about waist high.

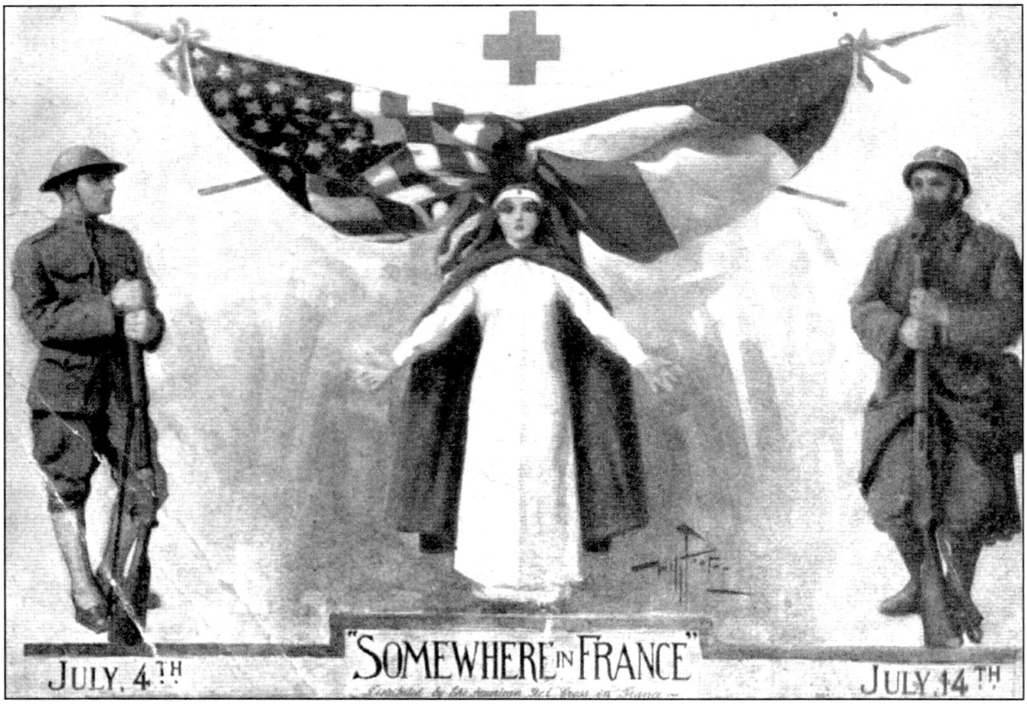

President Wilson called Company M to national service in 1916 to fight Poncho Villa during the Mexican War and again in 1917 to blunt the ambitions of Kaiser Wilhelm II during World War I. Most of Grove City was probably at the station to see the servicemen off after a parade through town. School children waited along the parade route waving flags. During both wars, Company M was under the command of Gen. John "Blackjack" Pershing.

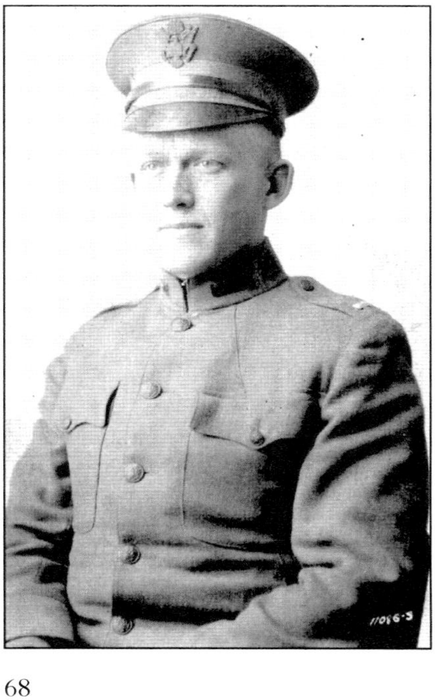

Folks sometimes sent photographs as postcards. This example is of James A. Welker, Company No. 9, ROTC Camp Lee, Virginia, and was taken March 1918. Ever since photography became widely available, soldiers have had their portraits made to send to loved ones back home. Communication during World War I between those serving in the armed forces and family and friends back home was only by letter or postcard.

In 1908, the United Methodist congregation in Grove City built a new church at the corner of Pine and Broad Streets in Grove City. The church in this picture was built after the congregation moved downtown from an earlier location near the intersection of North Broad Street and Cranberry Road, at the edge of town. The Methodist cemetery is located at the Cranberry and North Broad intersection.

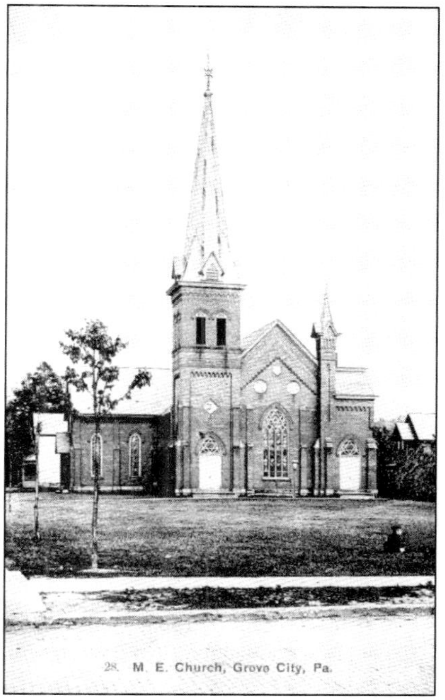

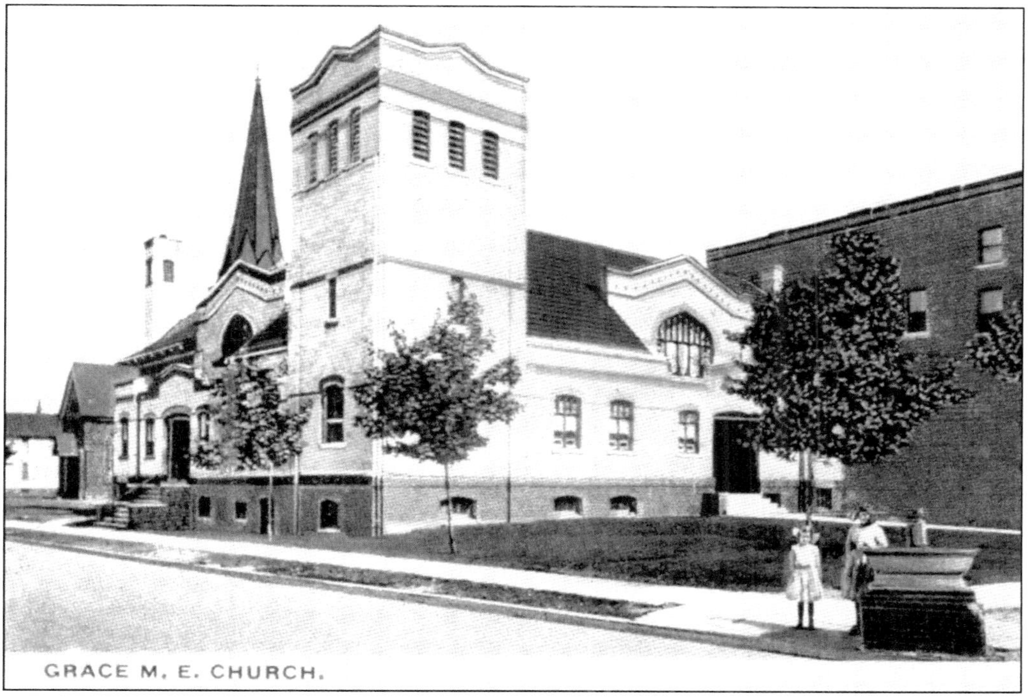

After the construction of the new Grace Methodist Episcopal Church was completed, the spire of the older church could be seen in the background. When the church was dedicated, I. C. Pershing—the nephew of the World War I hero and commander of the American Expeditionary Force in France Gen. John J. Pershing—gave the dedication address. The largest crowd the church ever had was 2,240 people when evangelist Billy Sunday preached in 1910.

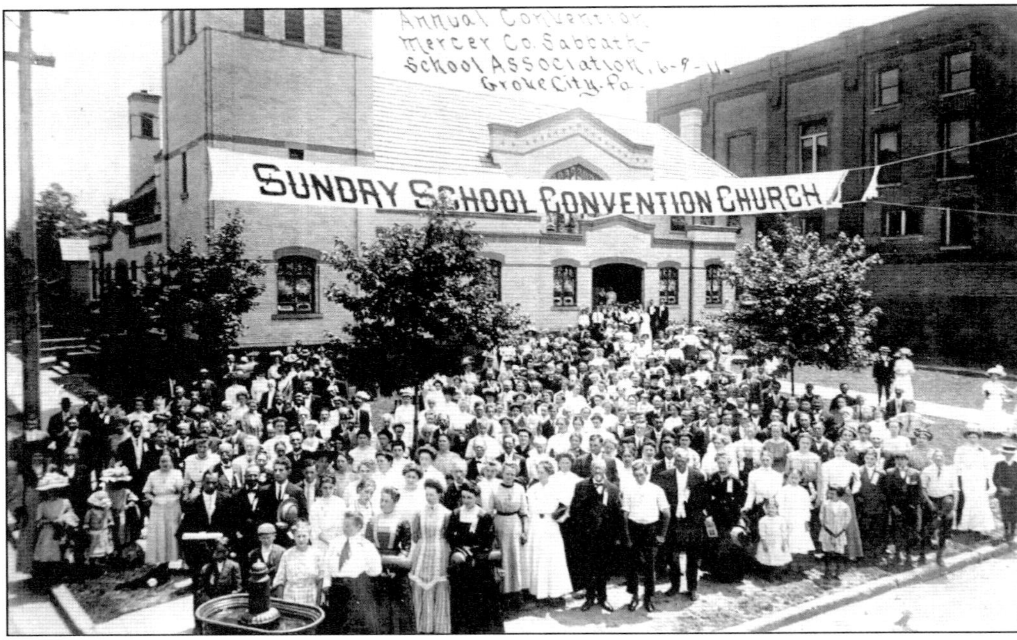

Probably taken from the roof of a building across Broad Street, this photograph is from June 1911, and the old Methodist Church was already razed. The image shows participants of the Mercer County Sabbath School Association's annual convention. Also shown in this picture is the side of the IOOF building on Broad Street and the watering trough and drinking fountain at the intersections of Pine and Broad Streets.

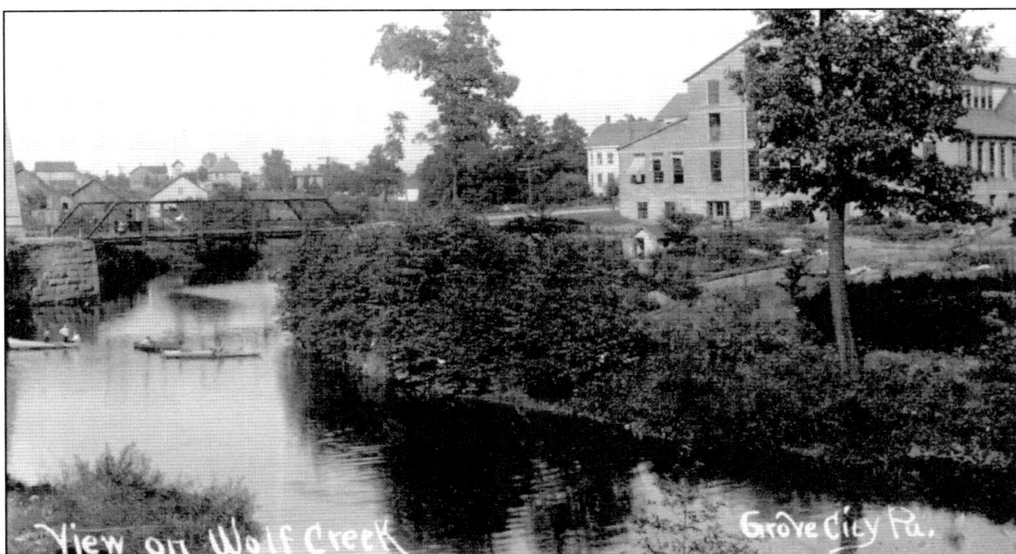

A few of the early buildings of the Bessemer Gas Engine Works—which was started by Edwin J. Fithian, who later ran for political office as a Prohibition candidate—can be seen to the right. On the bank in the picture upstream from the canoeists are barns where the state's demonstration creamery kept horses for milk deliveries. Wolf Creek, at this point in history, was used as a place to drain raw sewage and industrial waste products, such as oil and turpentine.

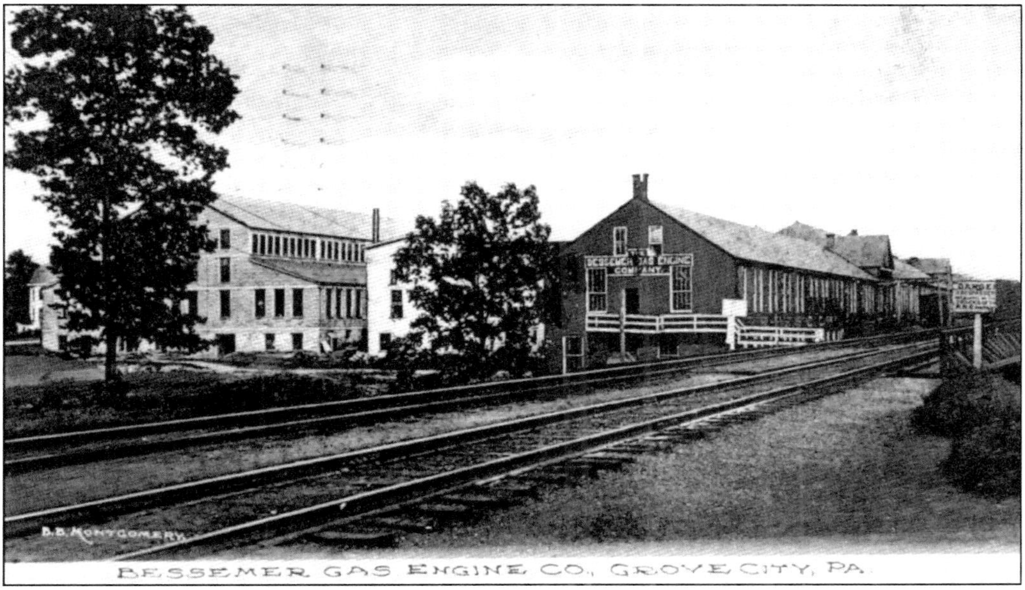

The railroad shown here is the Bessemer and Lake Erie line that ran to the port of Erie, where iron ore and coke were shipped to steel mills in Pittsburgh. Finished products were returned to Erie to be shipped through the St. Lawrence Seaway to the Atlantic.

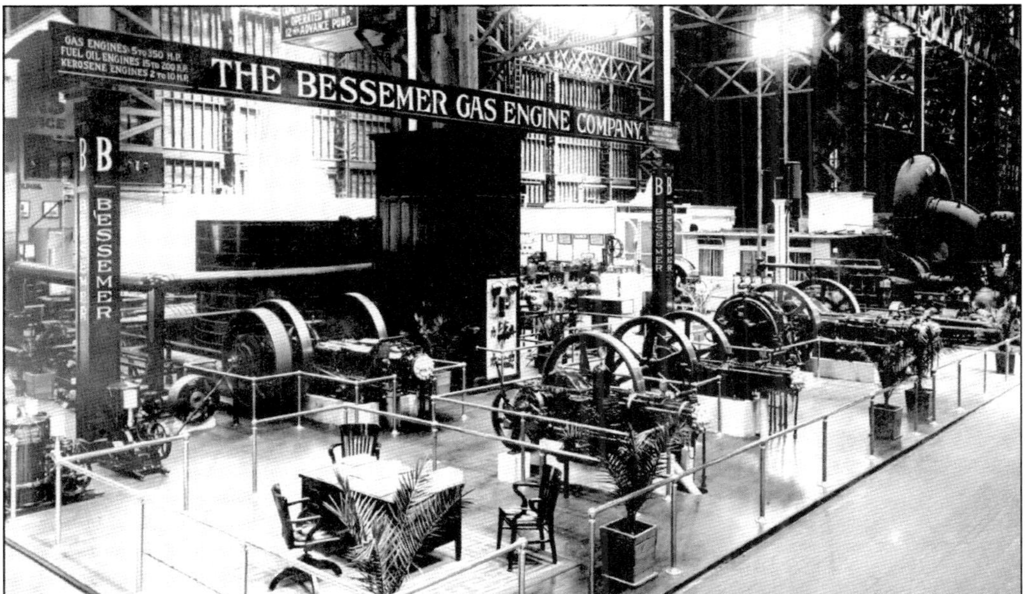

The Bessemer Gas Engine Company was awarded a gold medal at the Panama-Pacific International Exposition in 1910. Among its many applications of mechanical energy, the company made engines that were used to pump wells and to generate electricity. Grove City's water supply was pumped by a Bessemer engine from a well nearby. Another large engine produced electricity for the town. These working examples provided ready demonstrations of the power and reliability of the engines for customers visiting the plant.

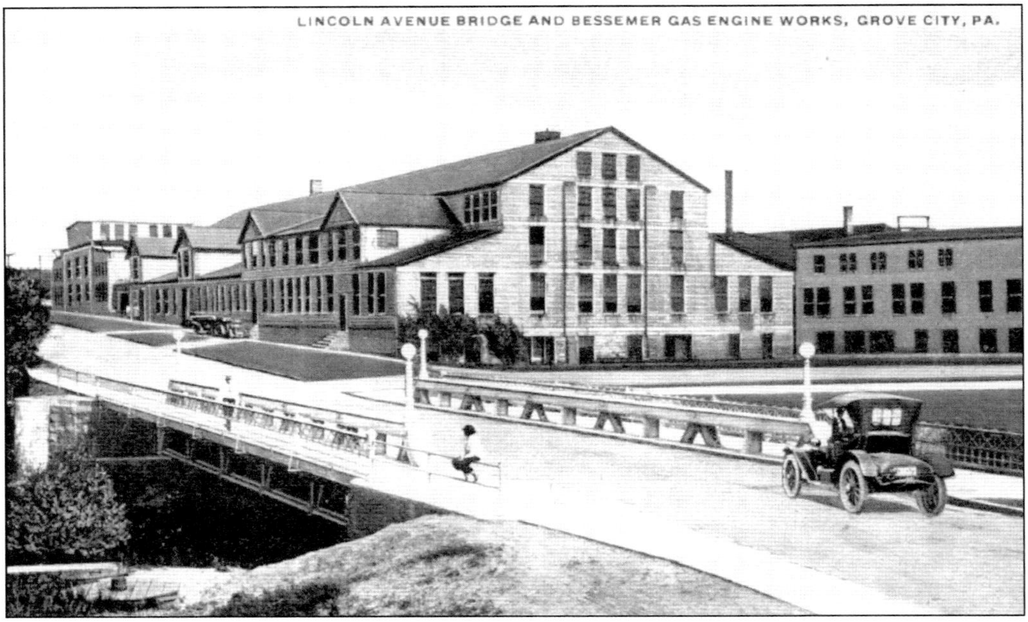

For nearly 100 years the company that began as the Bessemer Gas Engine Works and was later known as the Cooper-Bessemer plant was the largest employer in Grove City. Townspeople used to try to avoid getting caught in traffic when "the Bessemer let out." This *c.* 1915 picture shows the new bridge across Lincoln Avenue and the Bessemer's lower shop and office.

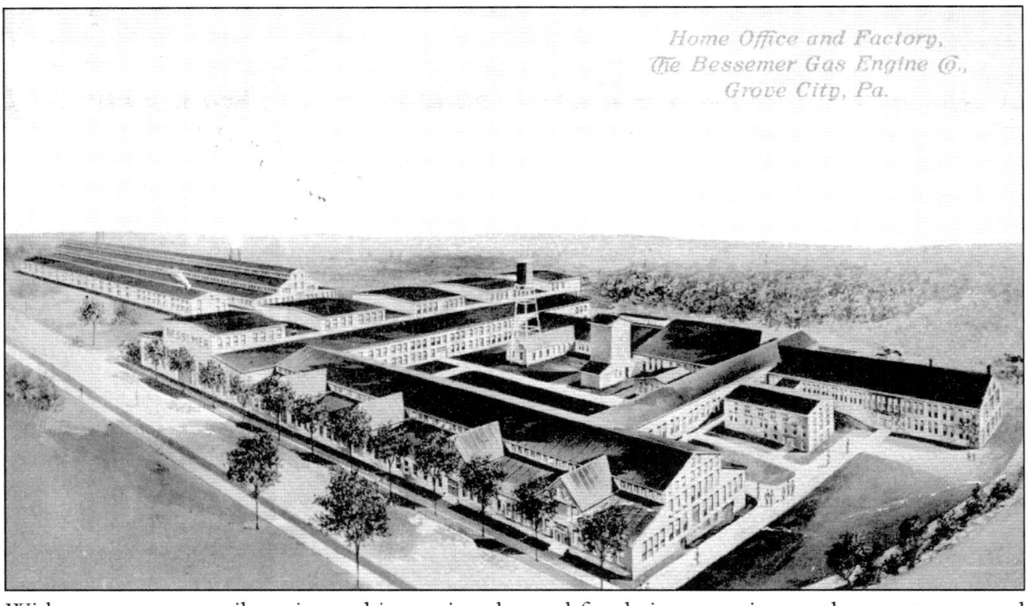

With easy access to rail service and increasing demand for their gas engines as the country moved toward an industrial economy, the Bessemer, as it was referred to by locals, expanded to cover more than 20 acres in the middle of town. So influential was the Bessemer that during one plant expansion, Monroe Street, which once met Lincoln Avenue, was simply closed and used as a building site. It was only decades later that the street was properly annulled by the borough council.

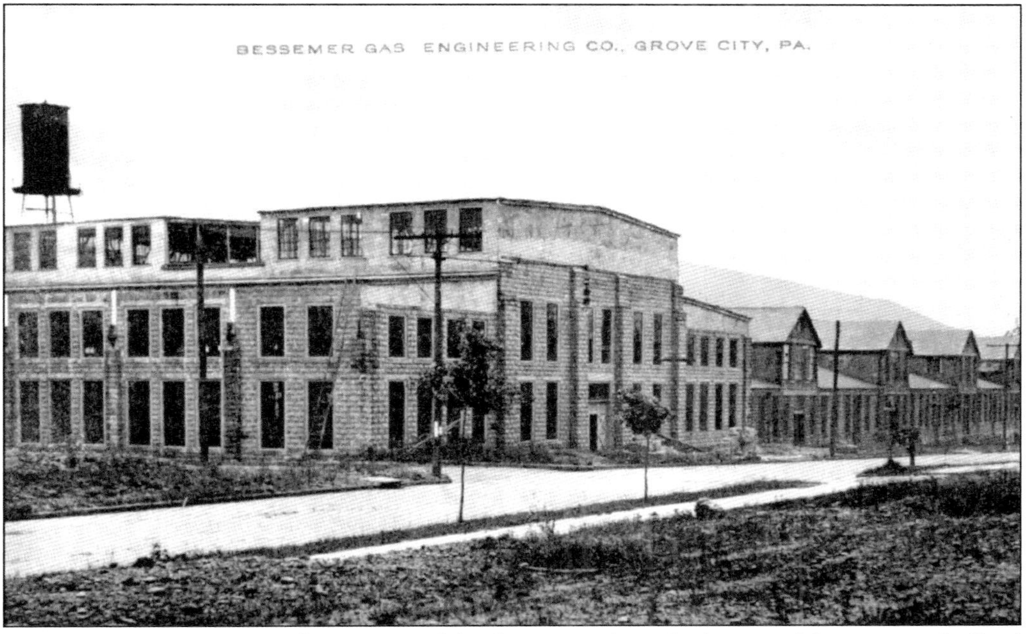

Known as "the Big Shop," this portion of the factory is where the largest of the company's diesel engines were manufactured. Fithian's influence followed workers home from the job. He was said to fire employees if he found out they drank alcohol at home. Bessemer engines were used on navy ships during World War II. Wendell August Forge could not get aluminum during the war, and the forge was turned it into a navy barracks. Seamen quartered there marched to the plant where they learned maintenance skills before being deployed.

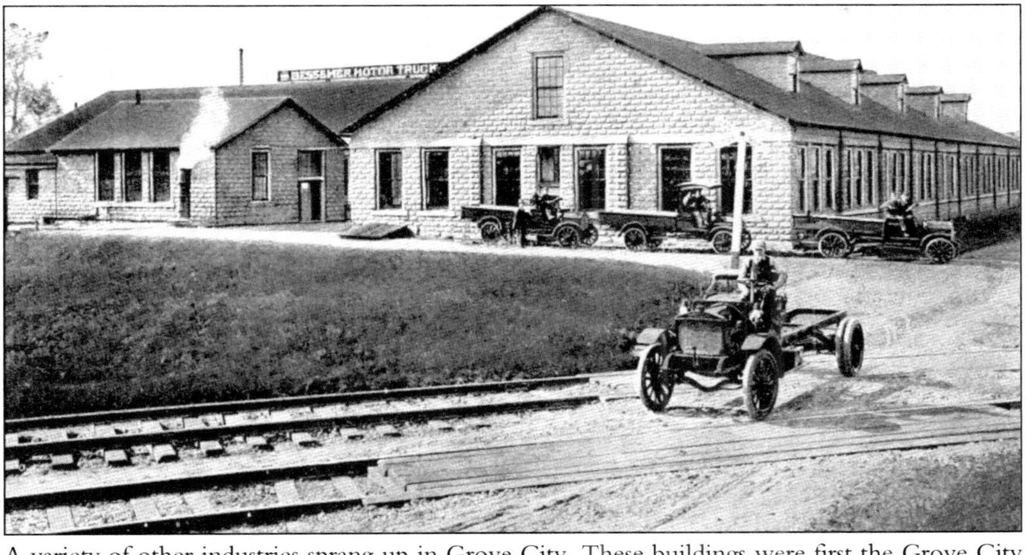

A variety of other industries sprang up in Grove City. These buildings were first the Grove City Novelty Works and later the location of the Bessemer Motor Truck Company. Motor vehicles were also manufactured by the McKay Carriage Company. When witnesses to Earl Sandt's airplane crash in 1913 say he was loaded into a truck when taken to the hospital, they probably were talking about one of these Bessemer trucks manufactured about a mile farther up Pine Street.

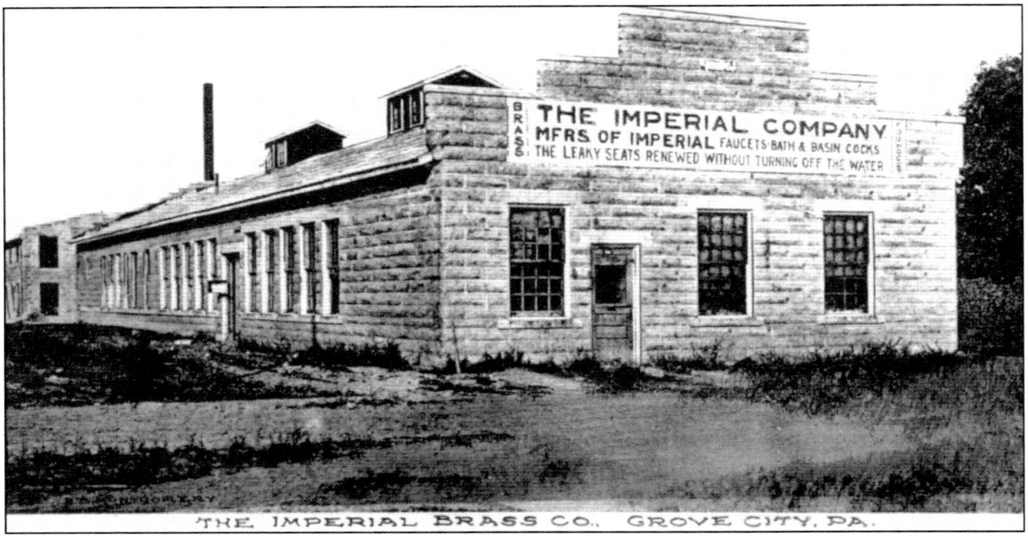

The Imperial Brass Company, later known as Grove City Brass and Bronze, was located at the intersection of Railroad and Second Streets. Railroad later became Erie Street and Second became Edgewood Avenue. The company manufactured sink and tub faucets. Their sign boasts, "The leaky seats renewed without turning off the water." Out of the picture to the right is the armory building.

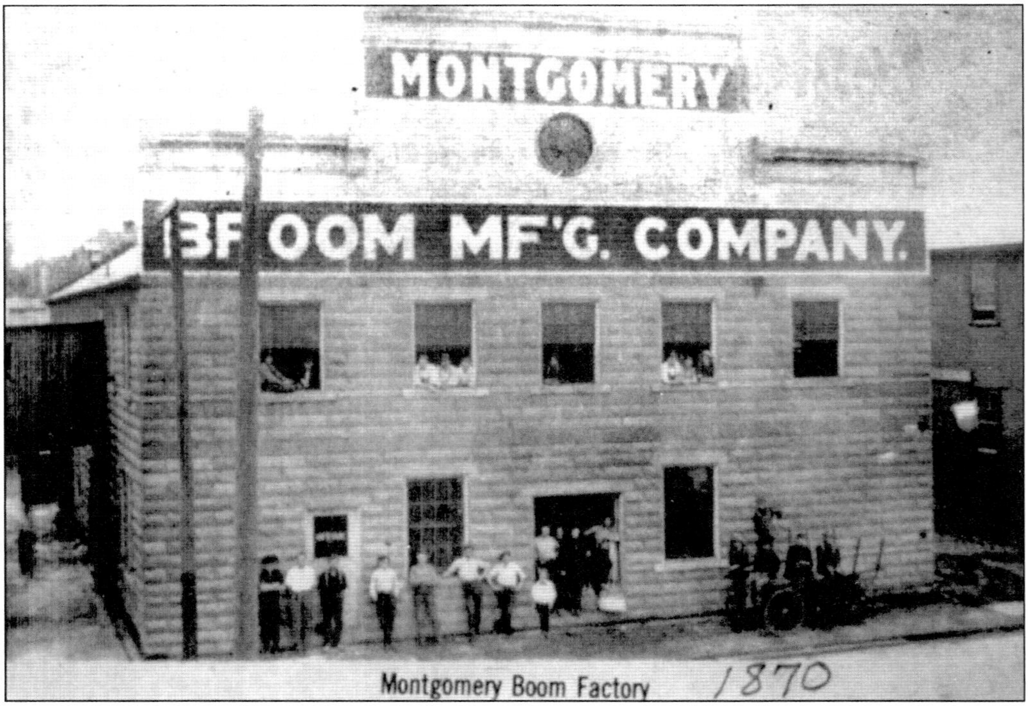

The Montgomery Broom Manufacturing Company was located on Blair Street along the railroad tracks where the VFW building is now. In later years, it was the storage for the Book Davis Lumber Company. On the other side of the alley from the old broom factory was one of the bigger and nicer bowling alleys in town.

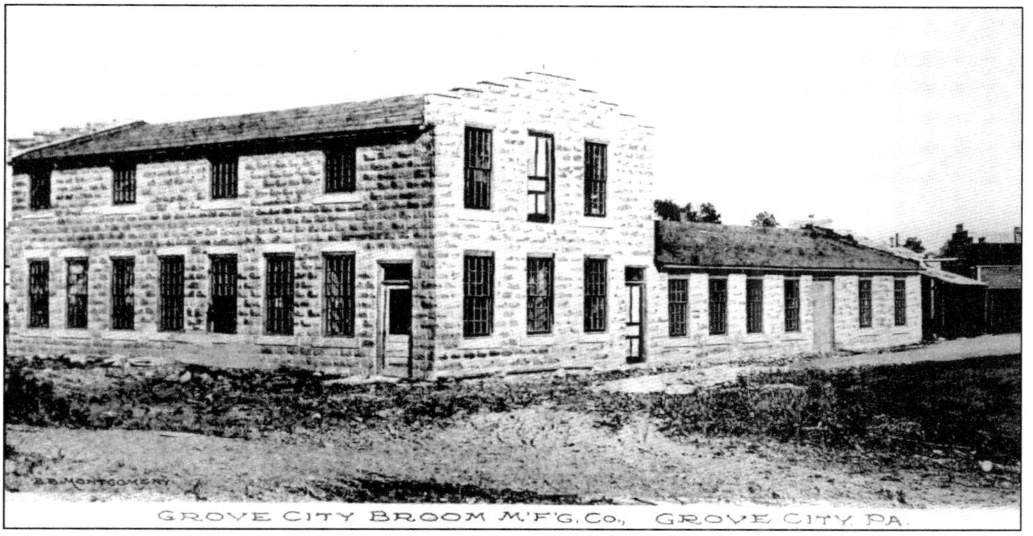

The Grove City Broom Manufacturing Company was behind the Brass and Bronze building on Edgewood Avenue. For a while, the small town of Grove City hosted two broom manufacturing businesses on opposite sides of the railroad tracks. W. E. Swart's eventually moved what had been the Montgomery Broom Factory to a small garage behind his house in Briscoe Springs, just north of Grove City.

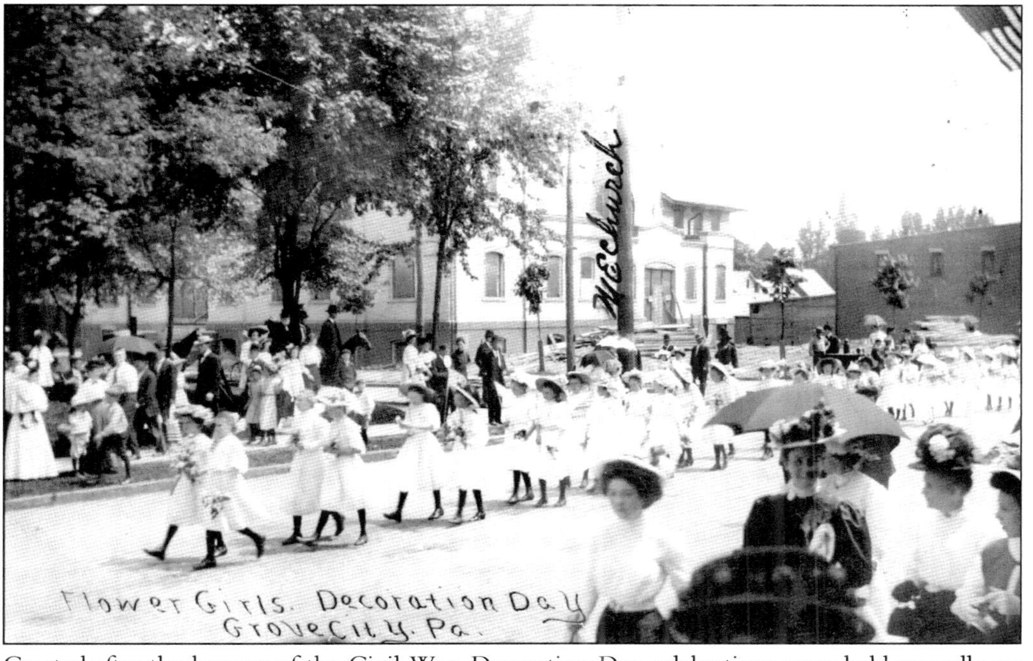

Created after the horrors of the Civil War, Decoration Day celebrations were held annually on May 31 to decorate the graves of fallen Civil War soldiers. In this 1909 photograph, this parade of flower girls is probably marching up South Broad Street toward Woodland Cemetery. They were probably holding flowers that bloom in Pennsylvania at the end of May, possibly lilacs, wildflowers, and spirea, also known as Bridal Veil. Notice beneath the flag in the picture that the IOOF building beside the church has not yet built.

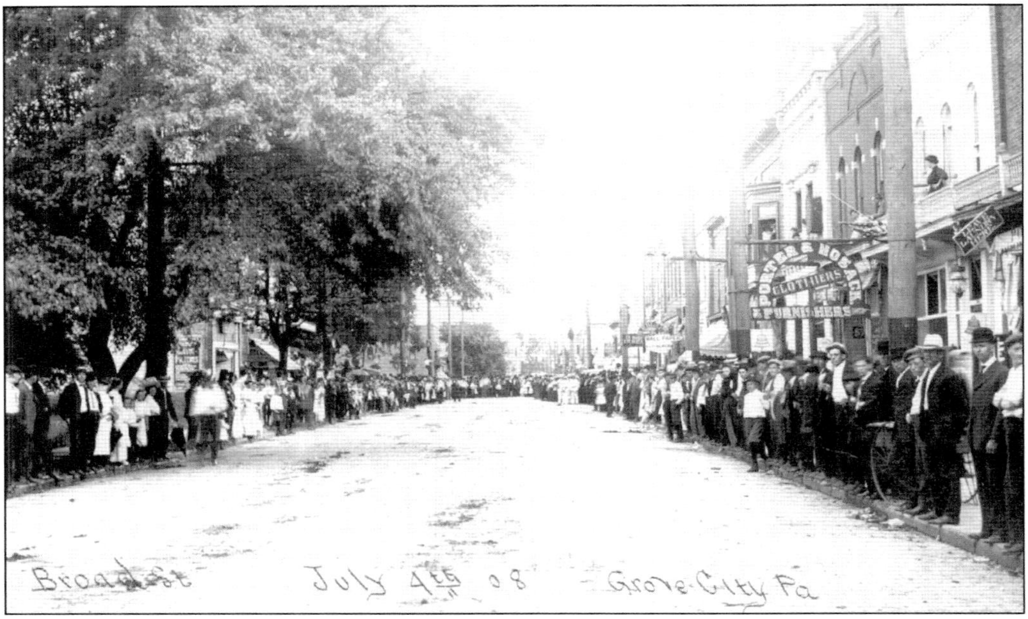

These two pictures appear to be two shots from up and down Broad Street before the Fourth of July parade in 1908. The photographer was standing in Broad Street in front of the Methodist church. In the picture above, looking south toward the college's lower campus, a store on the left advertises "moving pictures." To the right, signs include Rhodes and Redmond Hardware, M. P. Black, I. C. Black's Wallpaper, Porter and Hosack Clothiers and Furnishings, Porter's laundry, and the Bell Telephone Company. To get a better view above the crowd, boys climbed every telephone pole. Looking north, the Bessemer volunteer firefighters can be seen marching toward the photographer. To the left in the picture is De France drugstore, Filer House, Guthrie's Shoe Store, Dr. H. A. Kelly (dentist), and someone selling ice-cream cones for 5¢.

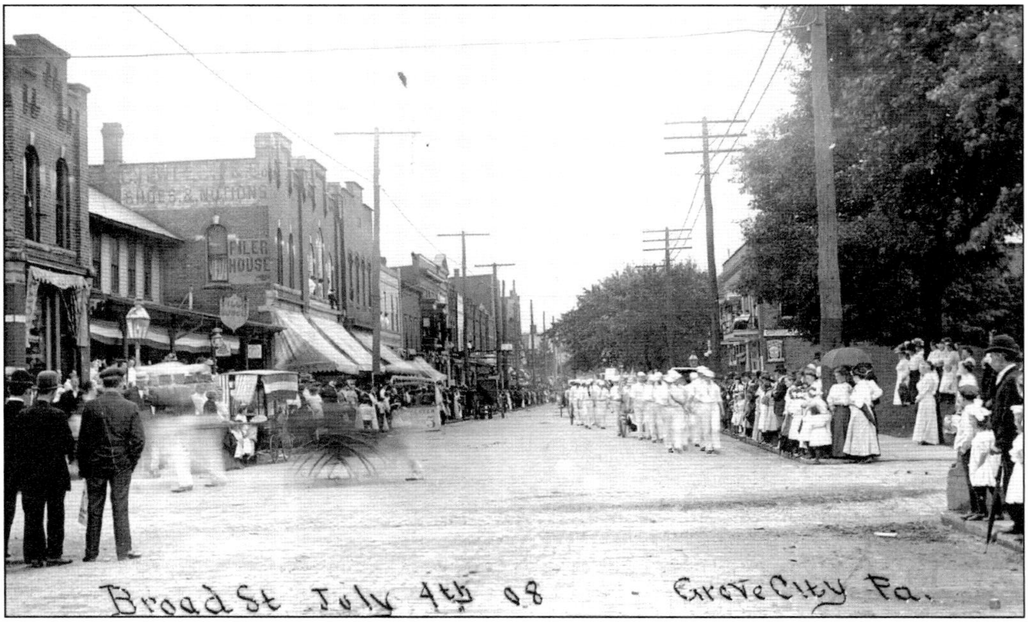

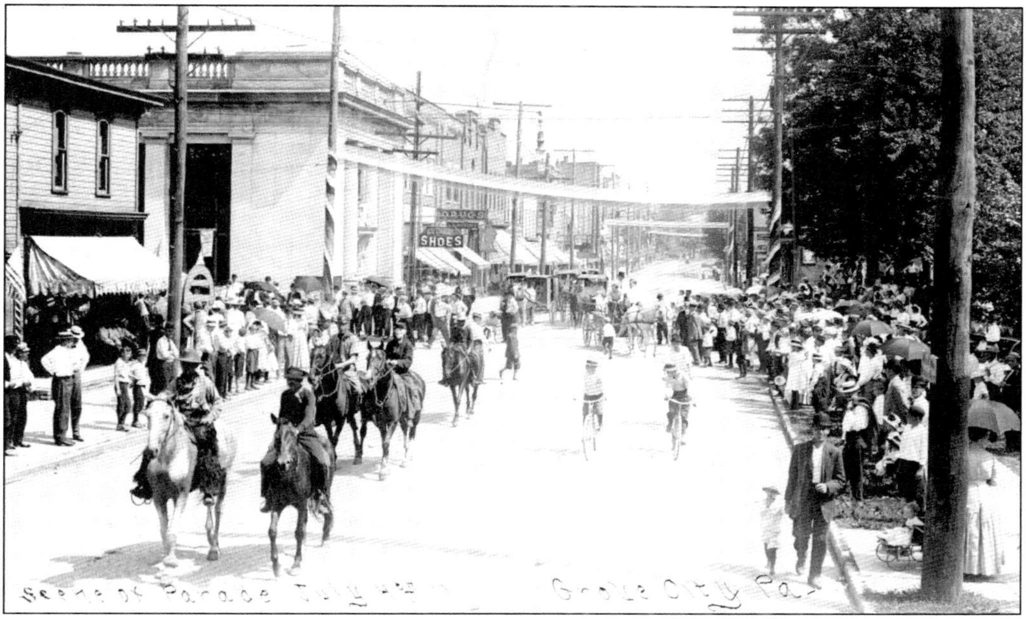

This Fourth of July parade from 1911 shows the new Grove City National Bank building at the corner of Pine and Broad Streets. The W. A. Young and Sons harness shop has not yet been replaced by a bank on the other corner. The light-colored lead horse has a badly swollen ankle. A sign on a pole to the right reads, "Hitch No Horses Here." The parade route has also been changed to turn from Pine onto Broad Street.

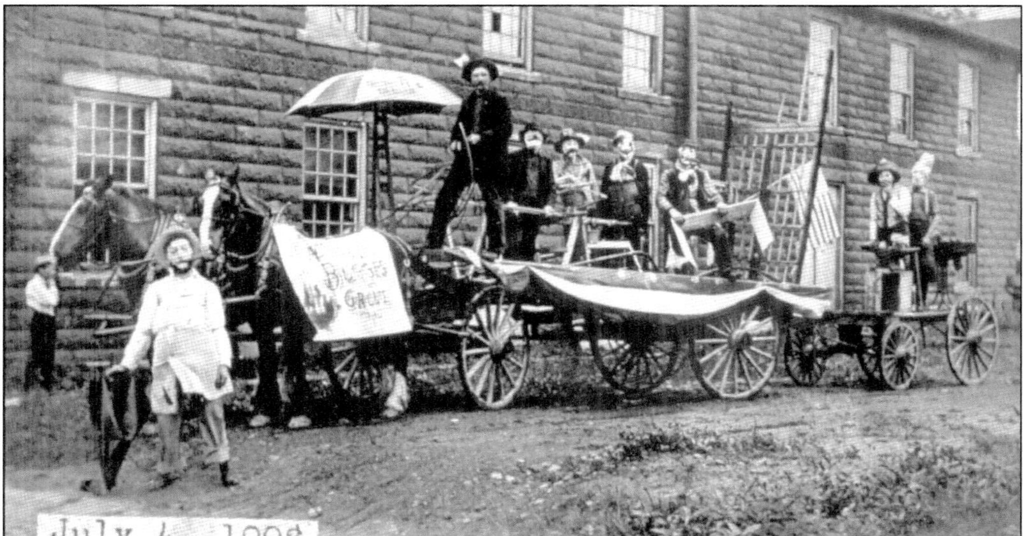

The 1908 Fourth of July parade is more evidence of the prosperity of Grove City at that period. This float was the McKay Carriage Works entry. The sign on the horse says, "Bugges' Grove." The umbrella says, "Douthett and Graham." All the characters are dressed like clowns, some with masks. They appear to have the tools used in the manufacture of buggies on the two wagons. The fellows on the second wagon are using an anvil and a hand forge.

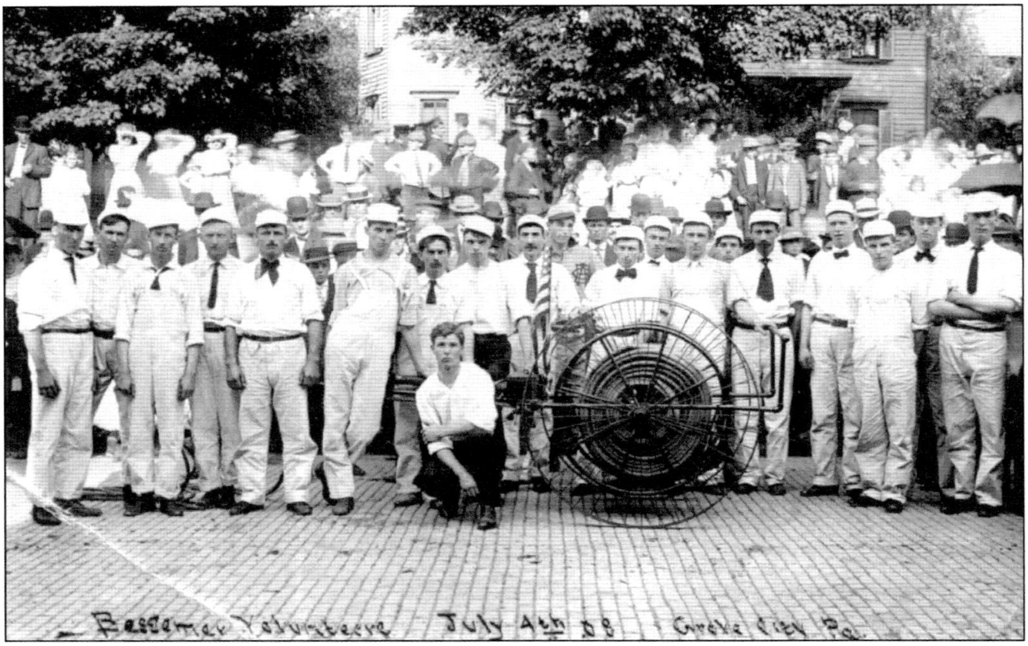

Part of the festivities in 1908 was a fireman's hose company race from the railroad tracks to the lower campus of Grove City College. The Bessemer Volunteers may have won the race because their's is the photograph that has survived. Because the factory was nearly a town in and of itself, there was a need for management to organize a fire company for internal use at the plant.

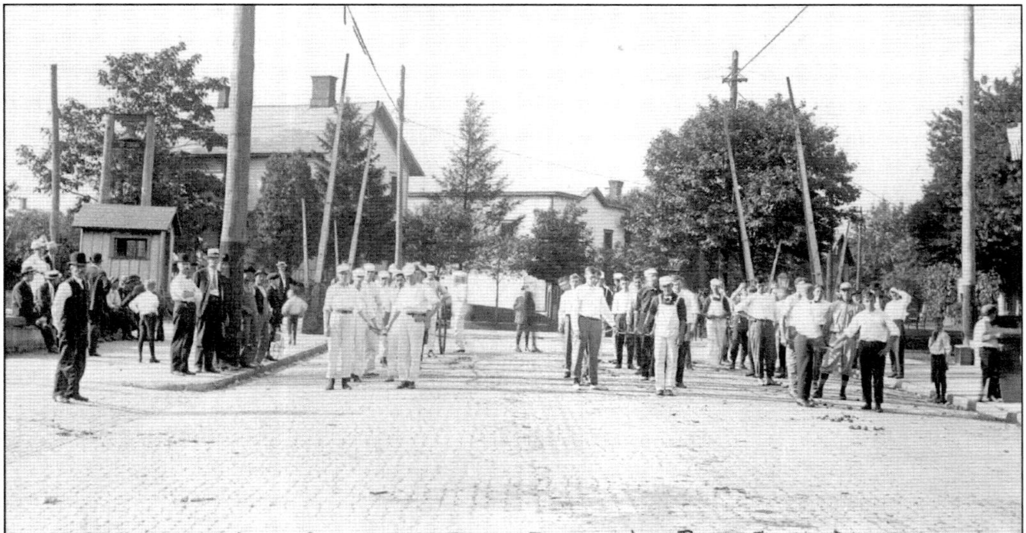

Teams of volunteers from three hose companies line up in this image to race down the brick-paved Broad Street to the lower campus of Grove City College. The race started at the railroad tracks. Behind the onlookers to the left is the little railroad crossing the watchman's building. The watchman raised and lowered the railroad crossing gates. In later years, the building was on a raised platform, and the watchman was Bailey Barnes.

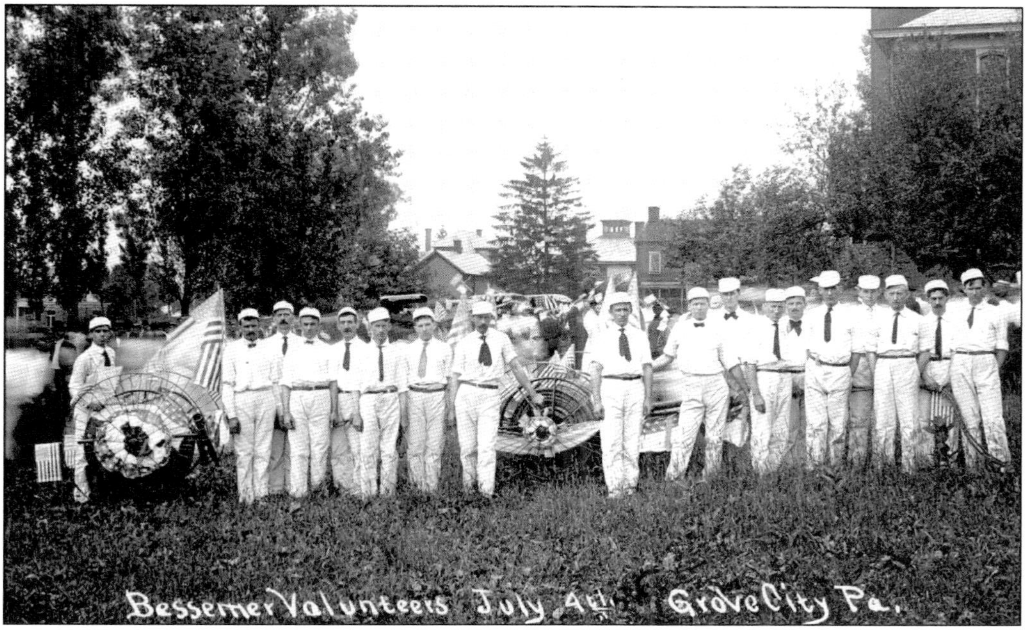

Shown here on the college's lower campus, the Bessemer Volunteers stand for another portrait after the race. Behind the hose company, the tops of buildings along Main Street can be seen. In the center, looking past the Cunningham house, a boardinghouse with a distinctive architectural feature called a belvedere crowns its roof. The back of the college's music building is to the right. When enlarged, the photograph reveals a man carrying a tuba in the background. It seems likely the photographer walked behind the firemen to take the below picture of the members of the Grove City Band under the poplar trees, which separated the lower campus from the college's athletic field in the background.

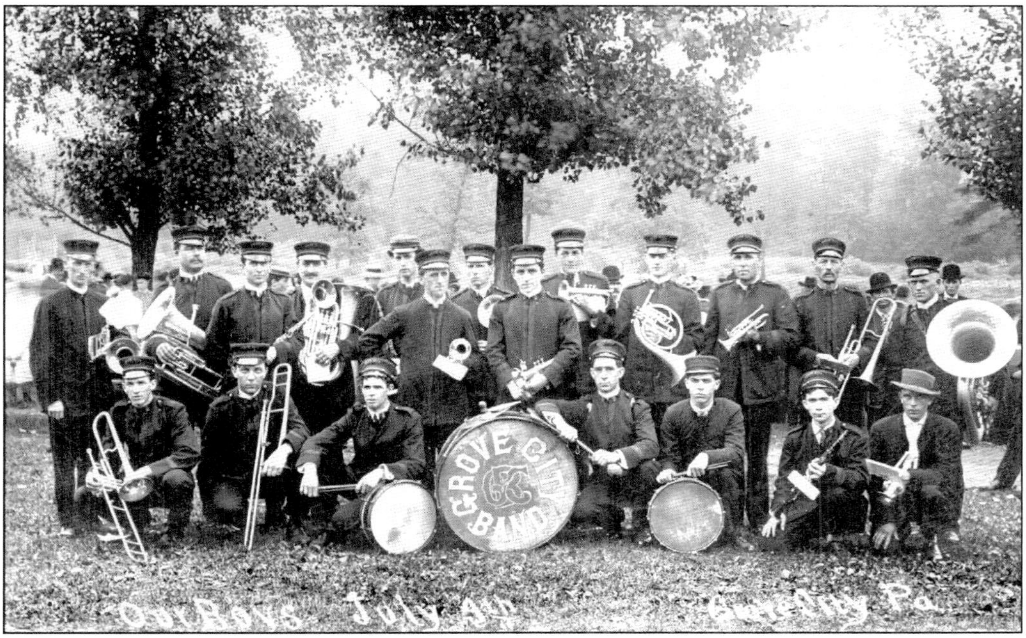

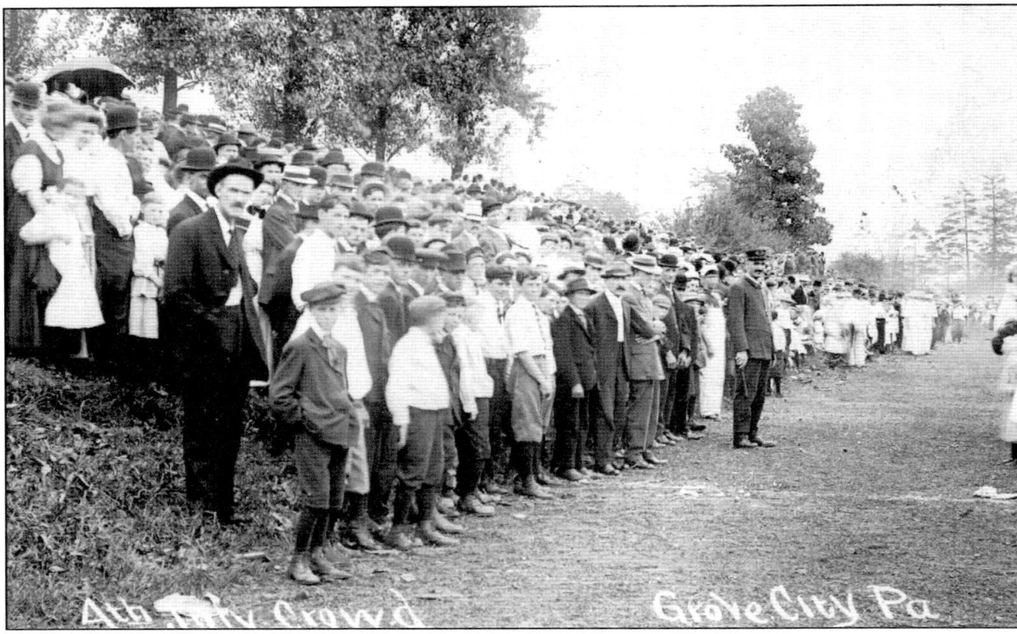

On the other side of the poplar trees, crowds formed to watch the judging of the Fourth of July parade entries. Note that there appear to be no bleacher seats at the athletic field yet—everyone stands. Boys wore knickers, jackets, ties, and hats to the celebration. So many people crowded the field that a policeman, or security guard, stands in front of the throng with his billy club in hand keeping everyone behind an imaginary line. In 1908, America's love affair with the automobile was just beginning. The car shown below has no front bumper, as there were not many other cars to bump into at the time. The college's old academy building was the first constructed on the lower campus and stands in the background. Above the roof of the car at the back of the photograph, the steeple of the old Methodist church can be seen.

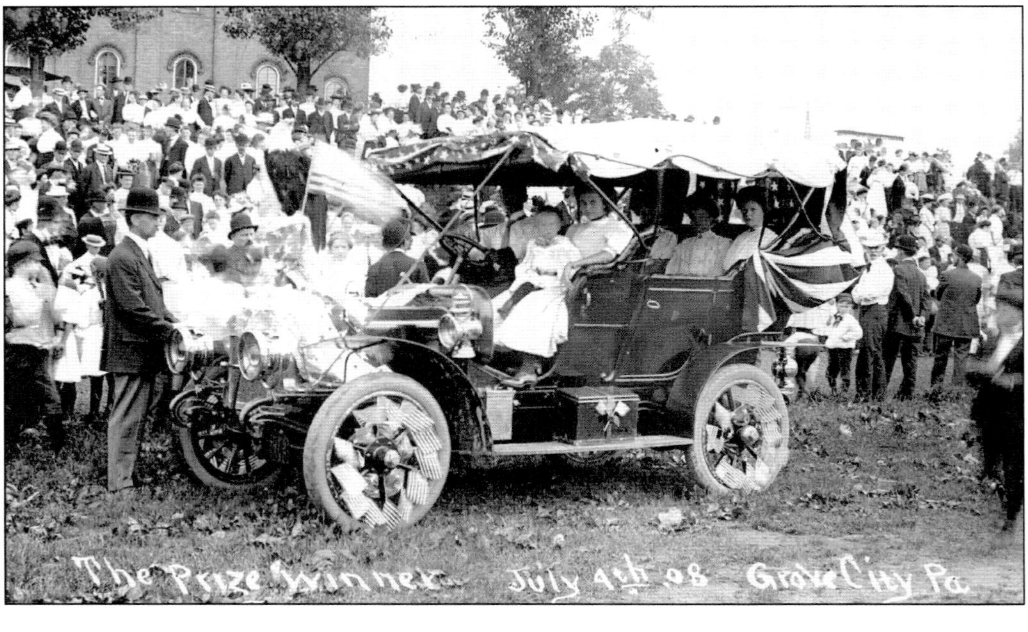

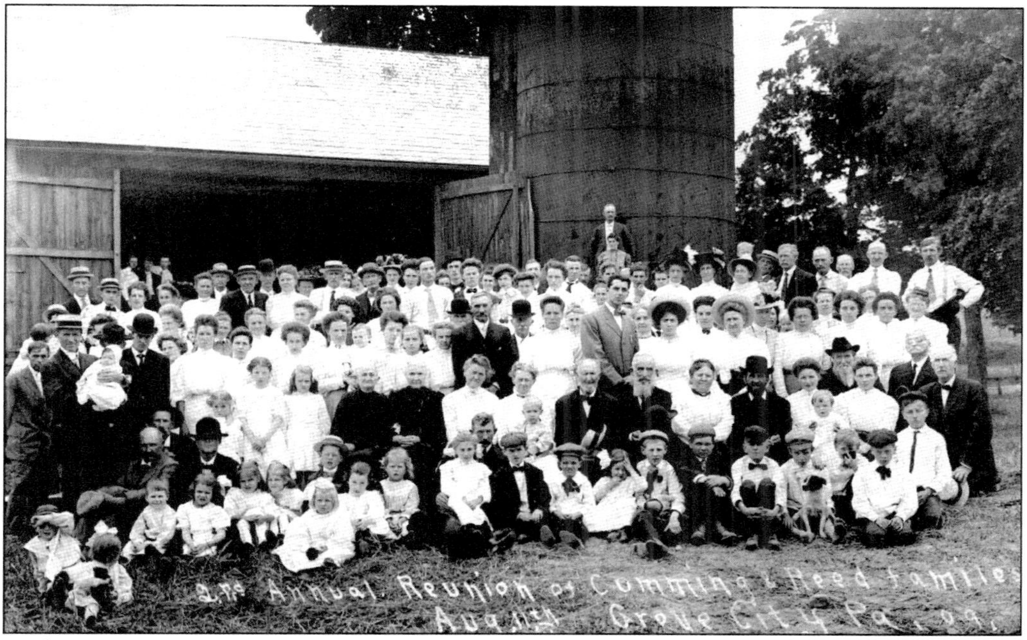

With prosperity came large families and large family reunions. A typical place to photograph more than 100 reunion goers at once was the inclined barn bridge. This crowd attending the Cummings and Reed reunion on August 11, 1909, contains at least 25 children, a dog, and a man who might be blind. A man sitting to the right, surrounded by children, has a hat that is pulled too far down over his ears, as if fixed by little girls while playing with a favorite uncle. Probably held at a different location, the Cummings and Reed family reunion the following year, pictured below, swelled to more than 150 family members. A child's wagon can be seen to the left in front of a crowd of children. Everyone attending a family reunion at that time dressed up in their best Sunday clothes. For such an army of people, the logistics of holding such a gathering must have seemed daunting, except for the fact that everyone probably jumped in to help.

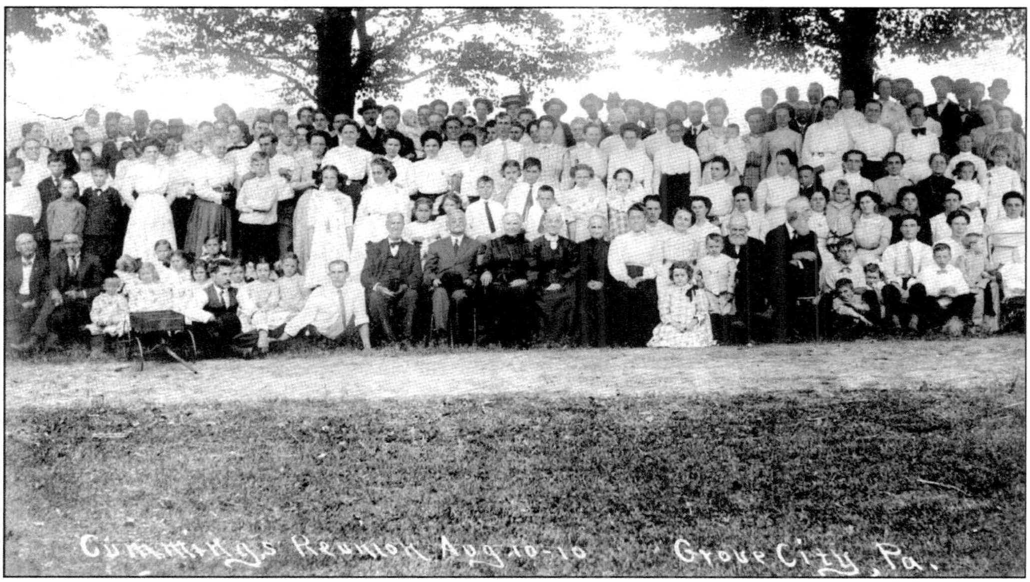

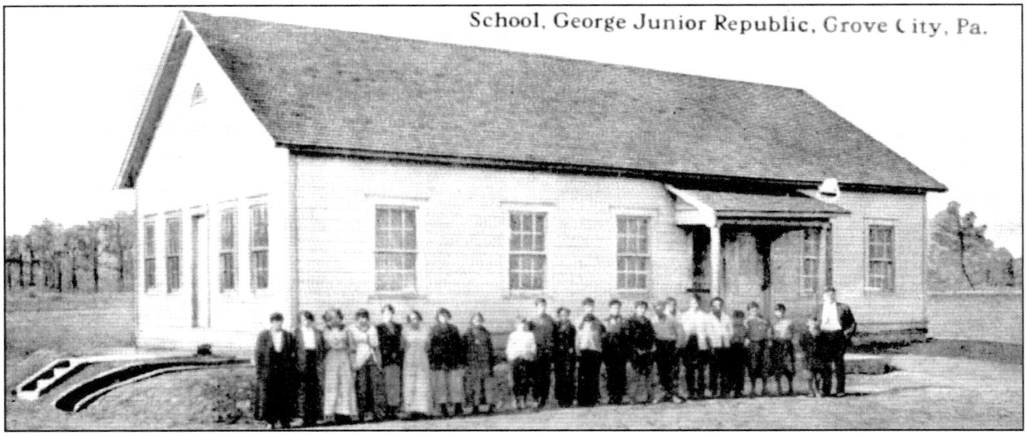

In 1909, philanthropist William Ruben George founded the George Junior Republic as a school and home for both boys and girls. It was at the intersection of George Junior Road and West Main Street. The school building shown above stood where the First National Bank of Pennsylvania is today. In present day, the George Junior Republic is a residential treatment facility for delinquent and dependent boys only. The goal of the facility is to create a community where young men can be guided to be self-sufficient and productive citizens in a democratic society.

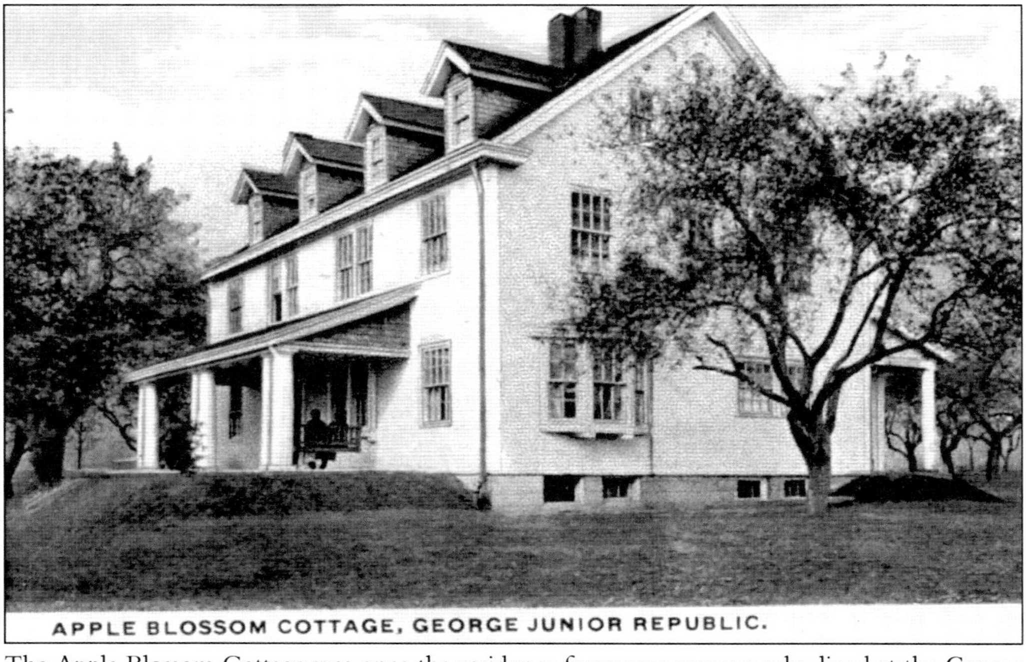

The Apple Blossom Cottage was once the residence for young women who lived at the George Junior Republic. Graduates of the George Junior program have gone on to successful careers. One student, Antwon Fisher, wrote an autobiographical book, which was made into a major motion picture starring Denzel Washington. Many former students credit the George Junior for turning their lives around.

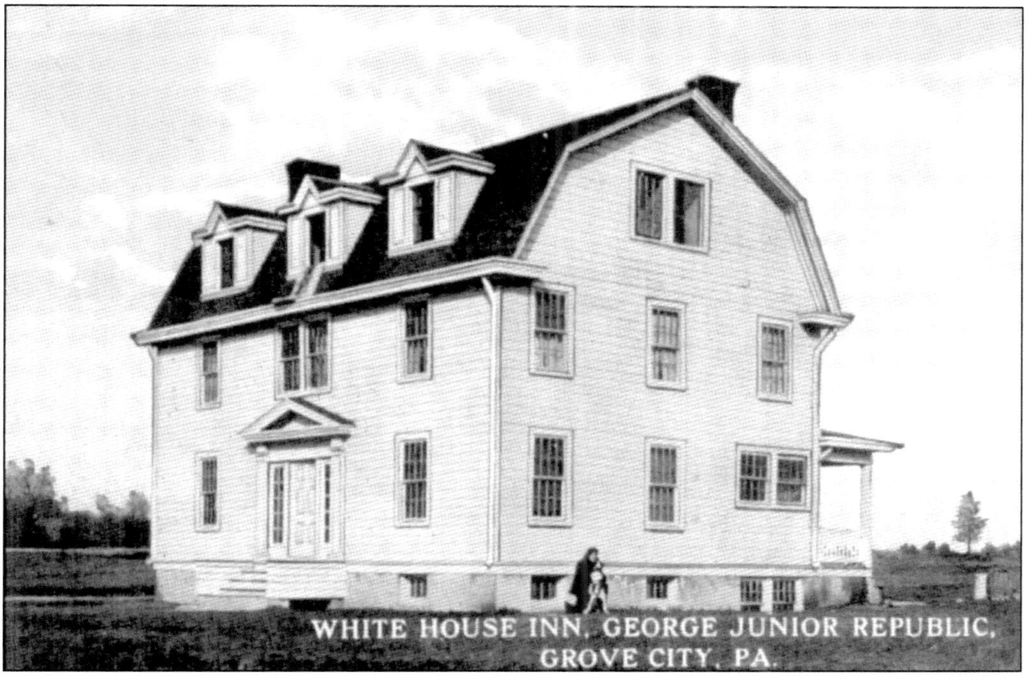

The White House Inn was a three-story residence for young men living at the George Junior Republic. Currently, the George Junior Republic provides an opportunity for positive and lasting development in a rural small-town atmosphere on its sprawling 400-acre campus. It is home to more than 450 young men from all over the United States. Creating a stable home environment serves as the foundation of the approach addressing the diverse needs of troubled youth.

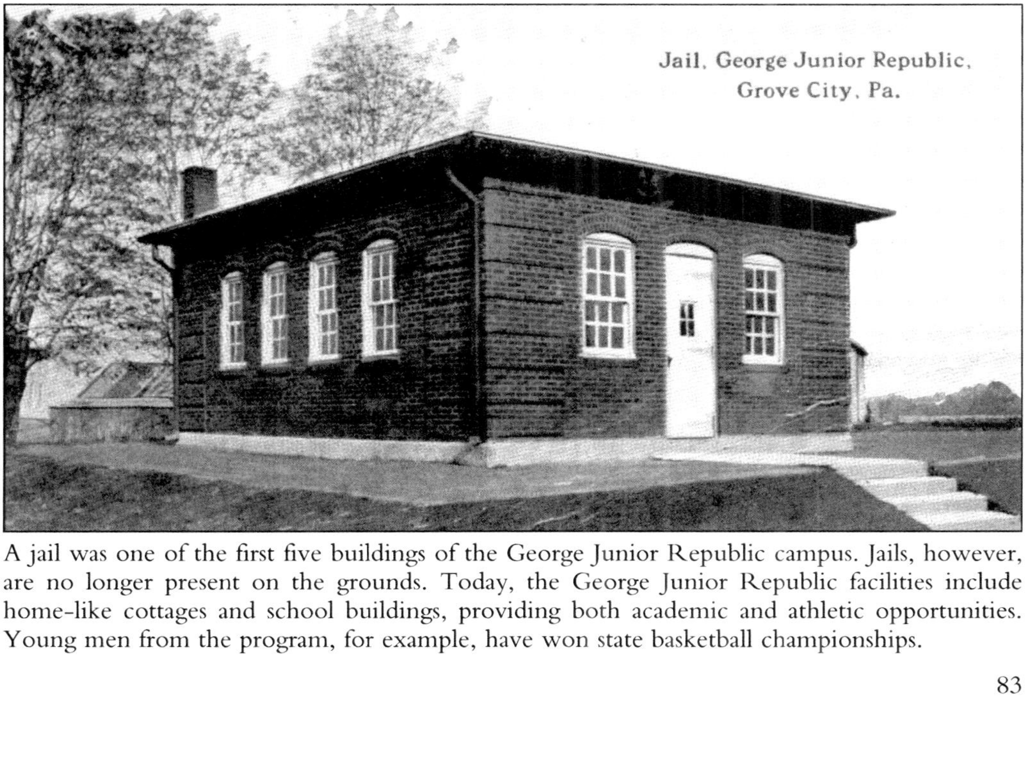

A jail was one of the first five buildings of the George Junior Republic campus. Jails, however, are no longer present on the grounds. Today, the George Junior Republic facilities include home-like cottages and school buildings, providing both academic and athletic opportunities. Young men from the program, for example, have won state basketball championships.

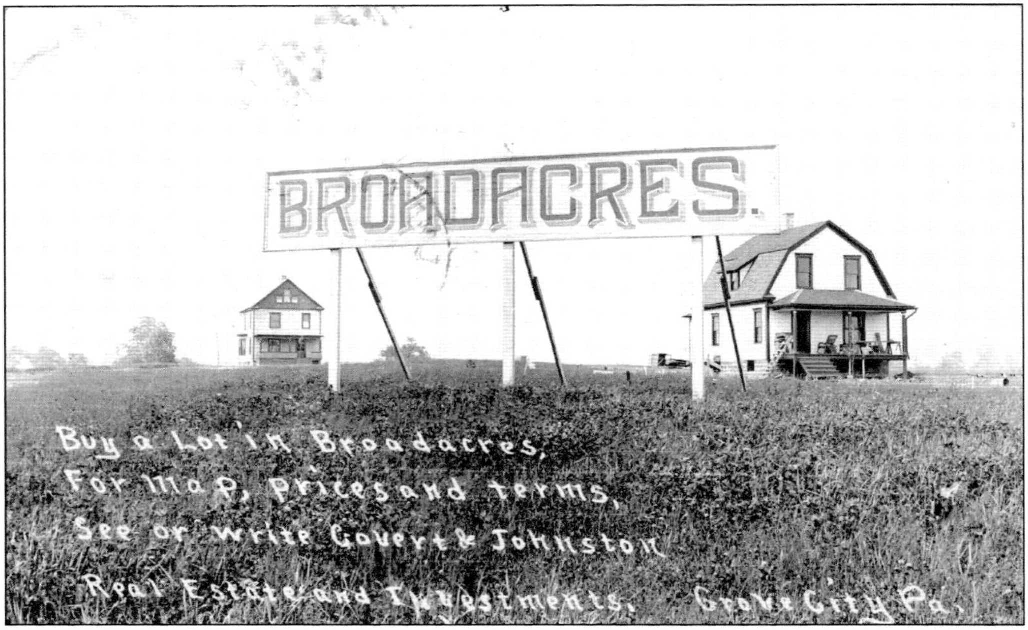

Along with an increasing industrial base and expanding educational services, the residential areas of the town grew also. Broadacres is a housing development north of town created by Covert and Johnston Real Estate and Investments. This area offered home lots for sale, but was also the site of two dynamite storage buildings for Grove City Hardware stores and a slaughterhouse where animal carcasses were washed in the Wolf Creek waters flooded by the upper dam.

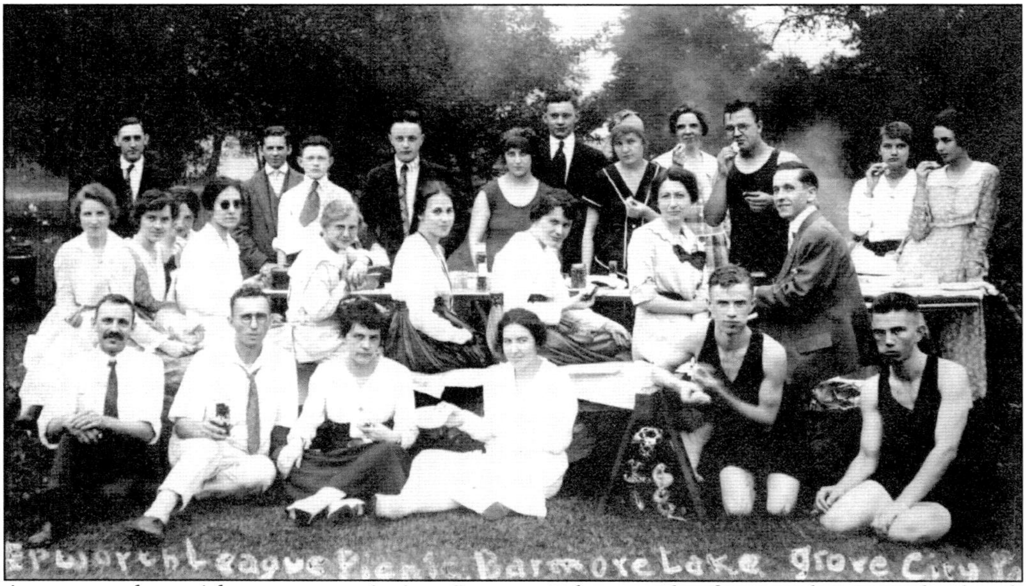

A very popular social event was a picnic at Barmore Lake, outside of town. The Epworth Church League picnic must have included swimming in the lake since there are several young people attired in swimsuits of the day. Several have food in their hands and one young man has stuffed his mouth full, right before the picture was taken. On the table are olives, pickles, and sandwiches. With no disposable tableware, glasses, crocks, and china were set out.

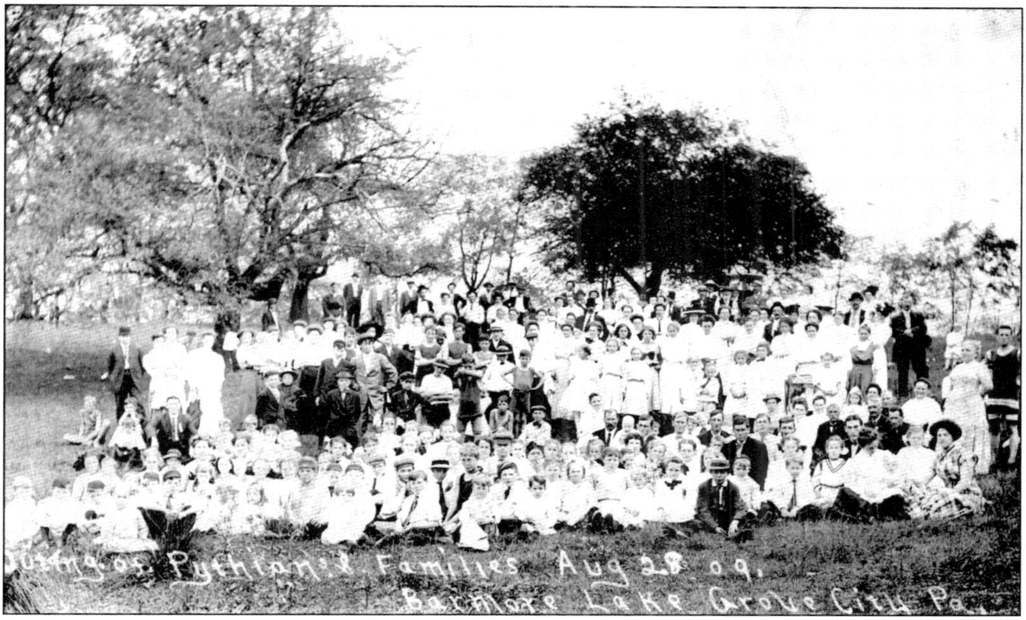

Grove City residents formed many social organizations, many of which had regular activities and annual picnics. Shown here are the Pythian Sisters and their families at Barmore Lake in August 1909. The Pythian Sisters is a sororal order that honors the Holy Bible and all religions and is affiliated with no particular denomination. Several men in this picture are wearing wool bathing suits; the most visible one is the fellow in the striped suit to the right. Today, Barmore Lake serves as the centerpiece for the Grove City Country Club.

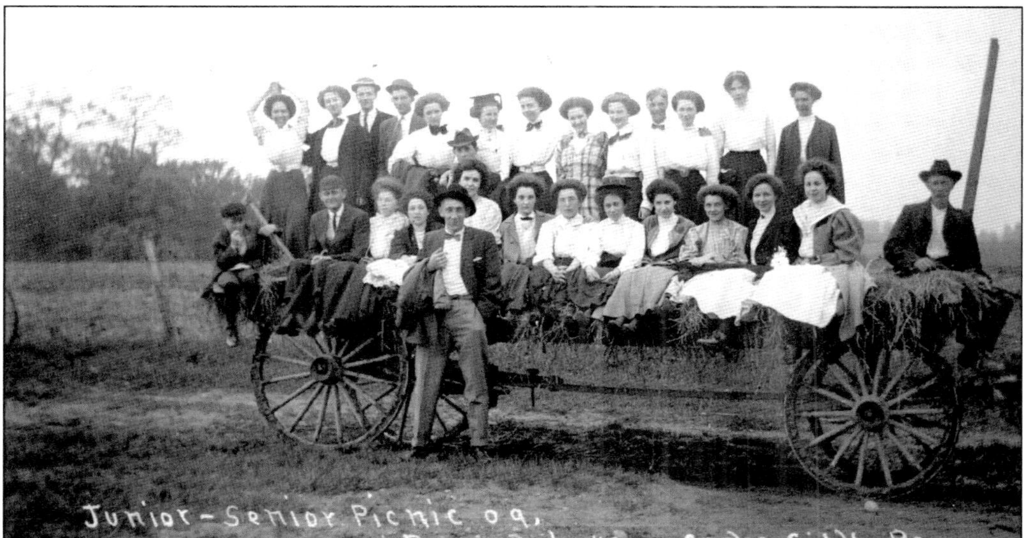

Because of the apparent age of the students, and because there are far more women than men, this is probably the junior-senior picnic of one of the Grove City College clubs, possibly the Philokalians or the Speedwells. This day was rainy, as most of the people in the picture are holding folded umbrellas and there is mud on the wagon wheels. One younger boy sits at the back of the wagon, and the driver is the gentleman in the dark coat in the front.

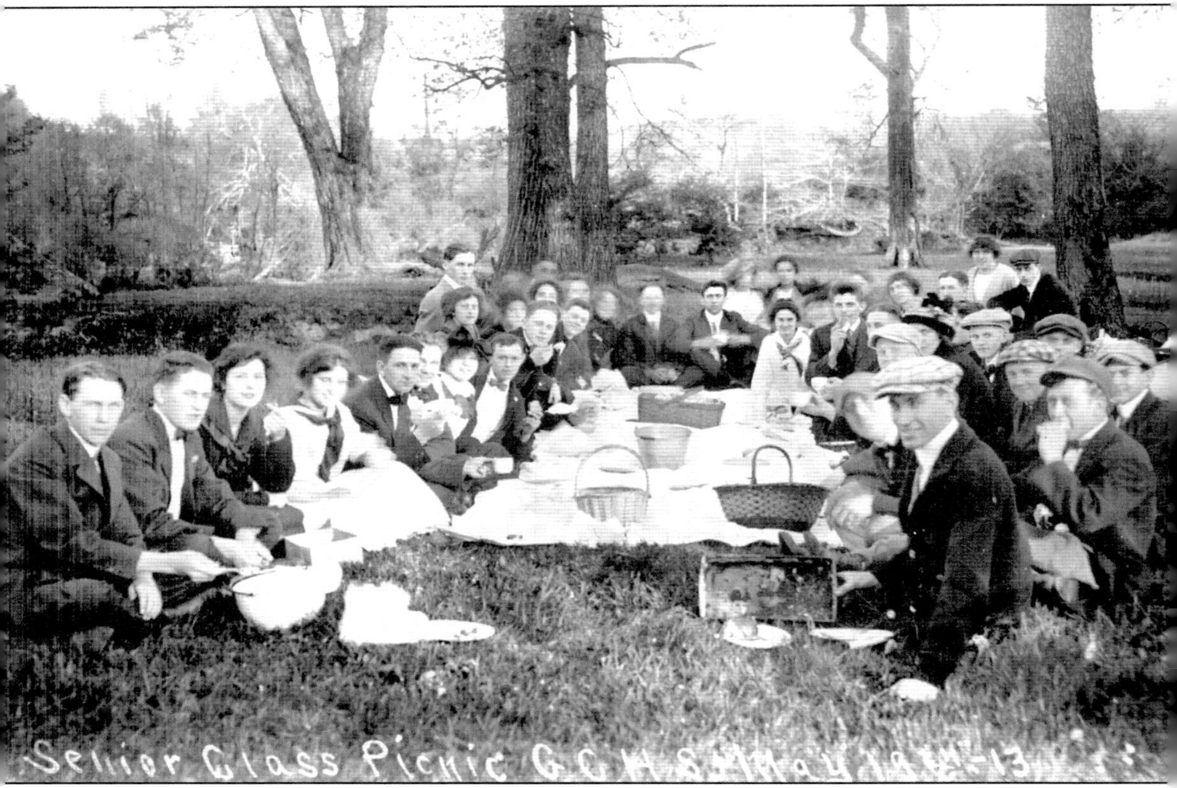

The Grove City High School senior class picnic on May 19, 1913, was no doubt held at Barmore Lake, a favorite picnicking spot. The men and women of the senior class have dressed up for this occasion. Men are wearing jackets and ties. The picnickers brought their food in picnic baskets, pails, boxes, and enamel pots and pans. Plastic was not invented for decades.

Six
SOUTH BROAD

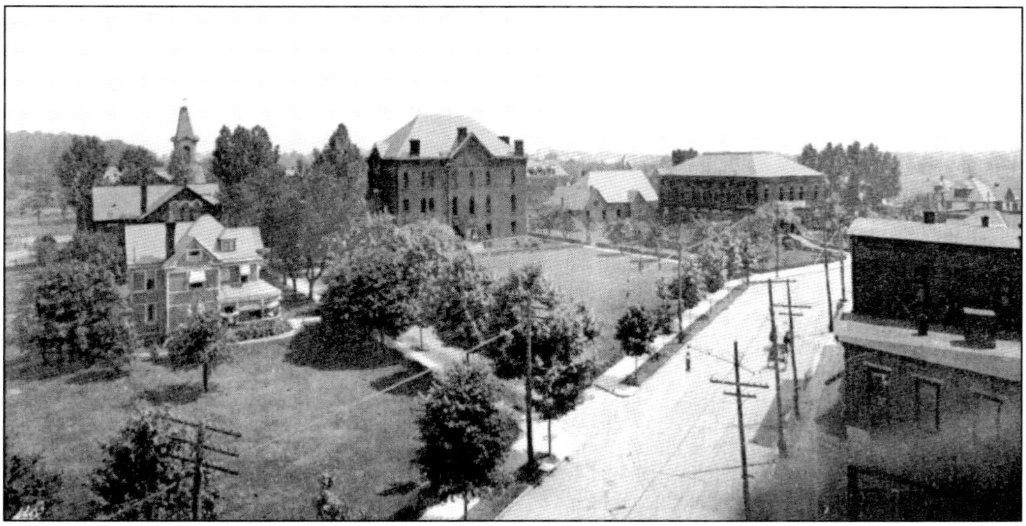

In 1879, when the first building on the Grove City College's lower campus was constructed; the site was at the edge of the town of Pine Grove. This area, next to the Carnegie building, is informally known as Strawberry Park because of a longstanding summer festival with the same name. It was not until after the death of founder Dr. Isaac C. Ketler that college buildings were constructed on the other side of Wolf Creek on what became the college's upper campus. Plans for the upper campus were created by Fredrick Law Olmsted, the same landscape architect who designed Central Park in New York City.

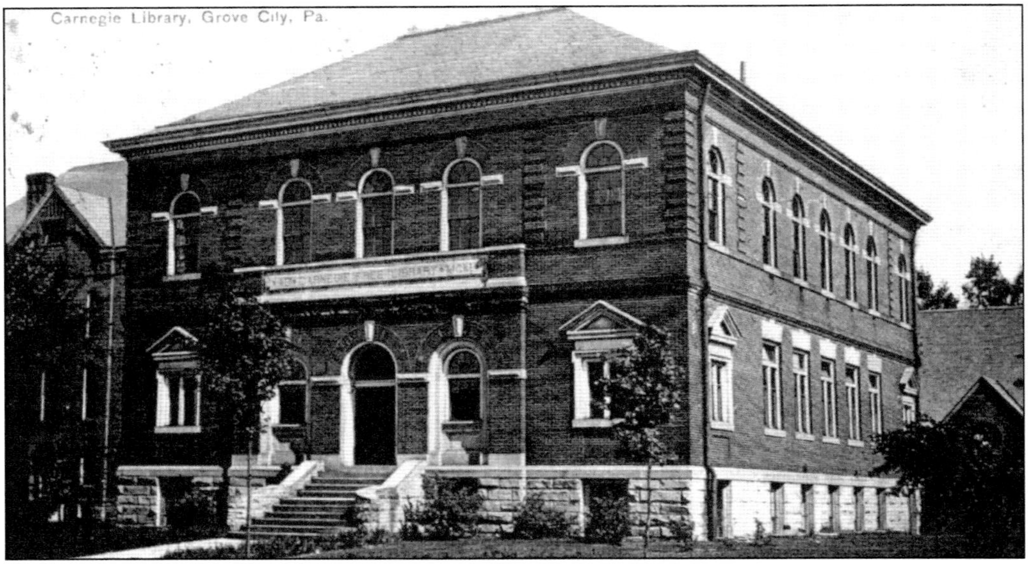

The Carnegie building was erected in 1901 as the Carnegie Library at the corner of West Main and Broad Streets. Steel baron Andrew Carnegie intended for the town and Grove City College to share his gift of a new library building. It was not long, however, before the borough decided it did not want the financial responsibility of maintaining a library and gave the facility to the college. It later served as a music hall and is now used as an administration building. When most of the buildings on the lower campus were torn down, the Carnegie building remained, allegedly due to complications of the entanglement Carnegie created by donating the original library to both the town and college.

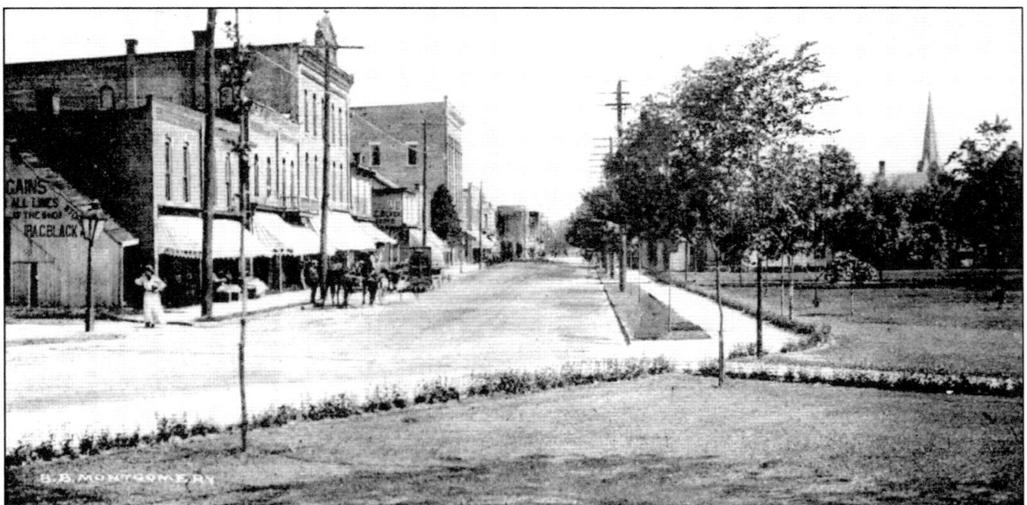

In this picture, the photographer is standing with his back to the Carnegie Library site. The buildings on the left side of South Broad Street, looking north, are where College View Towers apartment building now stands. On the wall of the first building in this section at the turn of the century is an advertisement for I. C. Black's bookstore: "Bargains of all kinds at the 5 & 10." In this block are H. S. Ross's Millinery Shop, Paganelli's Grocery, Ruffing Brothers' Meat Market, and the IOOF lodge, among others.

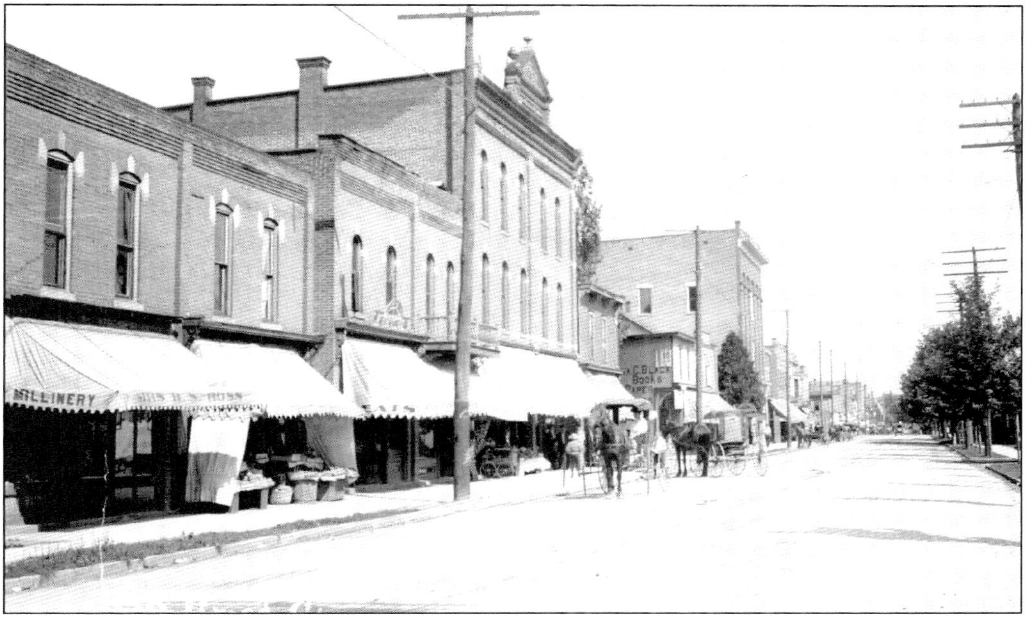

Most visible in this picture is H. S. Ross's Millinery Shop on the left side of the street. Millinery shops made elaborate women's hats that piled high on the heads of ladies in the 1890s and early 1900s. These hats were all handmade originals. Women emulated the hats of the rich and famous. Every woman wanted something better than every other woman. As a result, hats became increasingly elaborate creations that incorporated ostrich, peacock, and pheasant feathers into their designs, as well as silks, satins, ribbons, and bows. Some even included animal furs, and many had veiling. The woman drawn in this advertisement for the Grove City National Bank wears a hat that could have been made of velvet and ostrich plumes. Millinery shops probably also stocked items to match their hats, such as gloves, collars, muffs, and purses. Changing styles and manufactured mass-produced hats brought an end to the local millinery store.

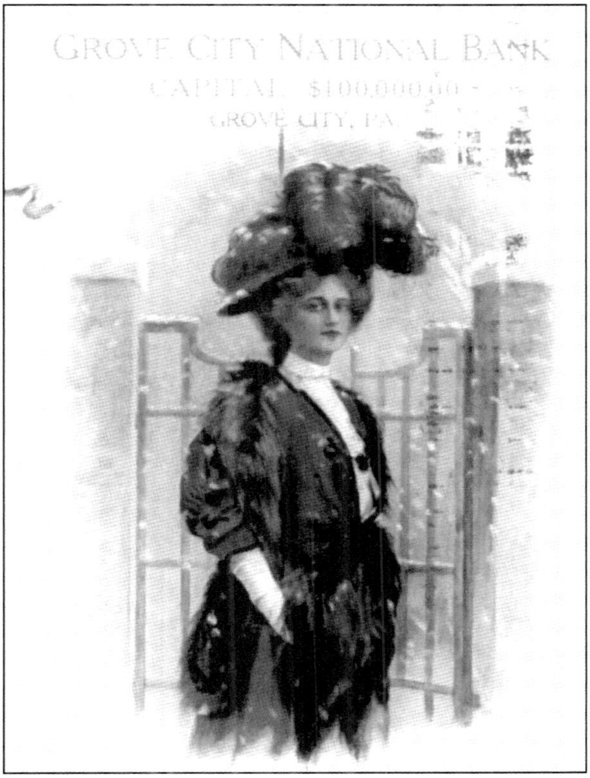

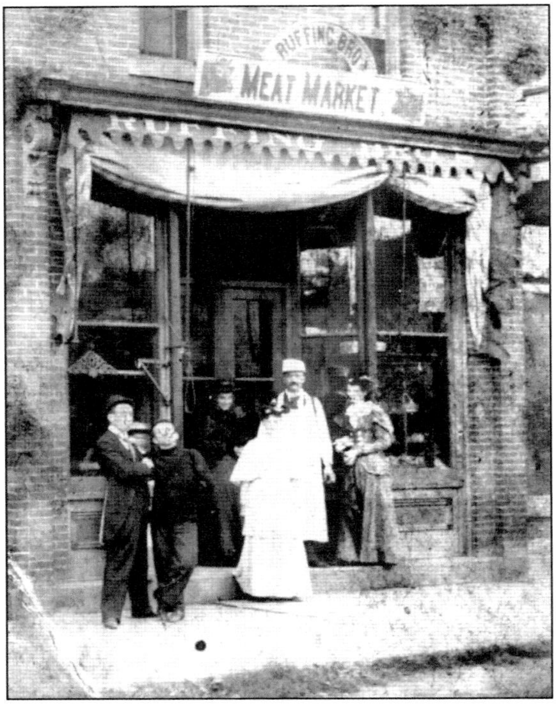

Down the street from Ross's Millinery Shop and across the street from Grove City College's lower campus was Ruffing Brothers' Meat Market. In the days before refrigeration, animals were slaughtered and consumed within a short time. Other preservation methods included drying, canning, and curing. According to Jennie Pearsall, whose firsthand account of the day survives in love letters found in her family home, part of the "Ruffing Block" had a room large enough to hold a hop, or a dance in 1900, thus shattering the local myth that dancing was not allowed in Grove City.

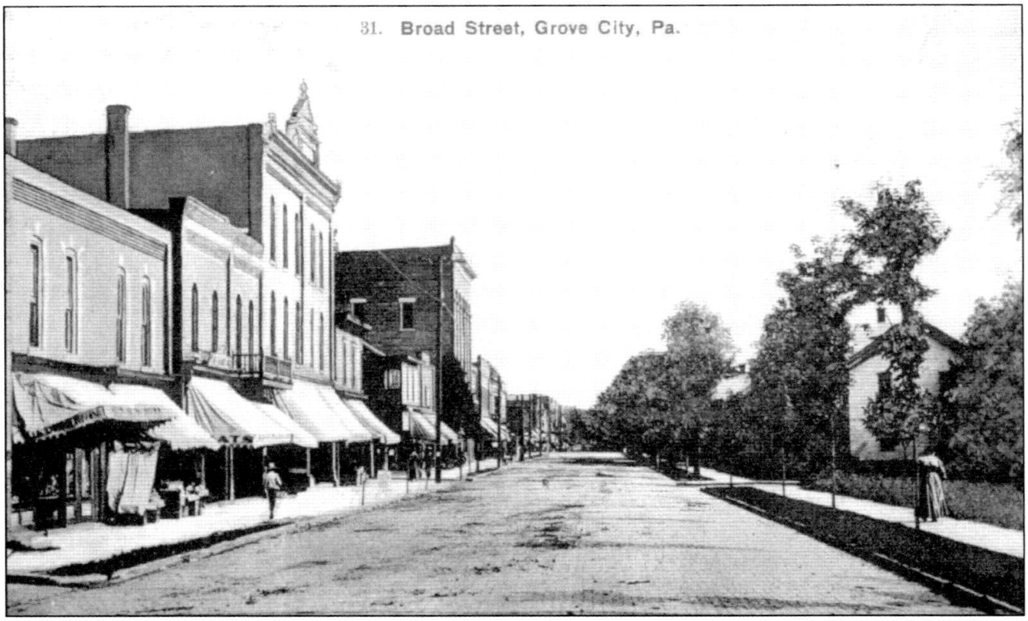

In this photograph of South Broad Street looking north, it is plain to see that businesses developed on the left side of the street far faster than on the right. It is possible that morning sun was desirable while afternoon sun was less so. Another possibility is that women's skirts touched the ground, and they may not have wanted to cross a street spotted with horse manure, as can be seen in this picture. On the right side of the street, where the house can be seen through the trees, is where the Tower Presbyterian Church was built.

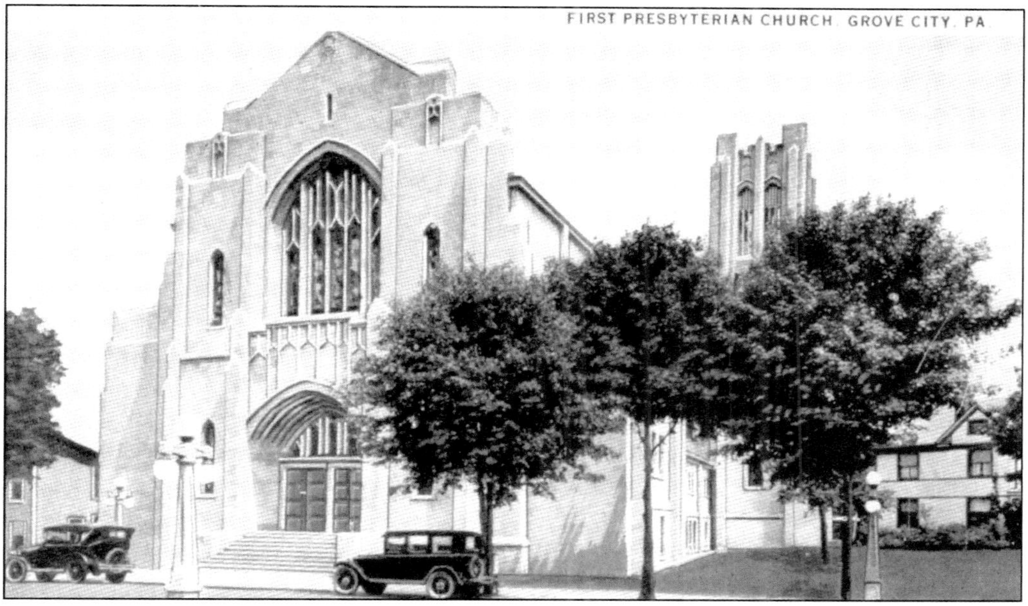

After the Presbyterian congregation outgrew their first church in Grove City at the corner of West Main and South Broad Streets, they built a new church a block away at the corner of South Broad Street and College Avenue. Stained-glass windows commemorating the sacrifice of the Simcox family, who were martyred during the Boxer Rebellion in China, are among those lining the sanctuary. Of the hundreds of artisans who worked to build this impressive structure was at least one out-of-work coal miner, Nicholas Wiand. The construction of the church was completed in 1926, just a few years before the stock market crashed and the Great Depression began.

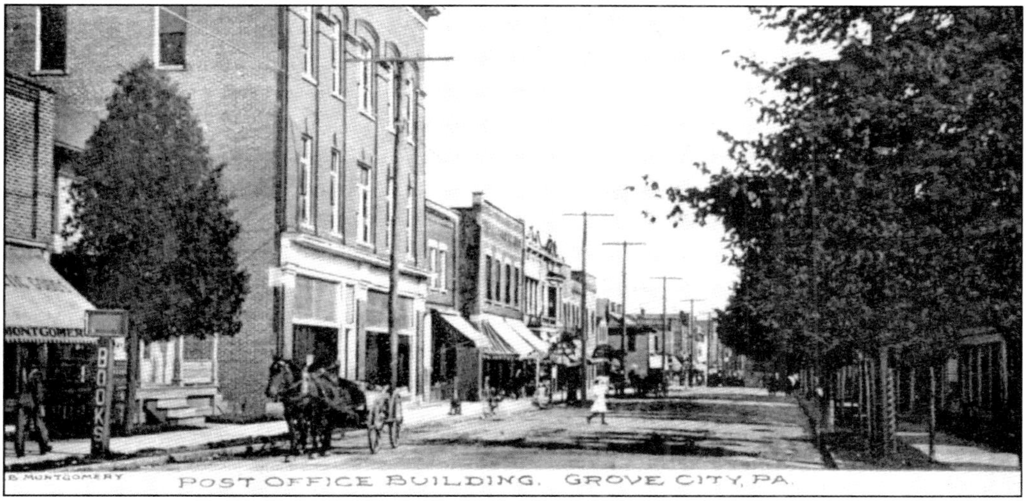

The businesses on the sunny side of the street were all reconstructed after devastating fires in the 1890s. An ordinance was passed limiting buildings to brick to reduce the risk of fire. One of the few wooden buildings remaining was B. B. Montgomery's bookstore, which is today the site of Marilyn's English Country Victoria shop. B. B. Montgomery published many of the postcards found in this book. The three-story building on the left once contained the Grove City post office.

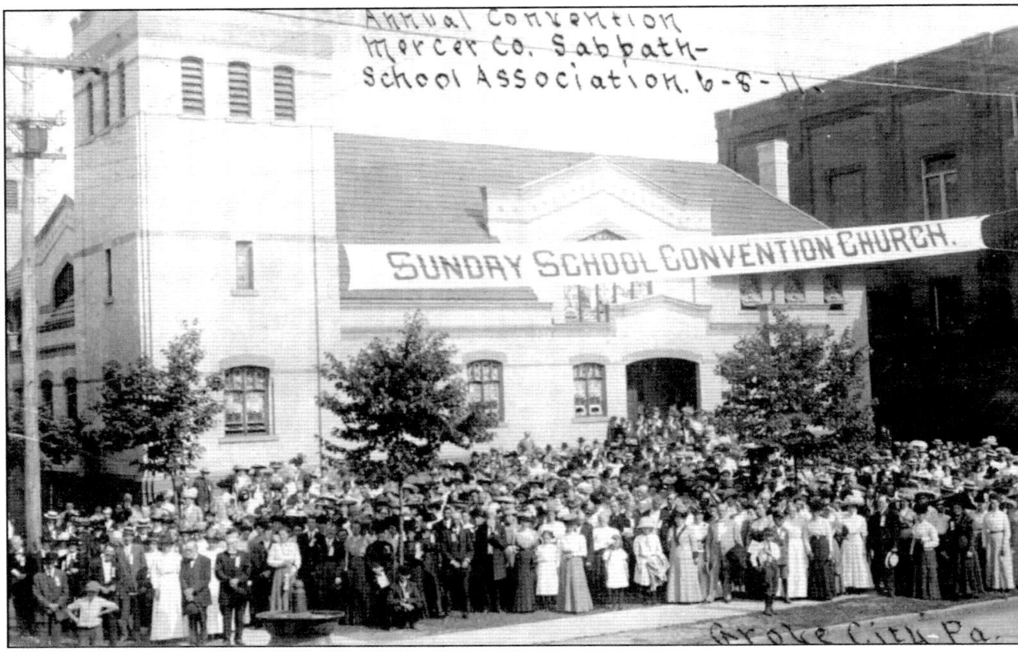

In 1885, the Methodist Episcopal flock dedicated a new church building at the corner of East Pine and Grace Streets. The building cost $9,700 and had 500 seats. The people attending services numbered 325 members. The fast-growing congregation outgrew the church in just 25 years and constructed their current building in 1908. The building and congregation are shown here on June 8, 1911, when they hosted the Mercer County Annual Sabbath School Association Convention.

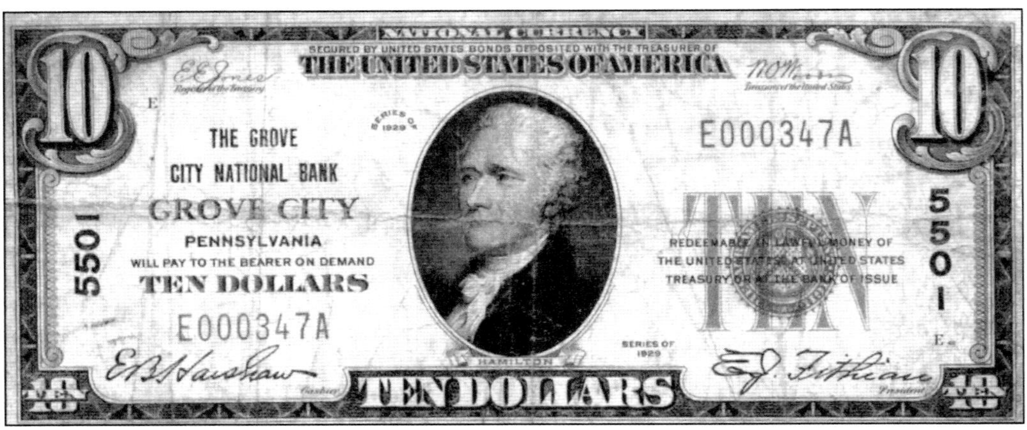

At one period of time, U.S. currency was printed bearing the names of local banks. This $10 bill was printed for the Grove City National Bank. The president at the time was E. J. Fithian, and the bank's cashier was E. B. Harshaw. The meaning of the word cashier has changed somewhat. Harshaw's title of cashier is closer in meaning to treasurer today.

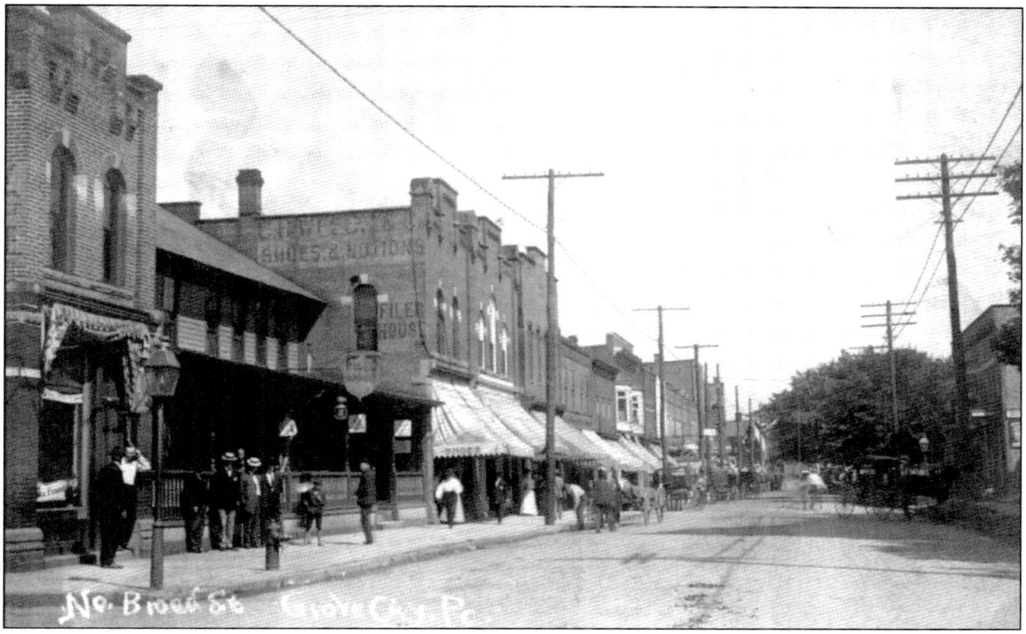

Diagonally across Broad and Pine Streets from the Methodist Church was the drugstore of Dr. Charles C. Campbell in the 1890s. In this photograph, the awning of the building reads, "Guy Emery," and the sign in the window, "Soda Fountain." Next-door was Filer House, one of several hotels in town. After the widow Filer, who last operated Filer House, died in 1907, the property was acquired by the Grove City National Bank, which built a new building on this most prominent corner in town. The J. C. Penney store in Grove City stood beside the new bank but later moved across the street, and the former Penney's location became Myers' Department Store. In the older photograph we see an example of Grove City's earliest gas streetlights. By the time the new bank building was erected, the town's streetlights were powered by electricity for the first time and were hung overhead, as seen below.

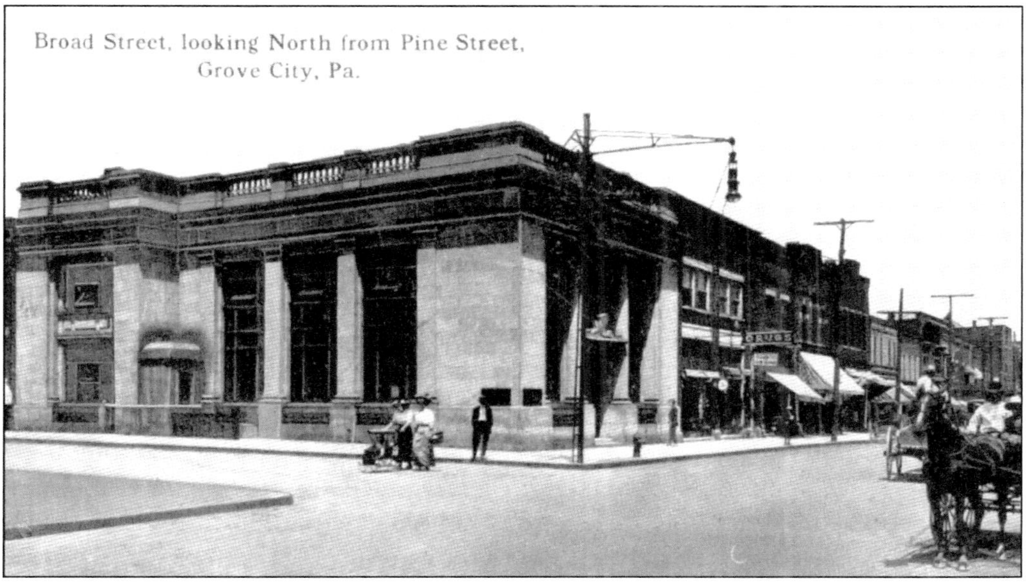

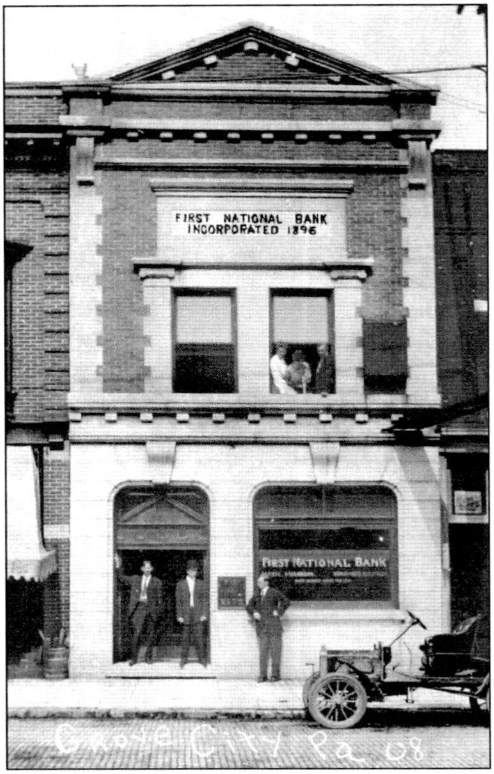

The First National Bank of Grove City, incorporated in 1896 and shown here at its first location a little farther down the street, was older than the Grove City National Bank. Once the Grove City National Bank built a new building at the corner of Pine and South Broad Streets, the First National Bank of Grove City built a new bank on the other side of Pine, also at the intersection. In the 1970s, the large columns in front of the bank were removed to install the first ATM in town. Bank machines now have signs that read, "no coins," but when first installed, one boy, who would like to remain nameless, did not realize it would cause any problems to put a roll of nickels into the deposit envelop and feed it to the machine. The ATM designers, expecting flat currency or checks, did not expect something so thick. The machine jammed, the envelope broke, and the nickels went everywhere inside.

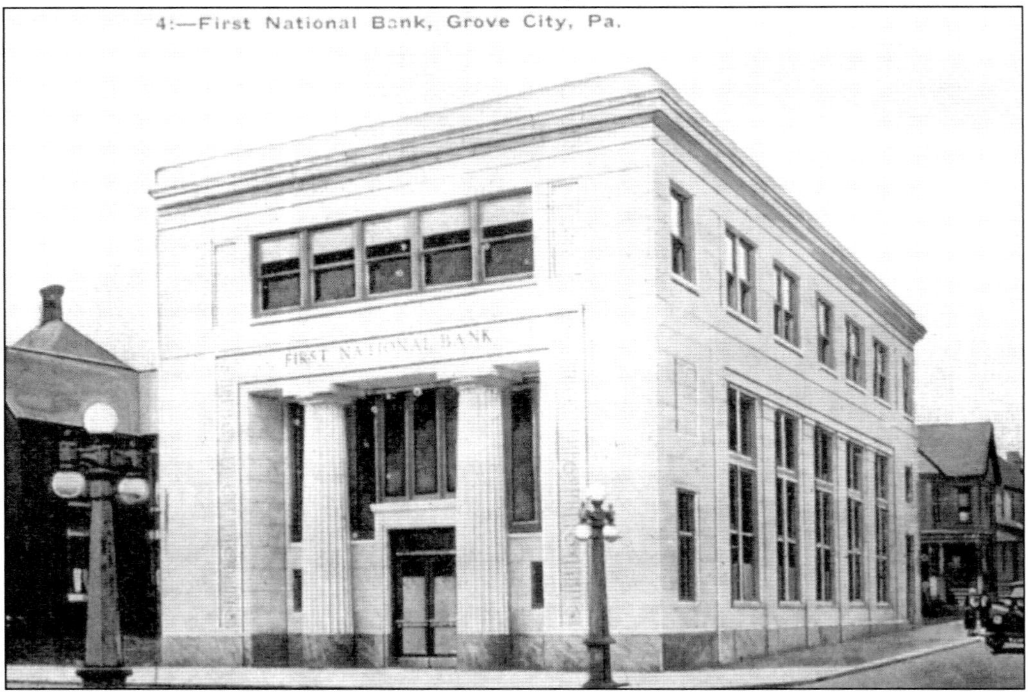

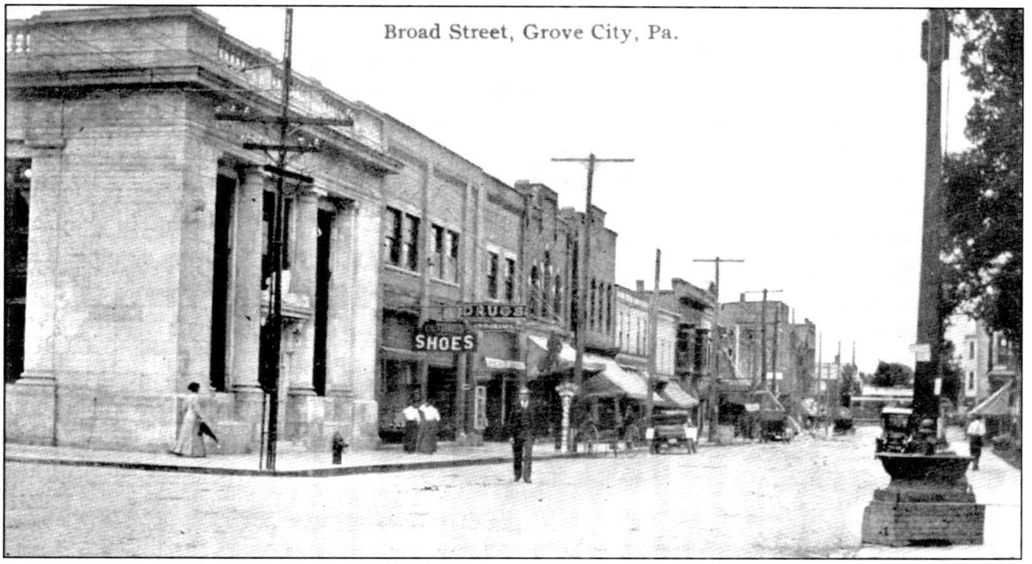

Broad Street runs nearly parallel to Wolf Creek. It connects the economic centers that grew up around the gristmills at the Upper and Lower Dams and then continues on northward through Mercer County. The new bank buildings and the many businesses crowding Broad Street reflect the growing prosperity of the town. Guthrie's Shoe Store and De France Drugstore are next to the new bank building. Guthrie also built the Guthrie Theater on Broad Street, near where Dad's Restaurant used to be, and a large yellow brick home at the intersection of South Center and Poplar Streets. The interior of the new Grove City National Bank shows all the elements banks have used to convey stability, wealth, and permanence. The polished brass and marble interior gives the impression of prosperity and that, if one deposited money in this bank, it would be safe.

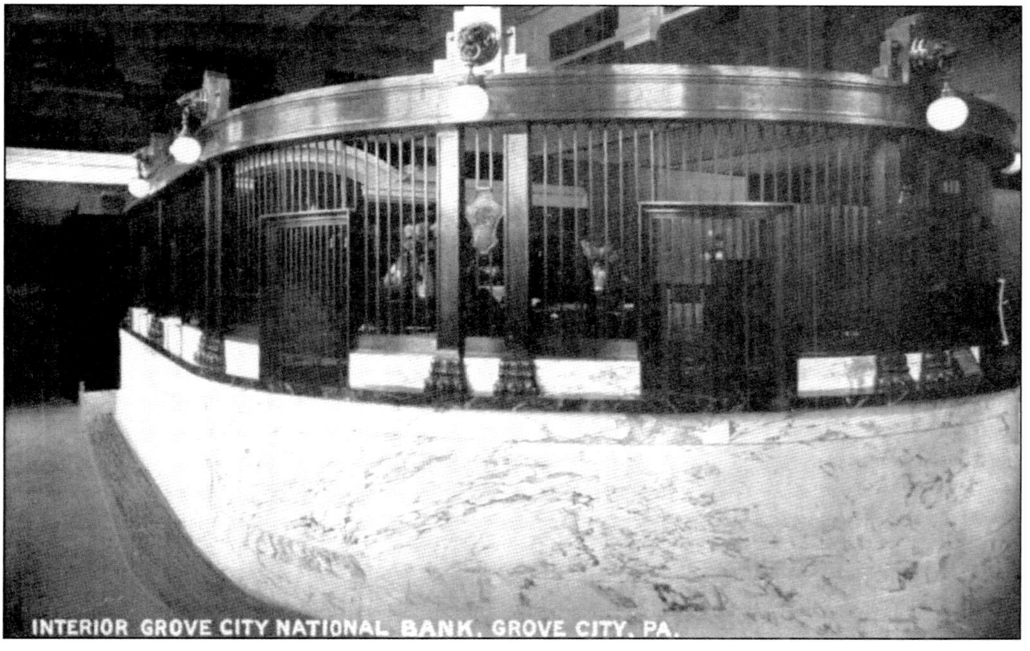

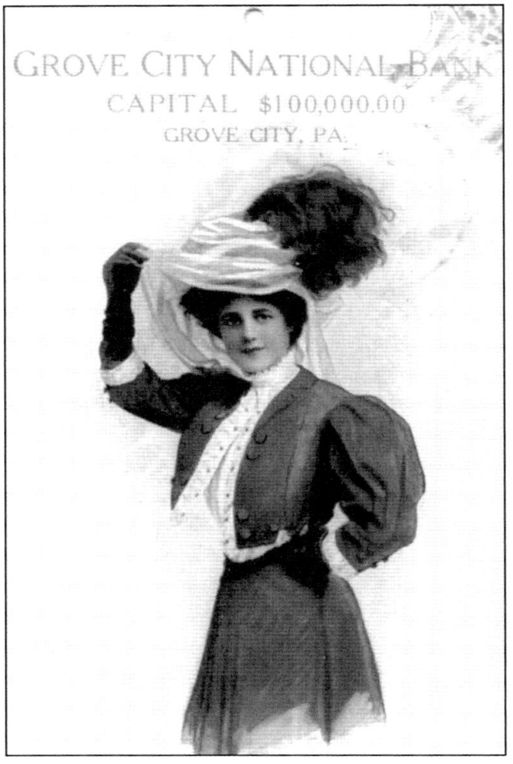

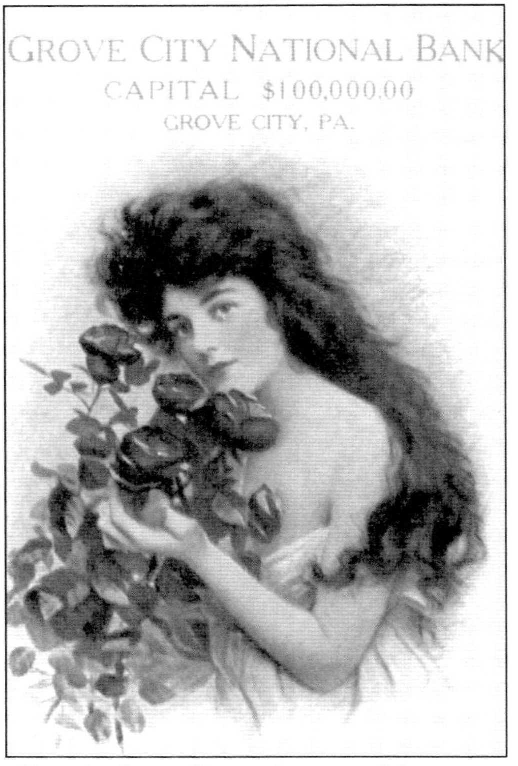

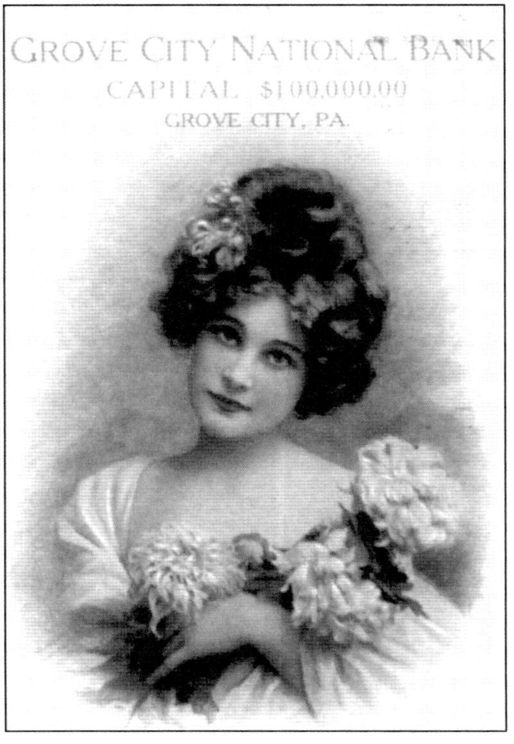

Even in Grove City at the turn of the century, advertisers used women in marketing materials to entice men to buy. In these examples, from the Grove City National Bank's 1908 calendar, attractive young women from the months of September, October, and November, flash coy yet inviting smiles leaving the rest to the observer's imagination. Miss October, who is holding a bouquet of roses, seems especially out of character for Grove City women of 1908. It was not proper for a woman to be seen with her hair down around her shoulders or for her dressing gown to likewise be heading south.

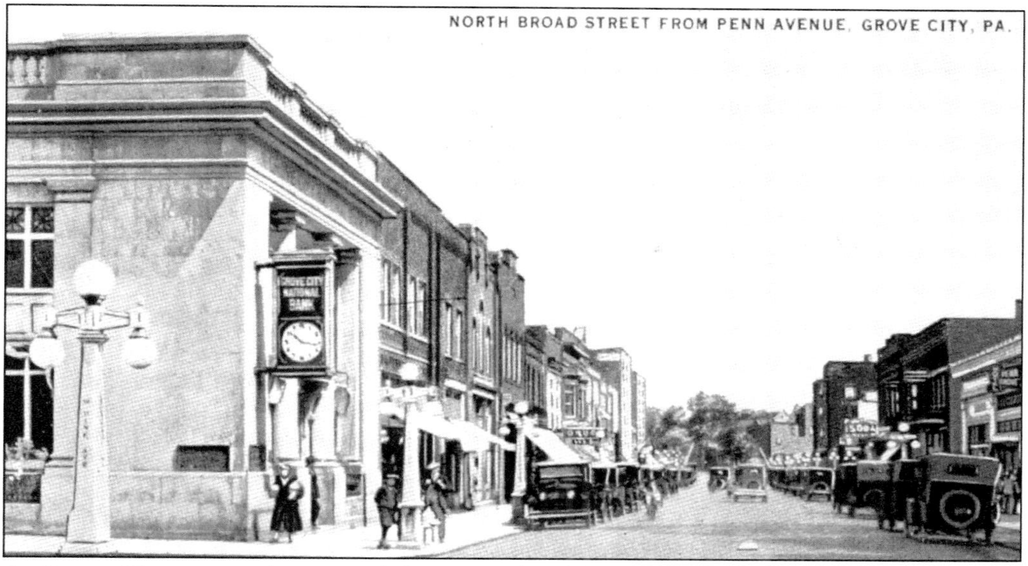

As Grove City grew and prospered, businesses lined both sides of Broad Street. New electric streetlights were installed, and the Grove City National Bank installed a clock on the corner of the building, which remained in service for more than 50 years. Interestingly, this card refers to Pine Street as "Penn Avenue." Past the bank on the left side of the street were King and Gilmore Shoes, formerly Guthrie's Shoe Store. De France Drugstore was next-door. On the right side of the street were Harshaw's Insurance, the new location of Guthrie's Shoe Store, and Burdick's, which was first a newsstand and soda fountain selling newspapers, magazines, clothes, and nickel candy. In the photograph below, probably taken a short time later, Dixie's Diner appears on the corner of South Broad and Pine Streets, where J. C. Penney eventually relocated. Notice that the streetlight on the corner in front of the bank is a different style. It is possibly a clue that the old one was ruined in an accident. Eventually, the street was lit with these fixtures.

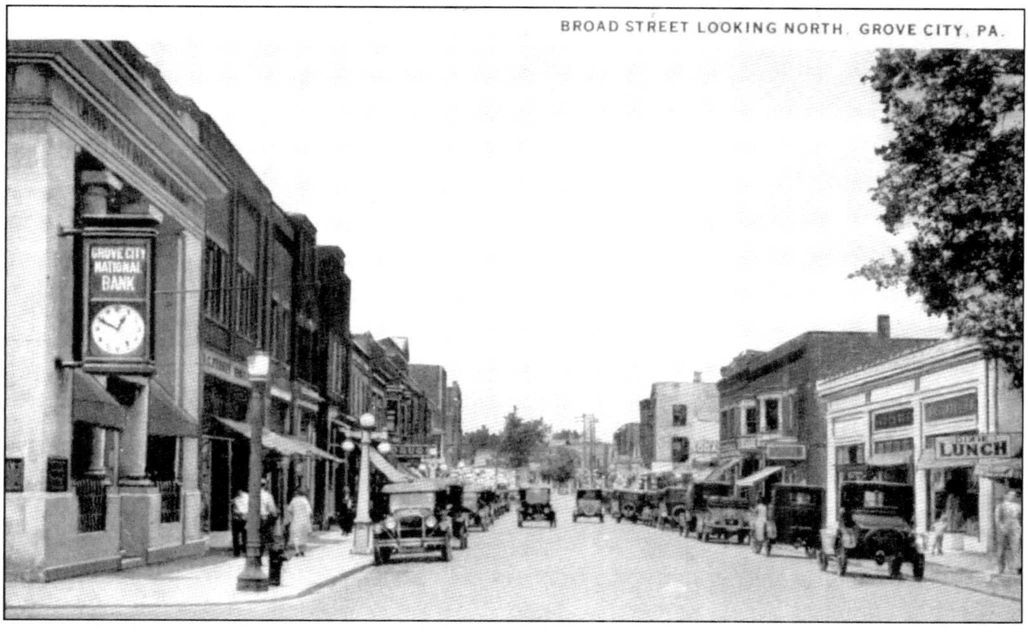

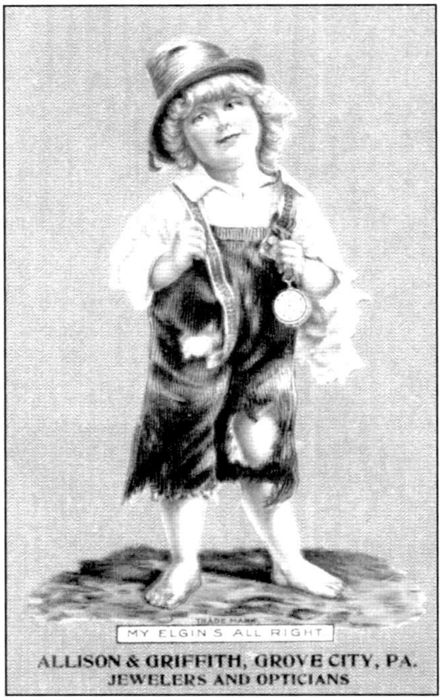

Businesses on Broad Street often moved up and down the street as circumstances and business conditions changed. In the 1916 *Ouija,* Grove City College's yearbook, Allison and Griffith have an address close to the railroad tracks. Later, however, the business had jewelers and opticians and a showroom and office in the vicinity of the Laurel Eye Clinic's present location.

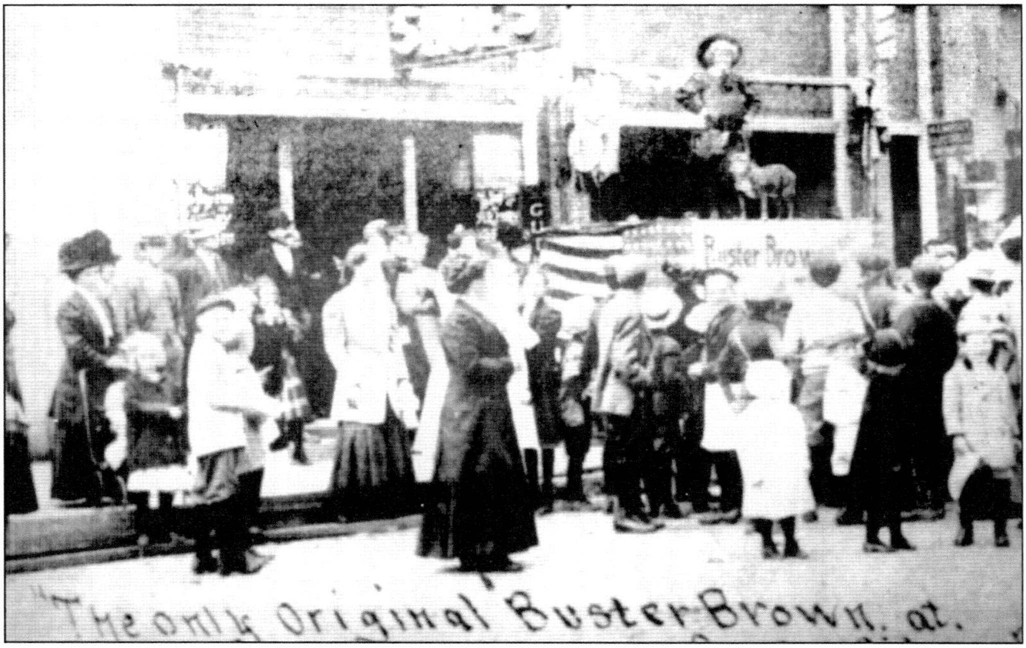

As a promotion, shoe stores hosted several visits by Buster Brown and his dog. In this photograph, the actor portraying Buster Brown stands on a stage erected for the occasion in front of Guthrie's Shoe Store. Although boasting "The only Original Buster Brown at Grove City, PA.," actors portraying the child in the Buster Brown advertisements visited Grove City several times during the following decades. The word "original" on the card hints that other Buster Browns might be around who were not the original.

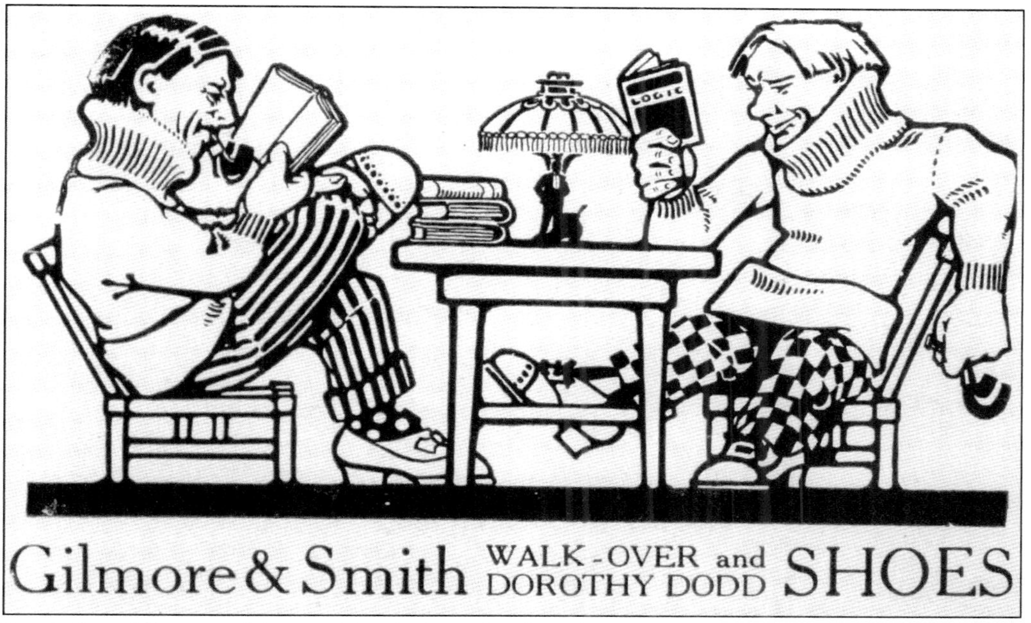

South Broad Street and Grove City College developed together. Regular train service on Broad Street began within a few years of the founding of the Pine Grove Normal Academy, the forerunner of Grove City College. The close proximity of the two meant businesses on Broad Street catered to the needs of students as well as townspeople. This advertisement from the 1914 *Ouija,* the college's yearbook, is for a shoe store downtown. It shows eccentric "college types" hitting the books while wearing shoes that were no doubt sold locally.

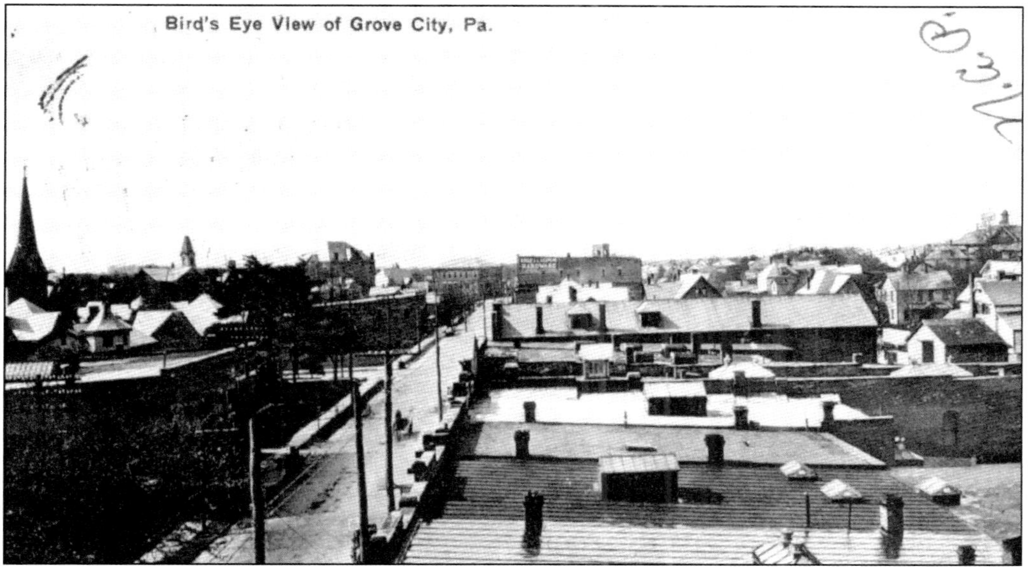

From this bird's-eye vantage point looking south on South Broad Street, the steeple of the old Methodist Episcopal church can be seen in the background, along with the tops of the buildings on Grove City College's lower campus in the distance. The tiny dot on the horizon to the right is the cupola of Central School at the intersection of Center and West Main. The ridges on the roofs, dotted with chimneys and skylights, indicate that they were likely made of soldered tin.

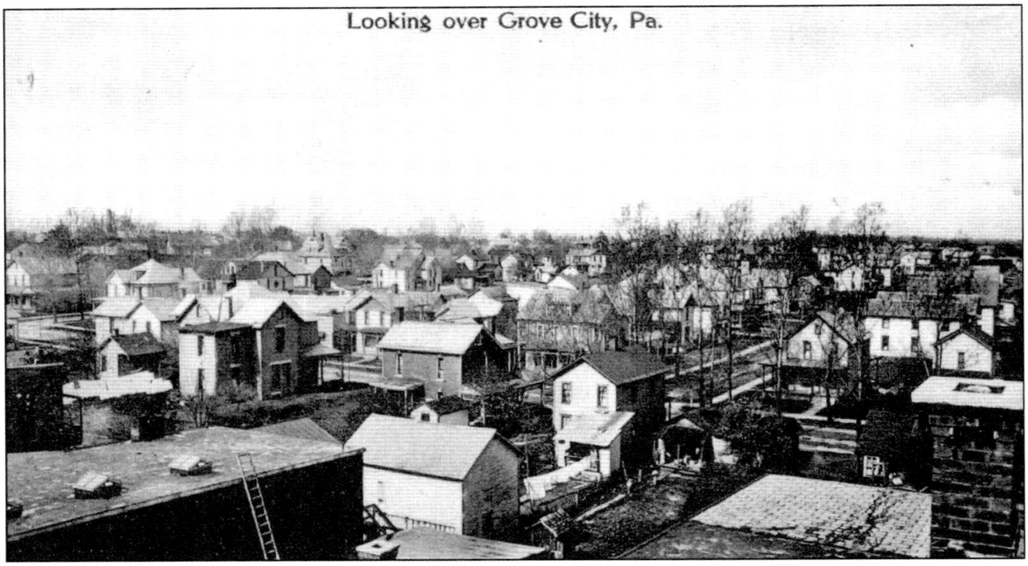

Shown here from approximately the same vantage point but looking west, a photographer captured this scene overlooking the intersection of South Center and Jackson Streets. While a few houses from this time period remain on Jackson Street, all the homes along Center Street have been replaced with businesses. In the center of the picture is a house with a barn in the back and laundry hanging on a clothes line. It was located approximately where the Moon Brothers built their garage on South Center.

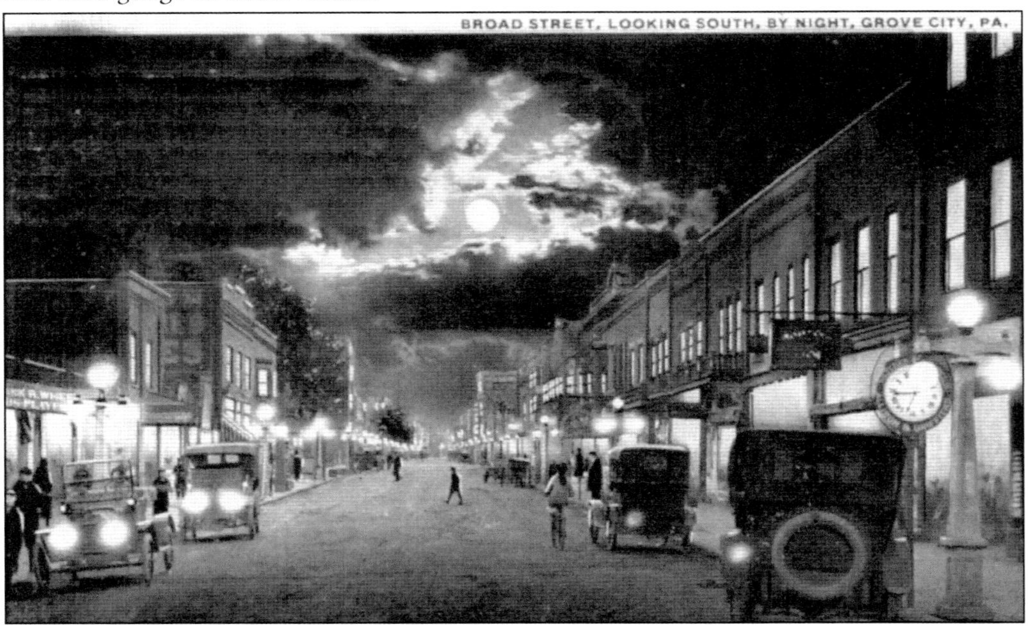

Shown from the street level, this card is unusual for presenting a nighttime scene. One clue that this is actually a daytime photograph colored to look like a scene after dark is that all of the windows on the second floors of all the buildings are lit; this seems unlikely. Most of those are apartments and would have had the shades drawn at night. In fact, in the Grove City College Colonial women's dormitory it was a rule that the shades be drawn if the electric lights were employed.

I. N. Fithian published this verse entitled, "A Hundred Years From Now." It was published in 1913.

A hundred years from now,
Where shall I be?
Asleep beneath the sod,
Or rolling in the sea?
Mystery hangs over all
And storms beat on.
Such things'll not bother me
When I am gone.
A hundred years from now
I'll be forgot.
No one will call my name
And I will answer not.
My image like the leaves
Shall fade away,
And all on Earth forget
My feeble day.

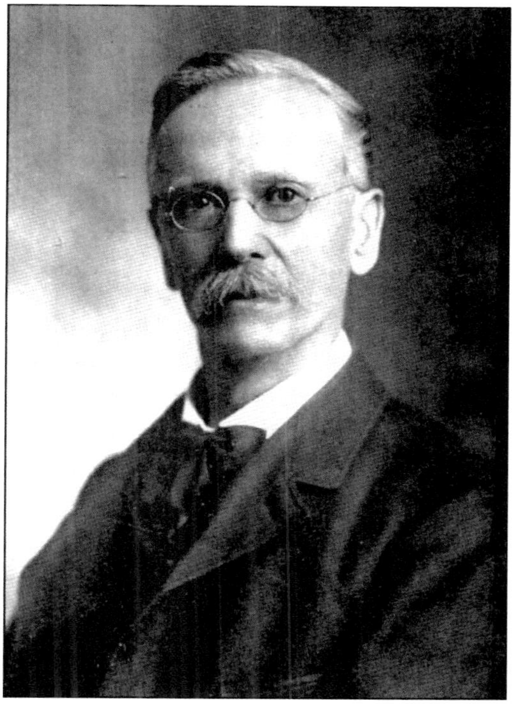

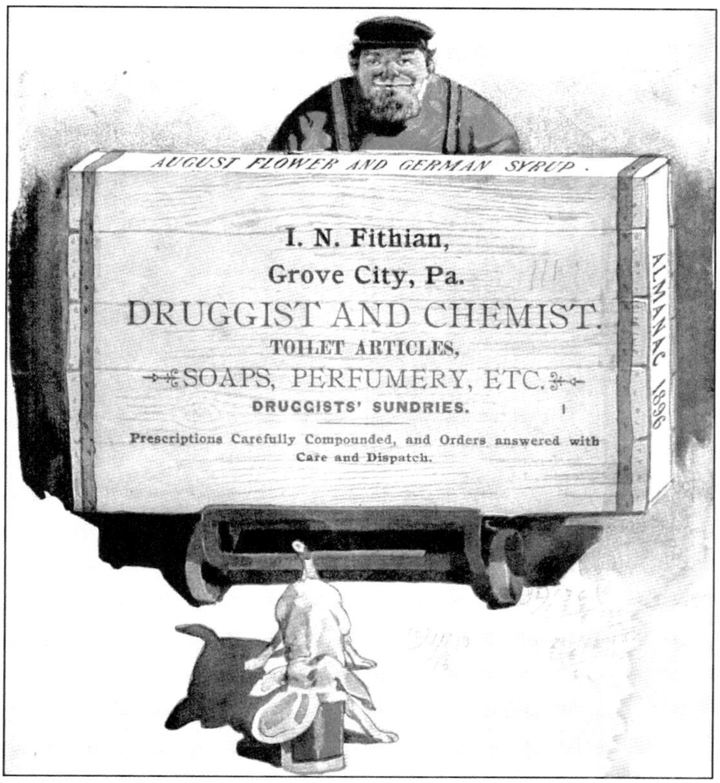

I. N. Fithian was the brother of Dr. E. J. Fithian, who ran the Bessemer Gas Engine Company, whose signature appears on the $10 bill as president of the Grove City National Bank, and who also ran for political office as a Prohibition candidate. I. N. Fithian operated a pharmacy in Grove City. One mysterious pill bottle from Fithian's Pharmacy, hidden beneath floor boards in the attic of the old hospital on West Main Street, said, "Poison: Use once or twice daily," on the label.

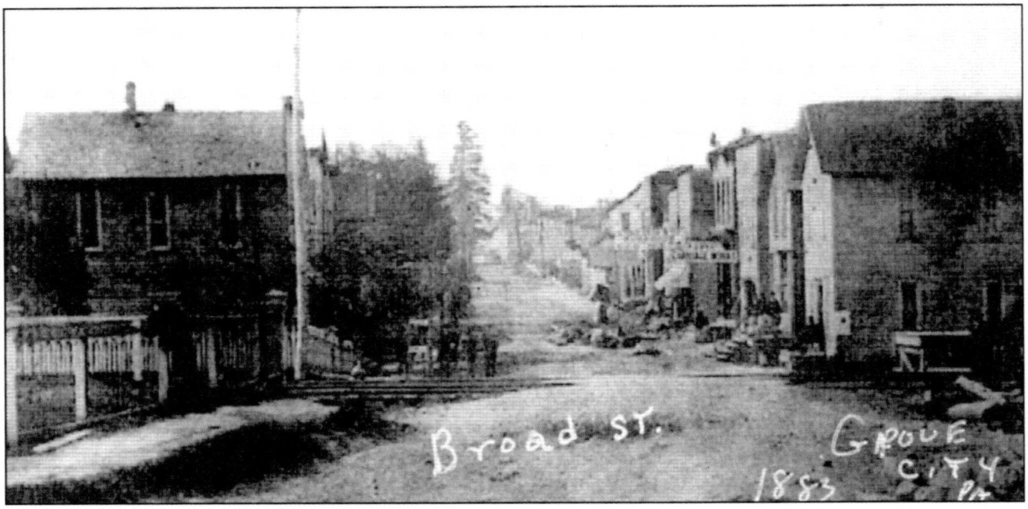

In this image of South Broad Street, the wooden buildings and dirt street can be seen past the railroad tracks looking south. Almost all the original wooden buildings were consumed in horrific fires just a few years later. The borough of Grove City was incorporated in 1883 from the village of Pine Grove. The name Pine Grove was already taken in Pennsylvania. Margaret Guinnip, the widow of a California sheep rancher and lifelong friend of Grove City College founder Isaac Ketler, lent the borough the money to get going.

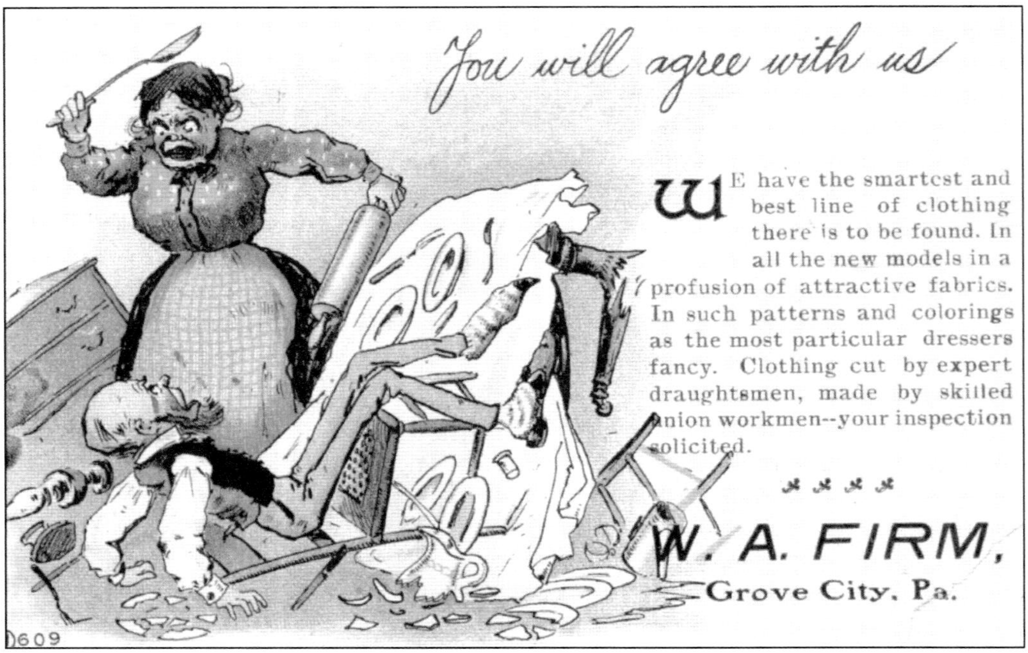

In contrast to the Grove City Nation Bank's use of alluring young women in its advertisements, W. A. Firm Clothier chose a slightly different tactic. Conventional marketing wisdom in 2004 would probably suggest not associating a product too closely with shrewish wives or battered husbands, and yet it is an eye-catching piece of advertising. W. A. Firm's clothing store was on Broad Street between the railroad tracks and Pine Street.

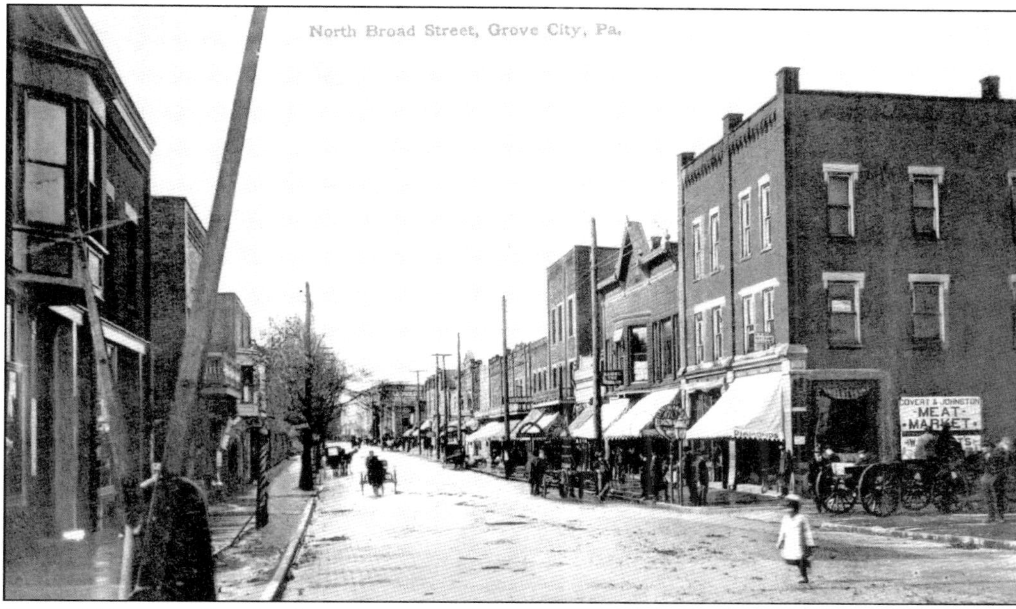

Around 30 years after the fires, the town rebuilt and acquired the streetscape it has today. The photographer of this picture was probably standing on the railroad tracks, as one railroad gate in the upright position is to the left. On the corner is the Covert and Johnston Meat Market. A sign on the wall discouraging loiterers reads, "Stand to the curb, or move on!" The meat market is currently the office of Grove City Realty. Covert and Johnston also developed real estate. They divided and sold the lots for homes along McConnell and Valley Streets and the Broadacres plan north of town.

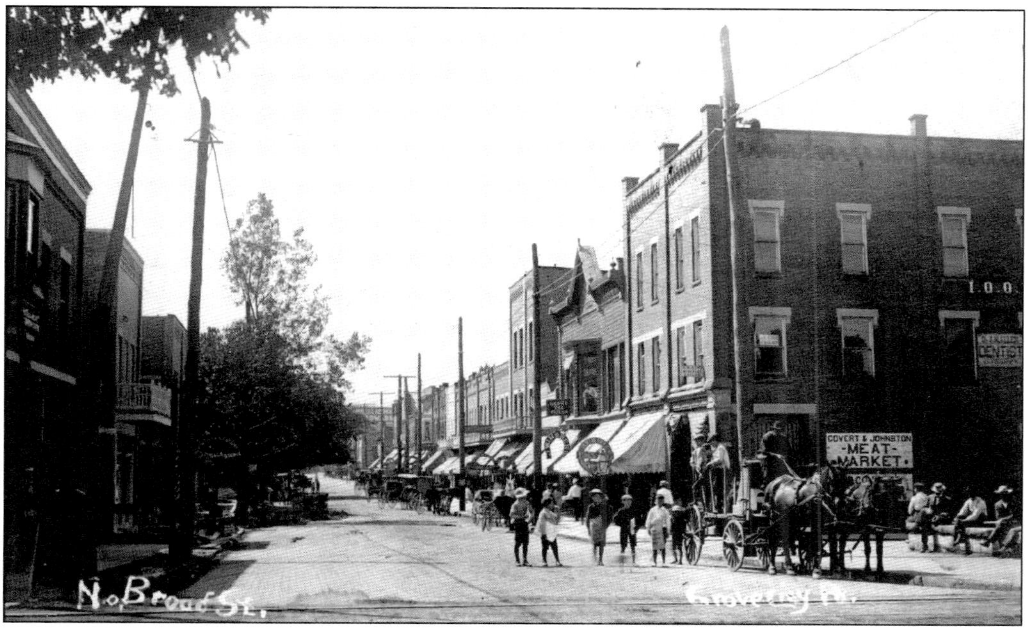

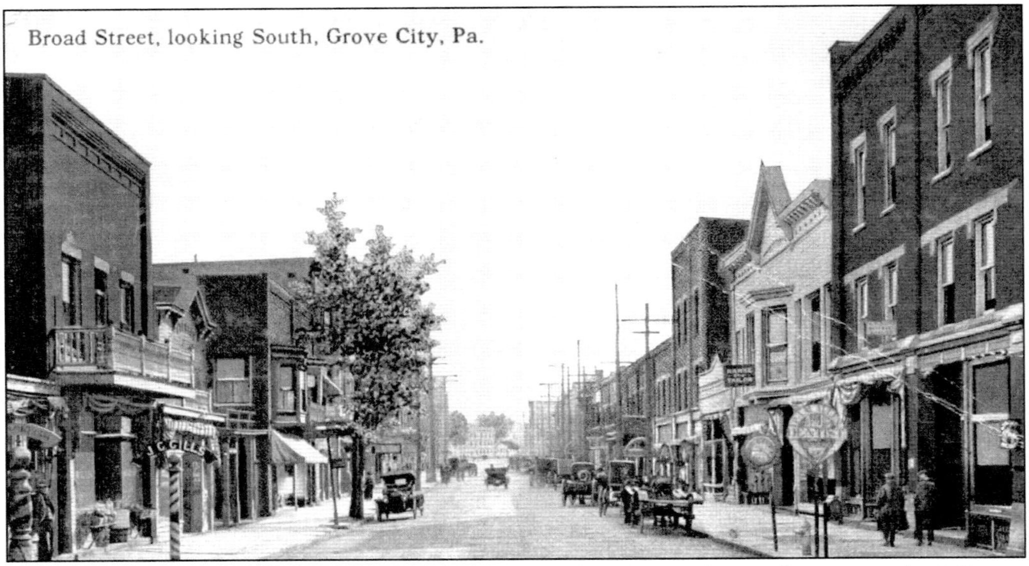

In this scene of South Broad Street looking south, barber shop poles can be seen to the left; one is advertising the services of barber J. G. Gills. This area of South Broad prospered due to its proximity to the Bessemer and Lake Erie Railroad Station, just out of the picture to the right. Businesses which depended on a flow of traffic and people suffered two severe blows in the early 1950s: passenger service ended and traffic became two-way, which made it difficult to get to this section of town. In 2004, Grove City Revitalization is raising money for a multi-million dollar renovation of this section of town. Included in the plans are burying most overhead wires, constructing new sidewalks, and planting trees. Compare these two postcards. Once again we see that an artist has enhanced the street scene by adding a vintage car and by removing the telephone poles visible down the street. While removal of the overhead wires from Broad Street has always been an ideal, there is finally a plan to remove them by 2006.

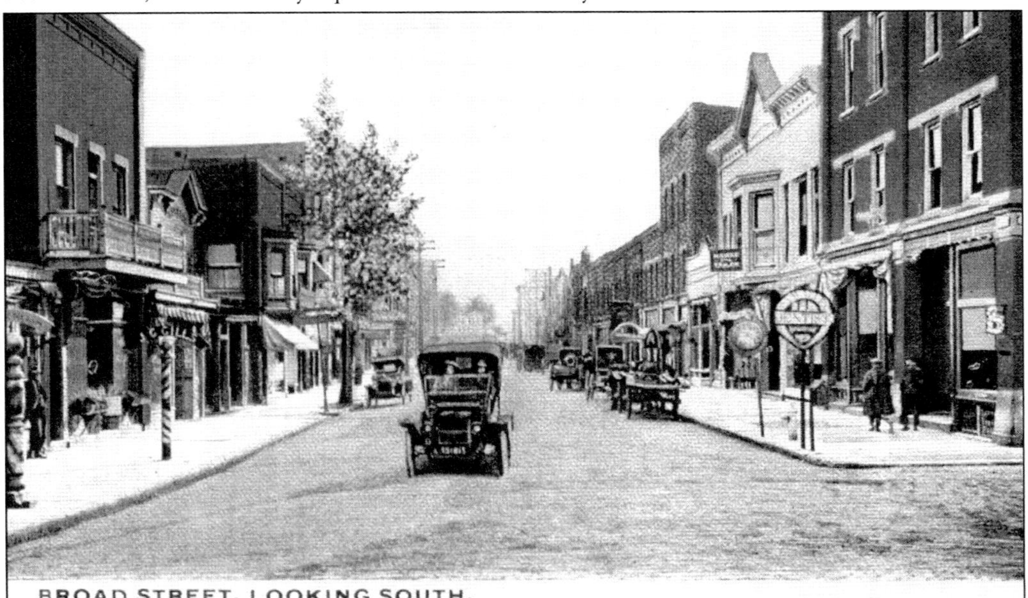

Seven

North Broad and North

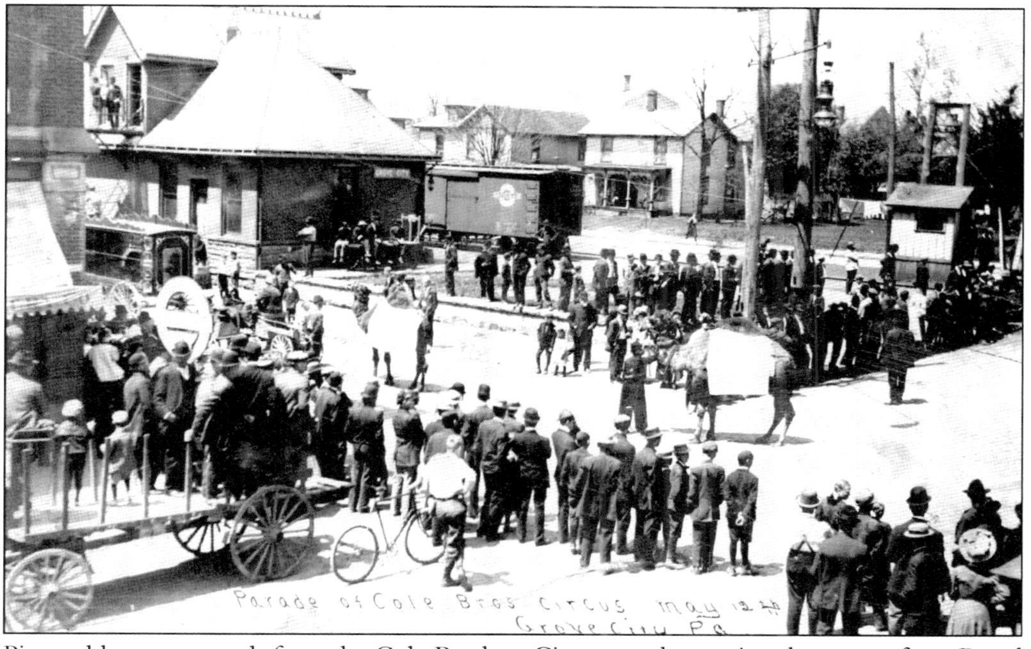

Pictured here are camels from the Cole Brothers Circus parade, turning the corner from Broad onto Blair Street. Sometimes things in the background are just as interesting as the intended subject of a photograph. Although the photographer thought he was capturing camels, he also collected images of a 1911 bicycle, the overhead electric streetlights, the train station, the signal house, a flat-bed wagon, and many bowler hats—the style of the day.

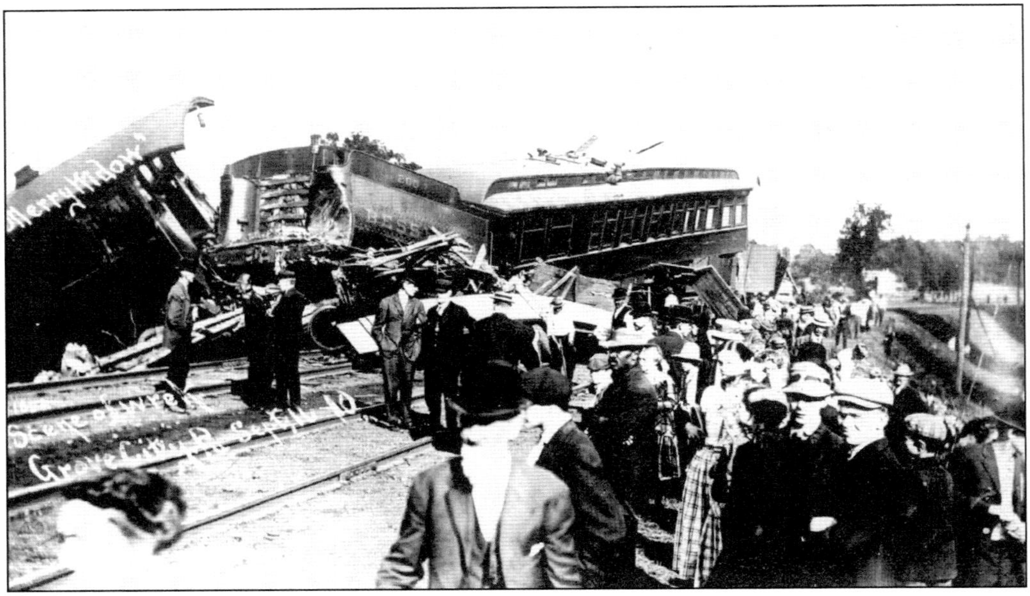

Because of Grove City's excellent high school and college, students commuted to class from miles around, including towns as far away as Branchton, Keister, Boyers, and Wick. These towns were several hours drive by carriage but just minutes by train. The Merry Widow was the short-distance coach used frequently by students traveling to school and back. On September 16, 1910, the Merry Widow jumped the track on the stretch between Madison Avenue and East Pine Street and was disabled and stuck on the tracks. The engineer of the oncoming Bessemer and Lake Erie Railroad did not see the crippled coach blocking the track. Fortunately, at the time of the accident nobody was on the Merry Widow, and few were on the colliding passenger train. There are no records of any deaths or injuries as a result of this spectacular train wreck.

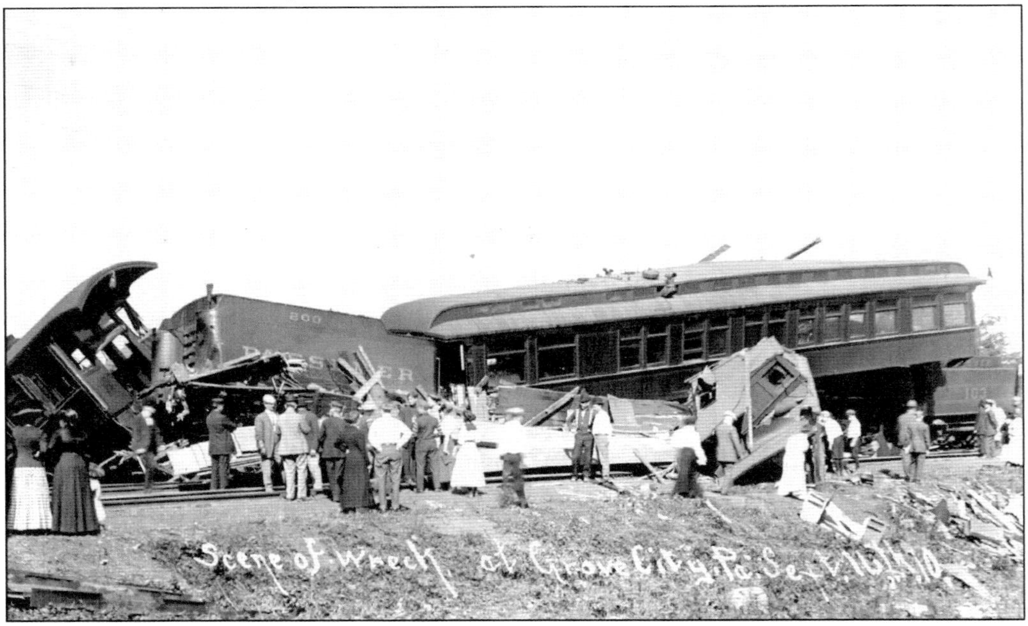

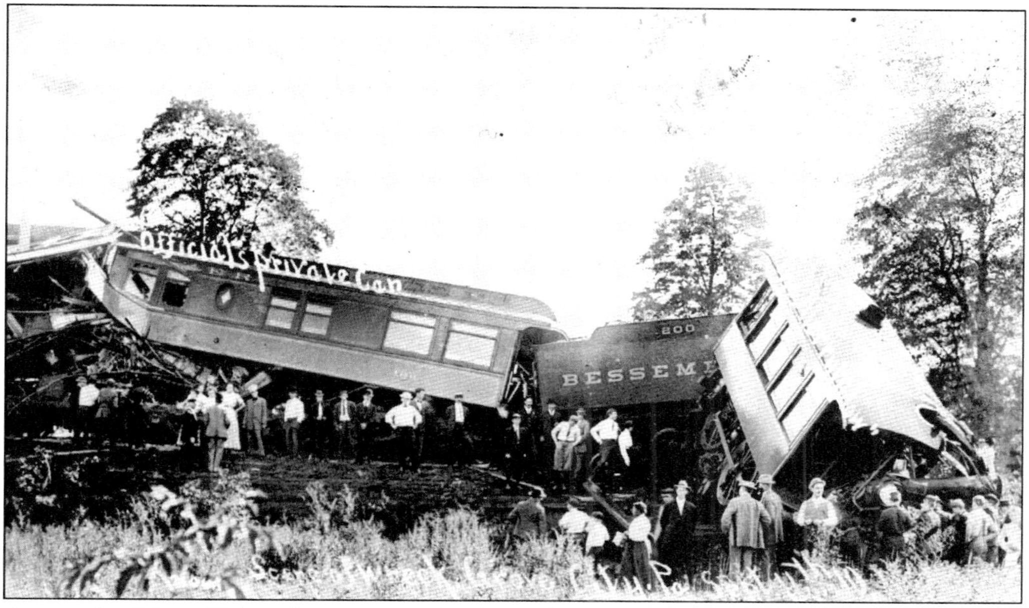

As a result of the collision, the Merry Widow's coach was completely destroyed. In January 2004, an automobile was struck by a train, and the wreckage came to a rest in about the same place as the Merry Widow crash. Fortunately, though injured, everyone survived. In another fool-hardy escapade, a young man from Grove City who got off work at the same time everyday would see the train at the Madison intersection and race it to the crossing on East Pine Street. Zooming down East Pine, he beat the train every time except in what proved to be his final try.

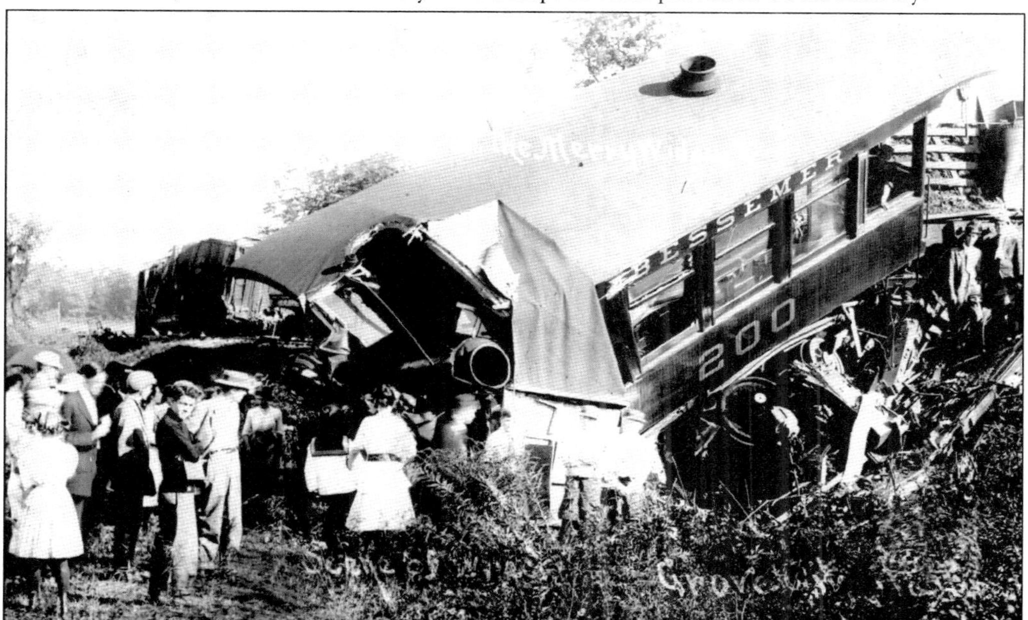

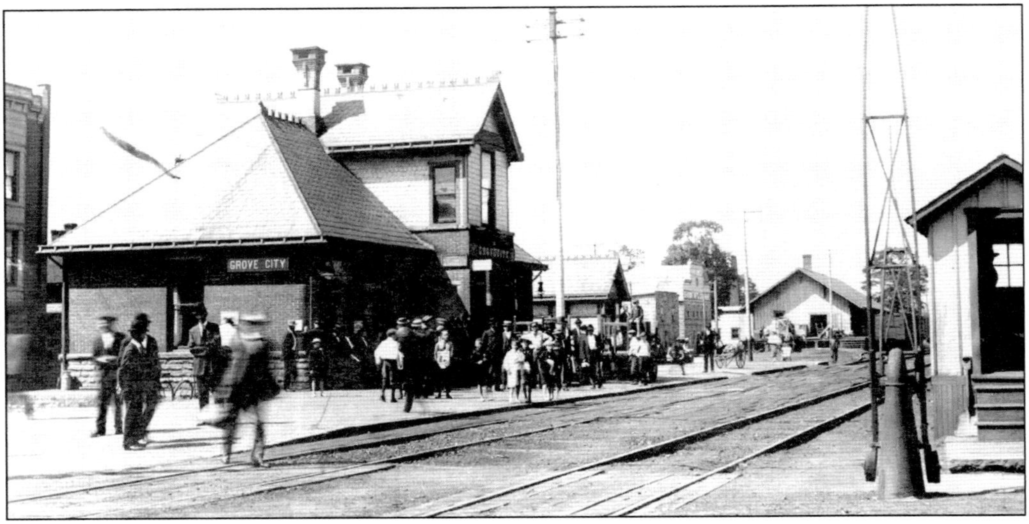

In the 1870s when the Shenango and Allegheny Railroad established a stop near the tiny village of Pine Grove, not more than a few hundred people lived in the area. It was operated by the Bessemer and Lake Erie Railroad at the time these pictures were created. Residents and businesses benefited by multiple trains per day, as Grove City was now on the main route between the ports of Erie and Pittsburgh. For example, by 1900, Jennie Pearsall in Grove City wrote letters to her boyfriend Edd Reed, in Mercer, inviting him to dinner the same evening. Easy access to railroad transportation was the catalyst that transformed the local Grove City economy from an agricultural base to an industrial base. For example, local coal mines depended on the railroad to get the coal to market in Pittsburgh once miners brought it to the surface. Working coal mines increased the demand for laborers, thus rapidly increasing the population of the Grove City area. Key to all this growth was access to rail transportation.

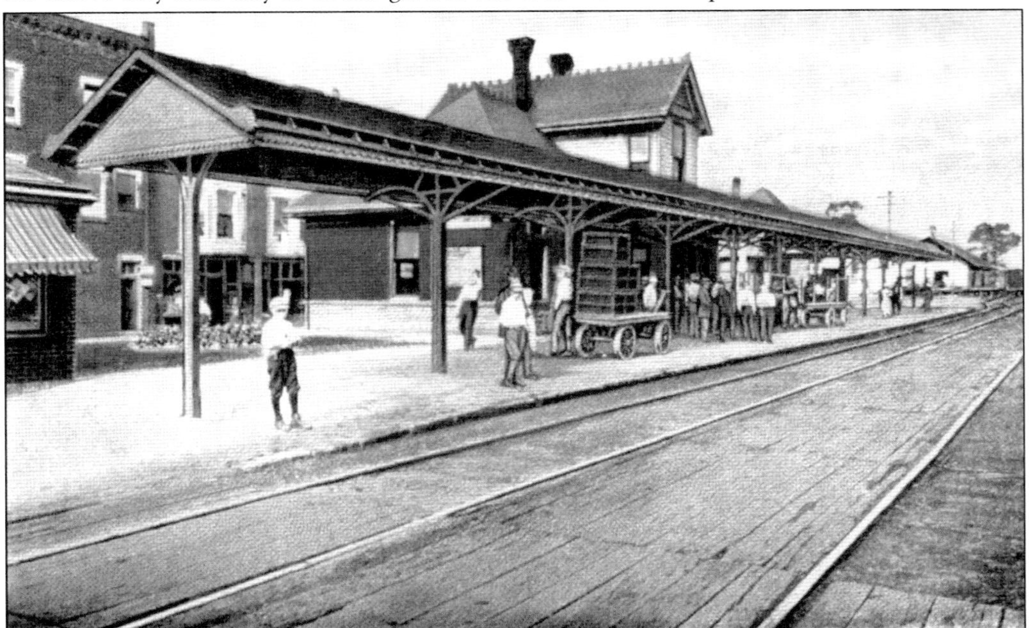

B. & L. E. RAILROAD STATION.

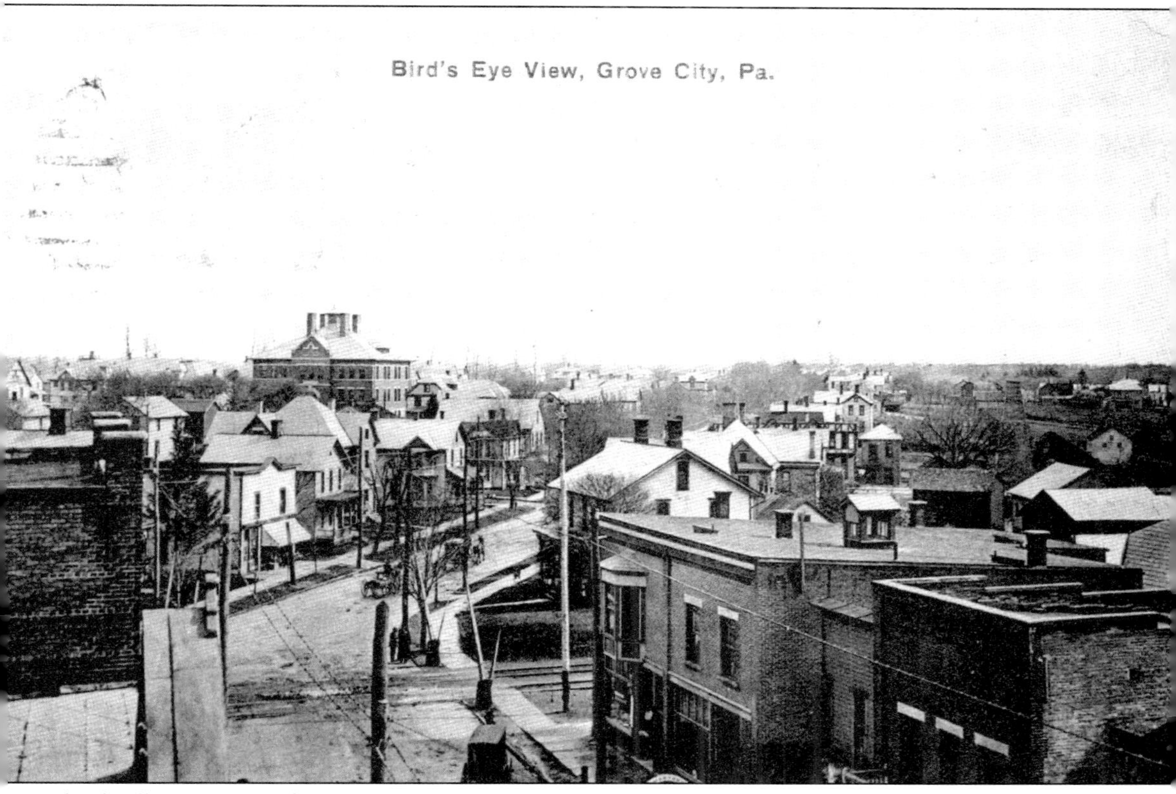

This bird's-eye view of Grove City shows the top of Lincoln School in the distance. The bend in the road is near the railroad tracks. The house beside the railroad tracks on the right with two chimneys is where the Broad Street Garage was built. The second store from the railroad tracks on the right was the location of George J. Howe's grocery store, where he began roasting coffee for his customers. Today, Howe's is a food industry innovator and distributes coffee, candy, and nuts across the country.

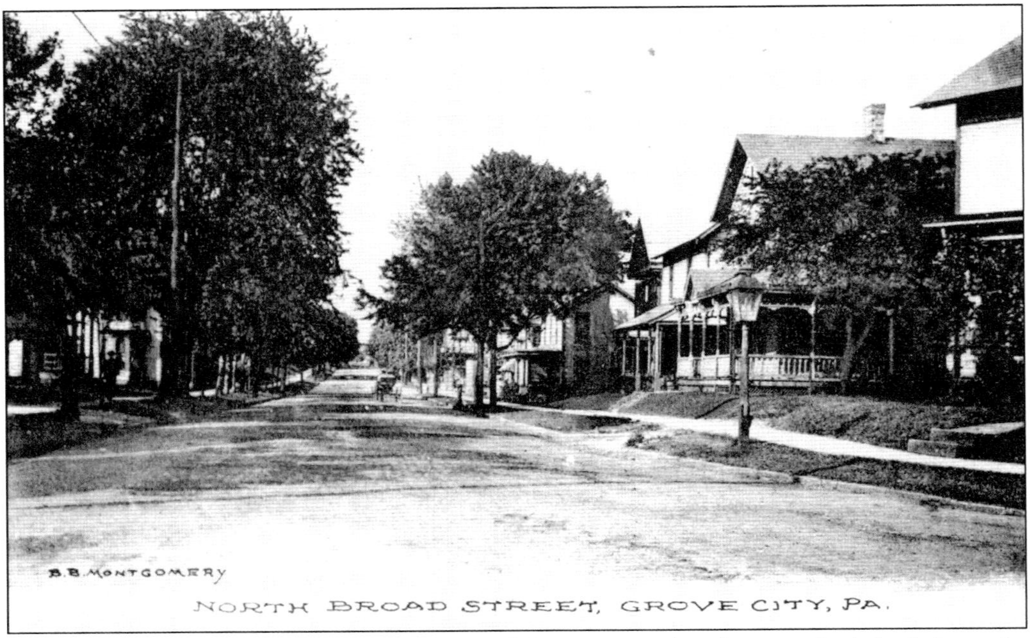

North Broad Street is shown near the turn of the century; the photographer's back is to the railroad tracks. To the left in the picture is a general store with a broom standing out front and an advertisement for an insurance and real estate office posted on the side of the building. On the right side is a nice view of an original gas streetlight. While both of these pictures were taken at about the same time, in the example above, the photographer has removed the telephone poles seen on the card below.

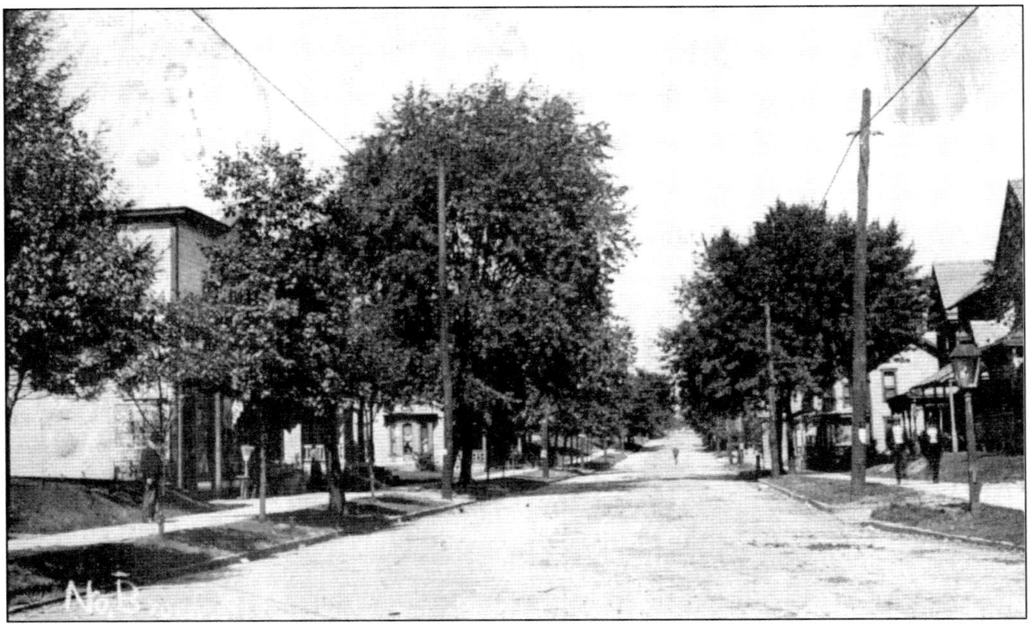

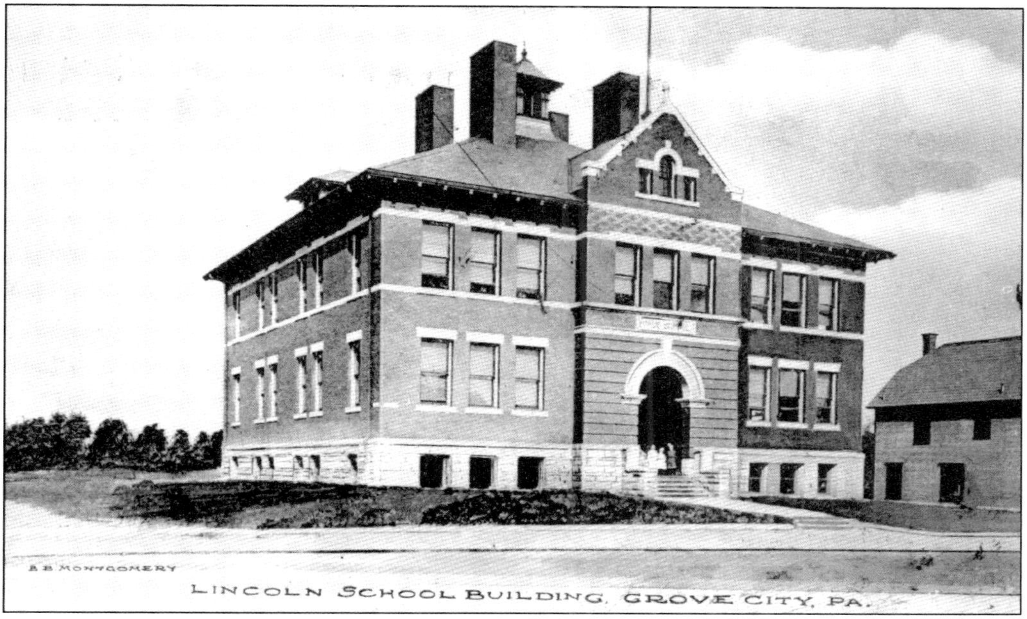

Author John Hummel attended Lincoln School where his teacher, Lois Jamison, taught him, "I may not be a Washington, a Lincoln, or a Lee, But I can be the very best there is to be of me." Lincoln School, curiously enough, is not near Lincoln Avenue but at the corner of North Center Street and Gilmore Avenue. Pictured below is Aletha Philpot and John Hummel's first-grade class. He remembers her finger being a foot long when she often pointed and said, "Keep of the grass!" Nevertheless, the kids all loved her.

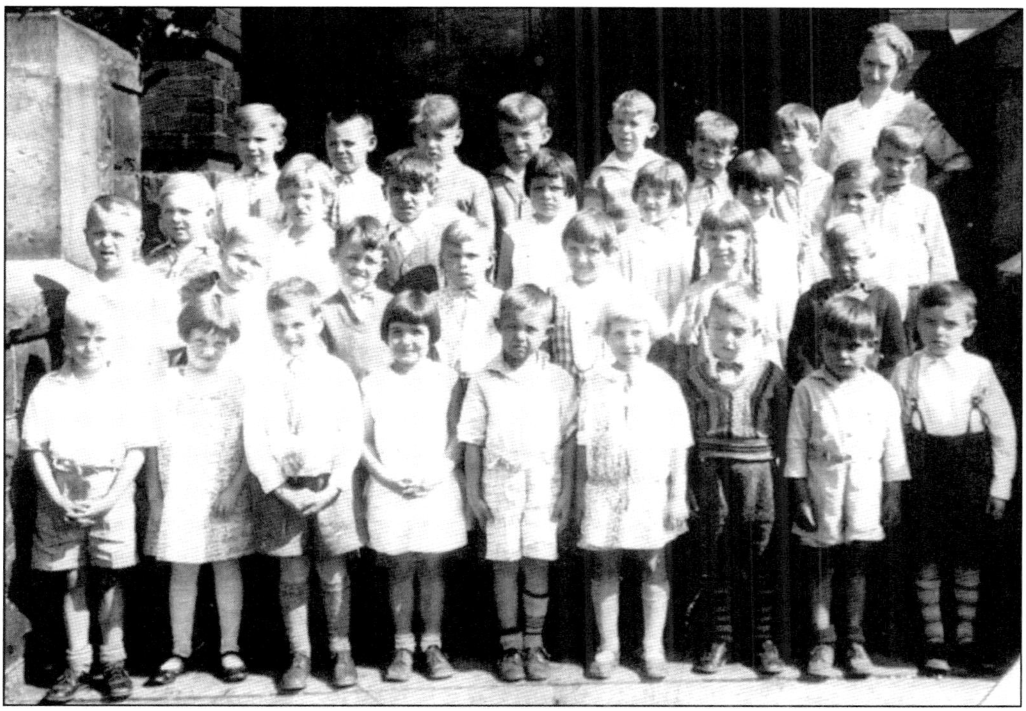

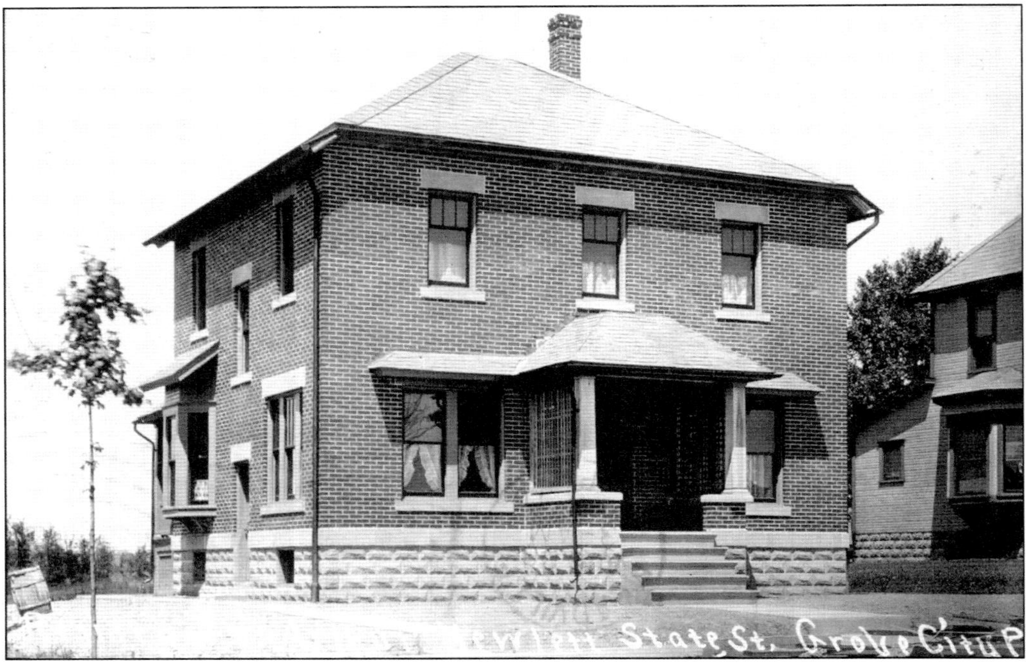

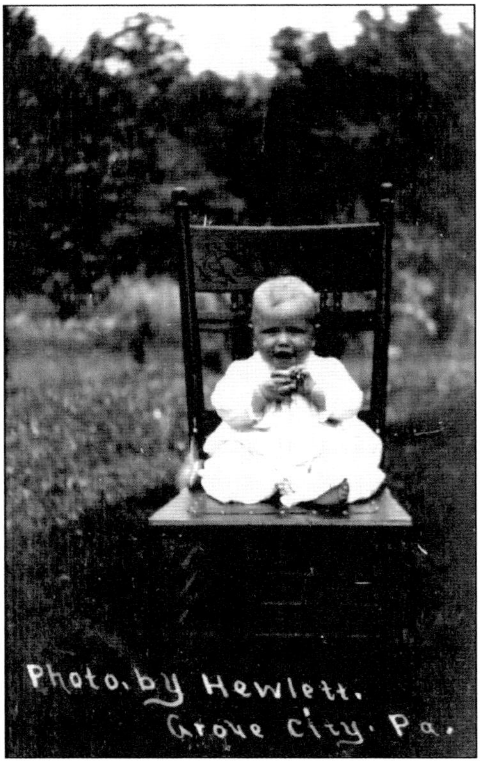

This photograph is of Arthur Hewlett's home, which still stands on State Street. The tantalizing clue, "Photo by Hewlett, Grove City, Pa.," on the picture of the child below, along with the similar handwriting found on many of the early-20th-century postcard images used in this book, points to the possibility that the photographer who captured many of these early images of Grove City was the same Arthur Hewlett. Other postcard publishers include the following: B. B. Montgomery, Grove City; Harry H. Hamm, Erie; I. Robbins and Son, Pittsburgh; G. A. Rogaliner, Pittsburgh; International Post Card Company, New York; Robert D. Young, Grove City; and Richard T. Young, Grove City. While their images live on, the names of the photographers who chronicled the Grove City of a century ago have not survived.

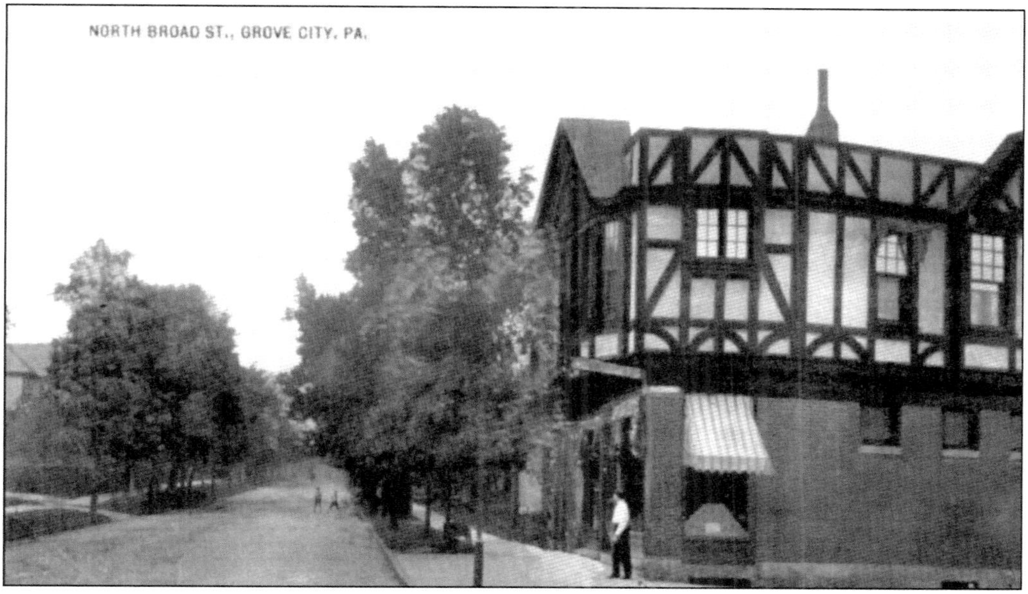

At the intersection of North Broad Street and Lincoln Avenue, one found Bobbitt's Grocery store on the northern corner. The faux half-timber style of architecture was used in the construction of only a few buildings in Grove City. Bobbitt's Grocery, the "Flat Iron Building" across the street, as the narrow triangular shaped structure has come to be known, and the demonstration creamery buildings built a block away on Lincoln Avenue make up most of the structures built in this style.

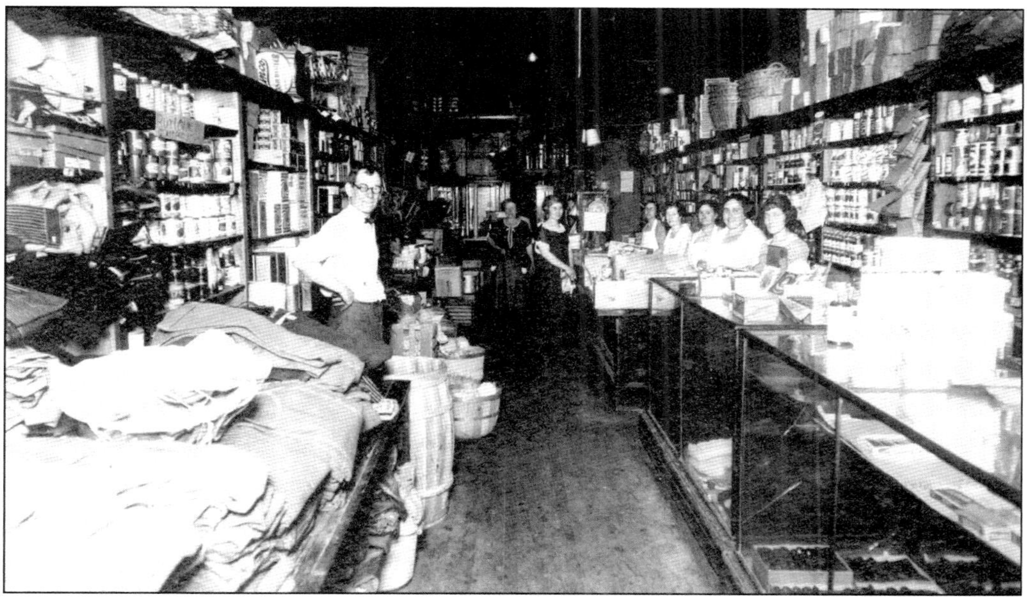

The interior of Bobbitt's Grocery is shown above. In the days before department stores and supermarkets, the corner grocery store carried everything. Bobbitt's carried chocolate, visible in the display case to the front, along with canned goods, some clothing items, laundry baskets, and what appear to be heads of lettuce or cabbage. In addition to locally grown produce, Bobbit traded merchandise for farmers' eggs and butter.

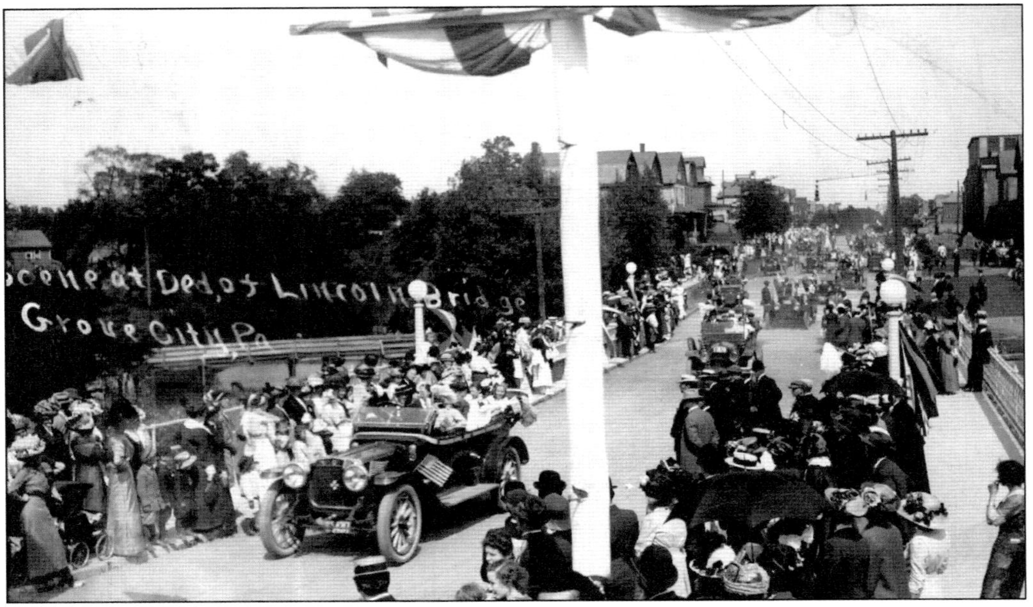

Bobbitt's store, just out of the picture to the left, is only a few feet from the Lincoln Avenue Bridge. The "new" Lincoln Avenue Bridge, shown here, was replaced a few years ago. In the picture above, taken during a parade of vintage automobiles crossing the bridge at its dedication ceremony, crowds of townspeople dressed in their finest look on. Although the style of women's hats soon changed, on this day in Grove City's history, the bigger they were the better.

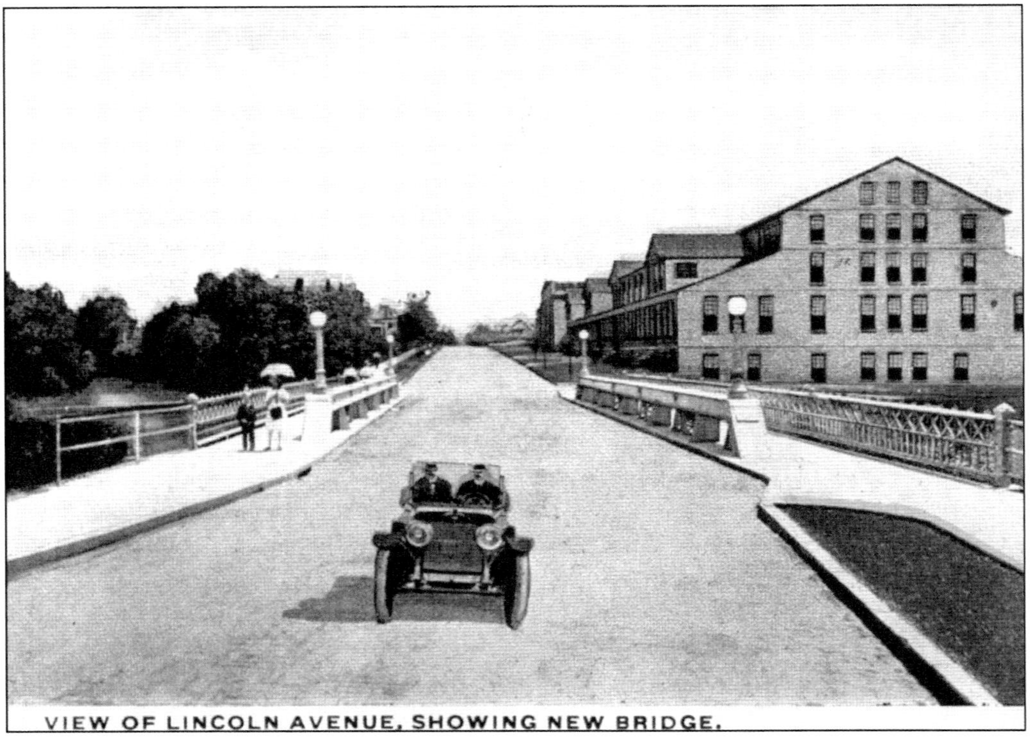

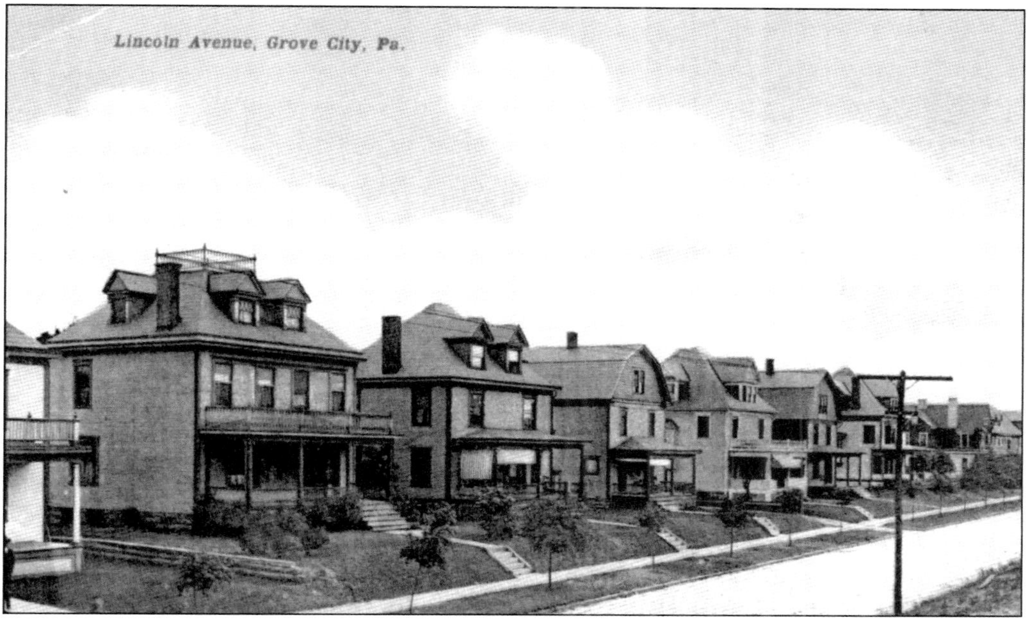

Lincoln Avenue across from the Bessemer Gas Engine Works was first developed as an upper-middle-class neighborhood. At the time these homes were built, it was not obvious that the Bessemer would grow to cover a large tract of land, consume part of Monroe Street, and develop as a site for heavy industry. In the years right after the turn of the 19th century, there was no urban or municipal planning used in small towns in Pennsylvania, and certainly not in Grove City. No efforts were made to locate industrial sites away from residential neighborhoods. And yet, it is not appropriate to judge the past based on what we know now, a century later. At the time these homes were built, the Bessemer Gas Engine Works might not have been as successful as it was. It might not have become the largest employer in town, providing tens of thousands of jobs over the next century. There was no way to know that heavy industry would dominate this area.

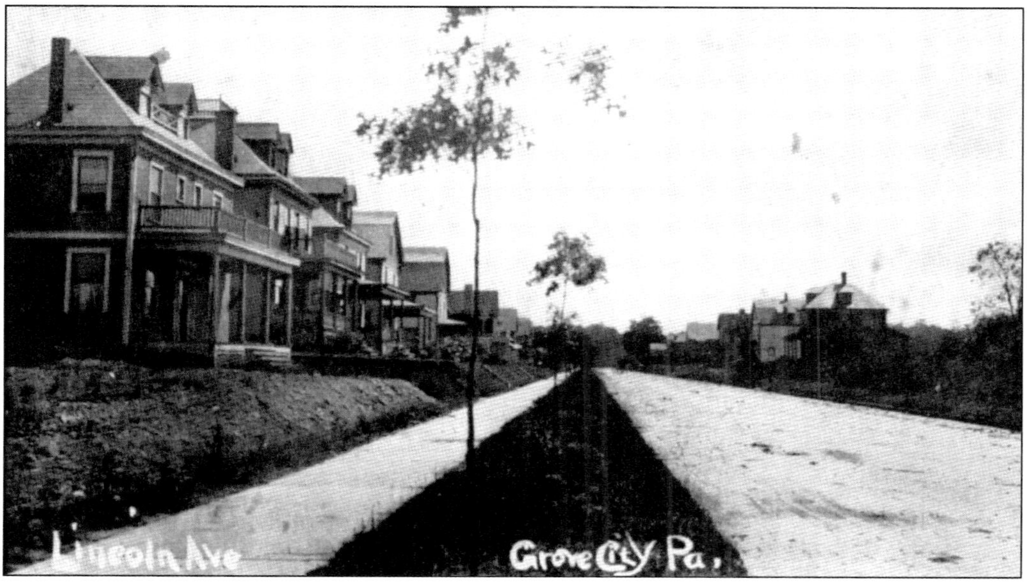

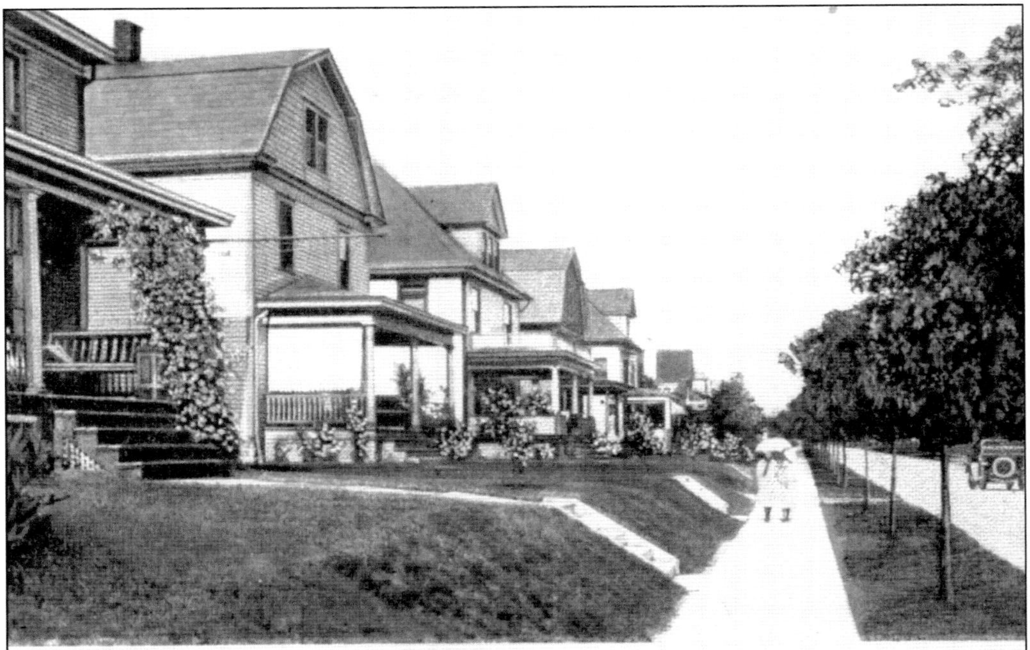

LINCOLN AVENUE, LOOKING EAST.

While homes similar to these still stand on Lincoln Avenue between Harvard and Princeton Streets, none of the homes pictured here or in the photographs on the previous page survive. If one looks carefully, one of the houses with a gambrel roof can be seen in all three pictures. In just a few years, however, in a curious combination of Grove City's agricultural past and its industrial future, the U.S. Government built a "demonstration creamery," which began to crowd out the residences pictured here. The first creamery building was close to Wolf Creek on Lincoln Avenue. Farmers brought their milk to the creamery to sell. In the picture below, a child watches the horses and wagons loaded with milk cans waiting in line. The creek is just down over the bank behind the trees in the background.

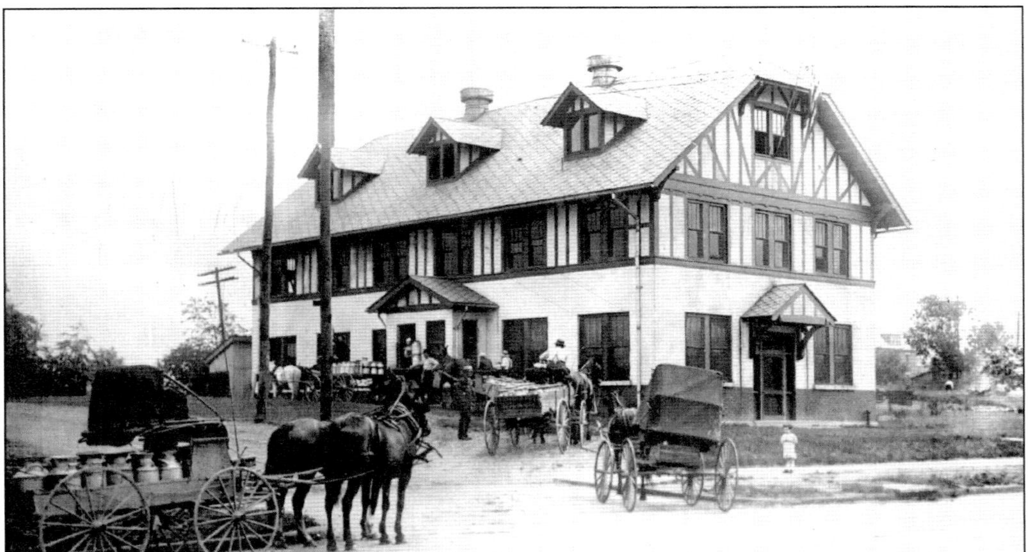

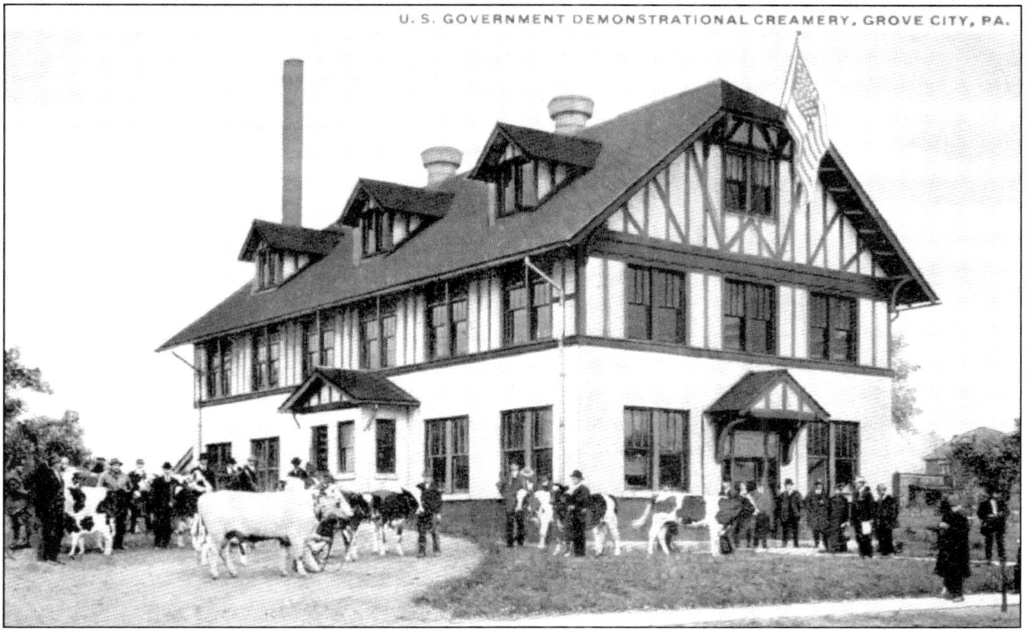

The creamery hosted dairy shows such as the one in progress above. In the picture below, the second creamery building is complete. Also visible to the right is part of one of the homes on Lincoln between Wolf Creek and Harvard Street. Although milkmen brought milk and cream to local homes, many residents remember visiting the creamery as children to get ice cream. At one time the ice-cream cups had lids with Superman images on them to the delight of little boys and girls. The Commercial Club takes some of the credit for bringing the creamery to town.

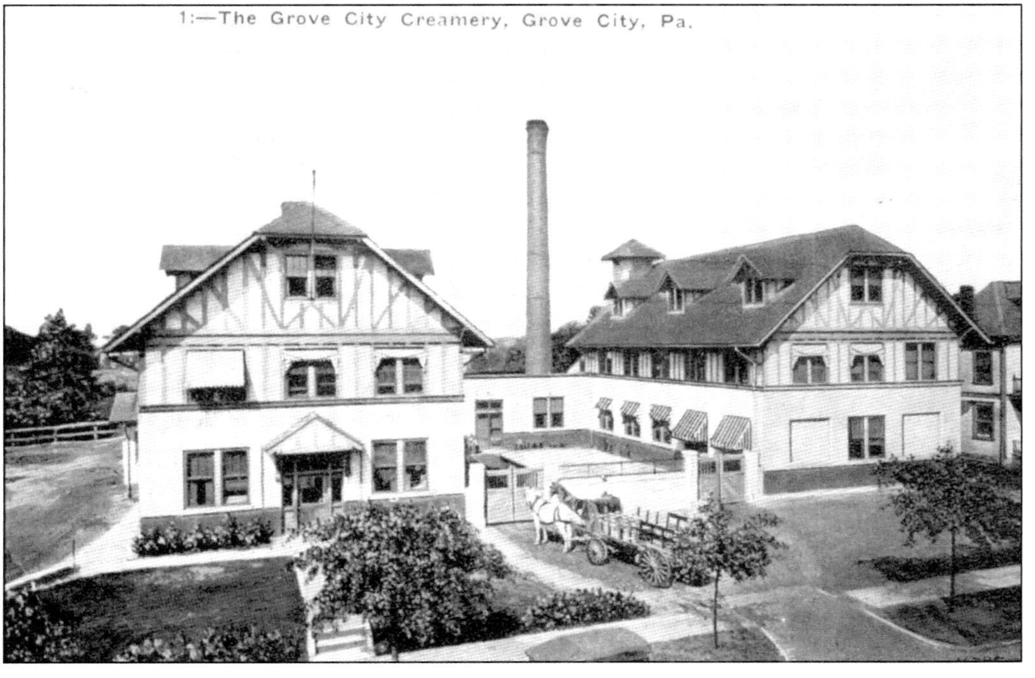

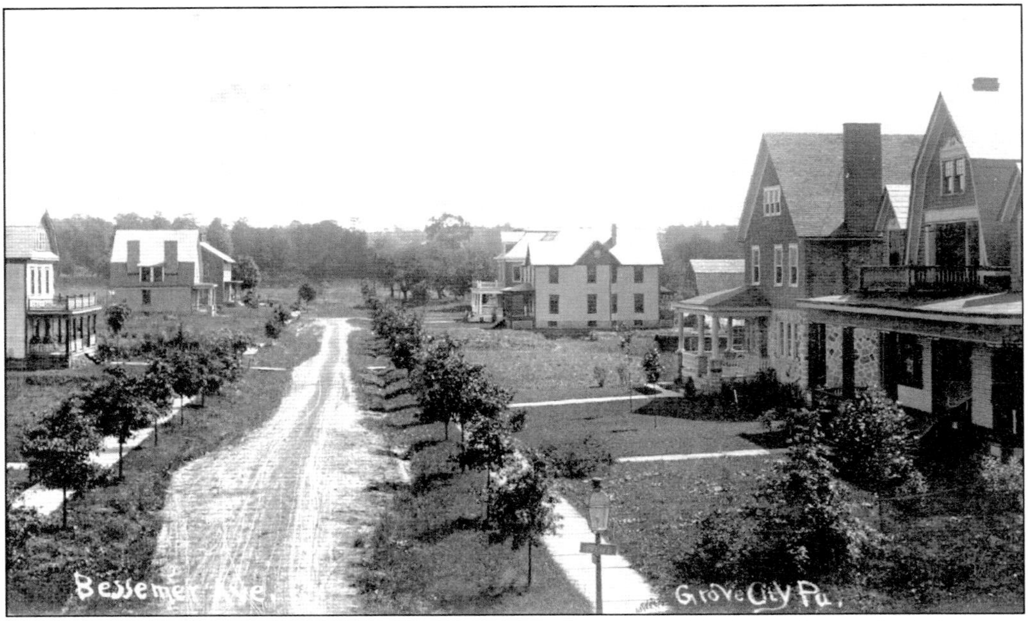

Bessemer Avenue, a street parallel to Lincoln Avenue and one block north, was built between 1910 and 1920 and remains a residential area today. Because the town and the heavy industrial plant just one block away grew together, residents were accustomed to the impact the plant had on their neighborhood. For example, when large engines were tested at the plant, the sound was deafening all over town. People standing in their yards talking to each other had to shout during the engine test runs.

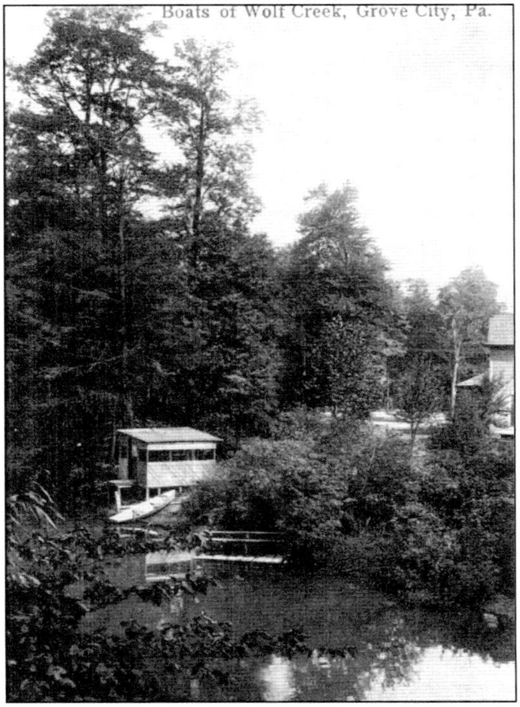

This boat house is, as the crow flies, west, in the opposite direction off the end of Bessemer Avenue and across Wolf Creek. From here, people could rent boats to paddle around the quiet waters held back by the Lower Dam. The house in this picture still stands at the end of McConnell Street. One curiosity about this neighborhood is that it is now inhabited by bank beavers. Because the water is already dammed up by the Lower Dam, the beavers do not commence building their own. This may change when the artificial Lower Dam is removed.

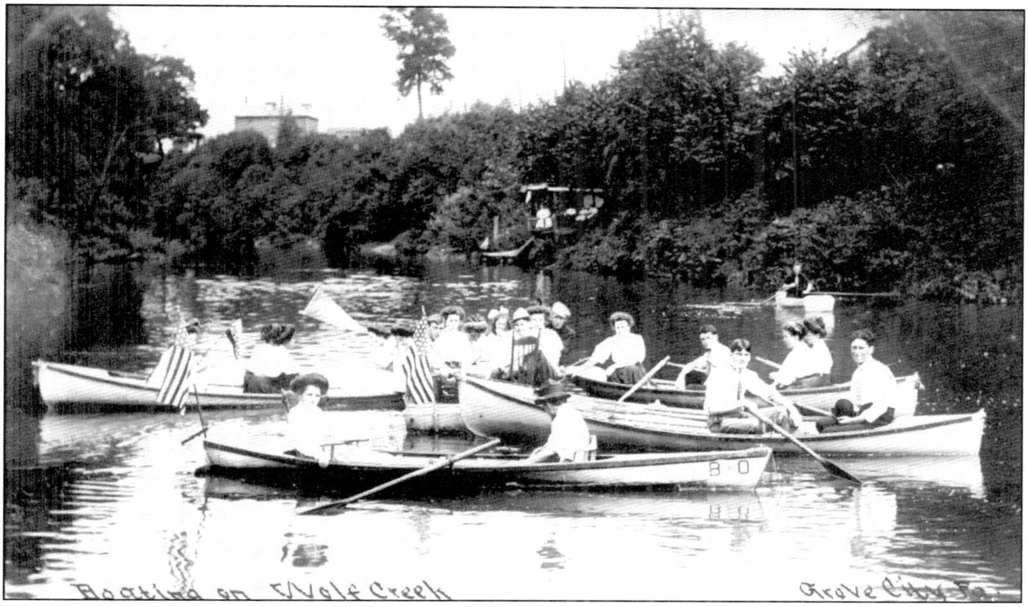

This photograph was likely taken from the dock of the boathouse on the previous page looking upstream. The square brick house in the distance still stands at the end of the Chestnut Street Bridge. This *c.* 1908 image appears to be of a group of Grove City College students out for a bit of summer fun. Many Grove City College students went on to professional schools after completing their studies in Grove City. A Yale pennant on one boat gives the clue that one of the young men in the middle might be Weir Ketler, son of Grove City College founder Isaac C. Ketler. Weir attended Yale Law School for a time, and after his father's death in 1913 and the death of Dr. Ormond (the second president of Grove City College), Ketler, at the age of 27, became the youngest college president in the United States. In the photograph below, taken from the same location, the season is fall judging by the warmer clothes and the leaves missing from some trees. Notice a second boathouse upstream on the opposite bank.

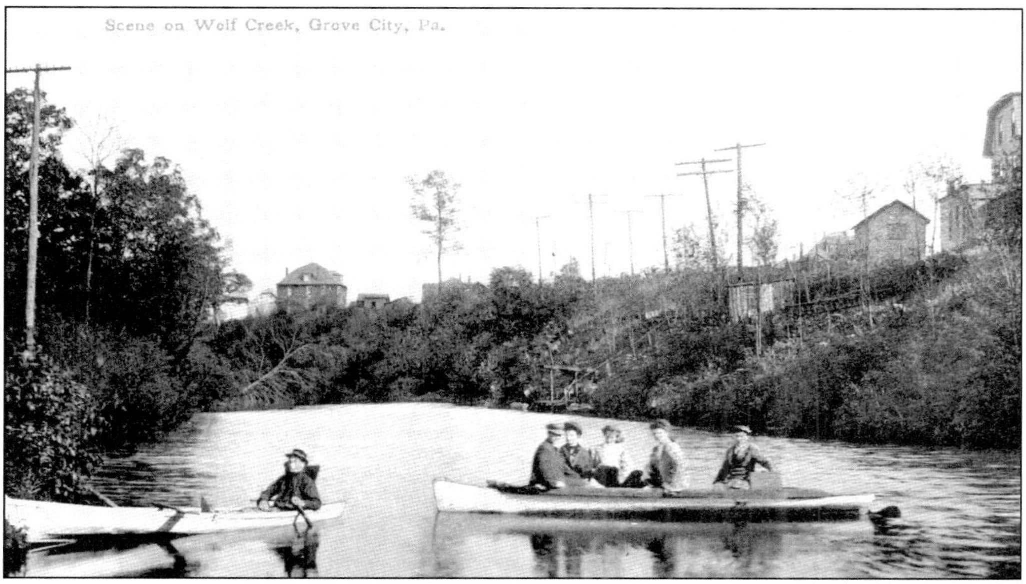

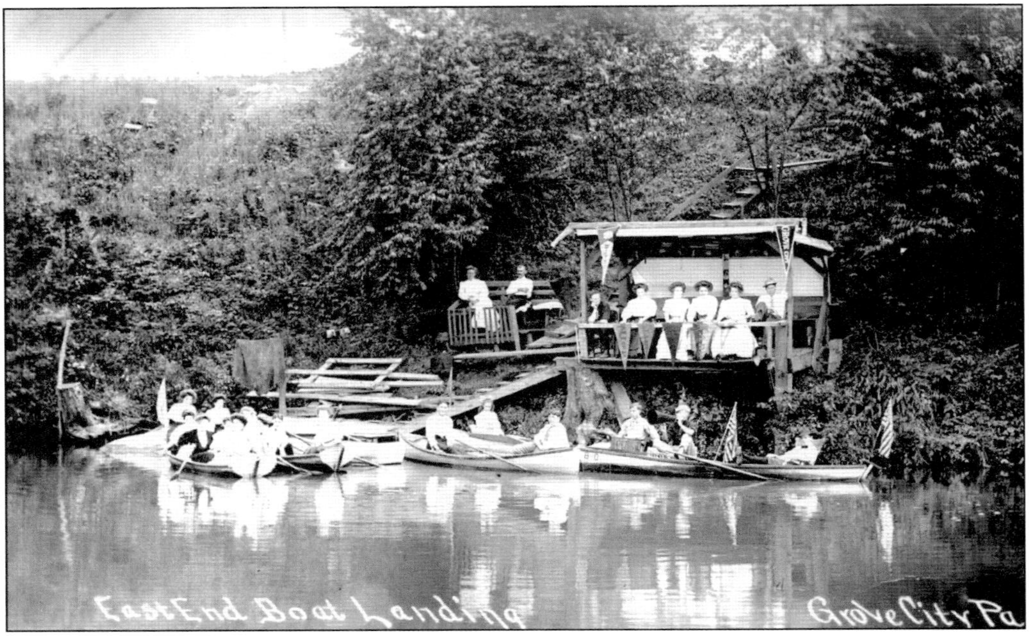

The East End boat landing would have been down over the hill from Bluff Street, which now exists on maps only. Currently up the bank from these boaters is the U. S. Investigations Service parking lot, which at the time was also one of the locations of the Nemo Bottling Company. Nemo bottled only soft drinks.

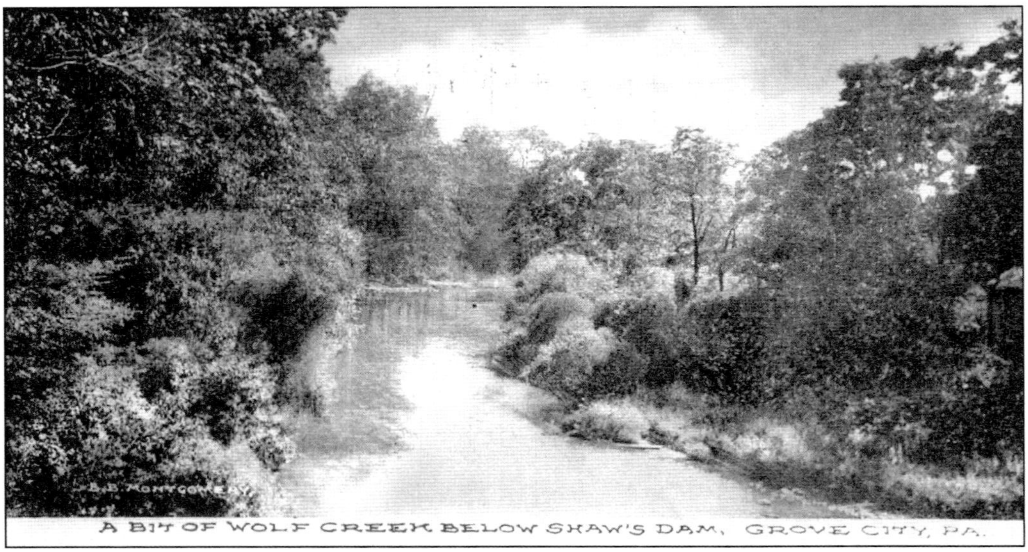

For a large part of Grove City's history, Wolf Creek was simply a drain into which all sorts of unwanted liquids flowed. The first homes with indoor toilets discharged their raw sewage and waste water directly into the creek. Except for a few boaters, most people did not use the creek for recreation. Picnics were held at Barmore Lake outside of town away from urban and industrial sights, sounds, and smells. As a result, the banks immediately along Wolf Creek were the backside of town, consequently remaining *relatively* wild and undisturbed.

Trinity Lutheran Church, which was located on North Center Street, has been torn down. The congregation moved to a new church building at Columbia Avenue and Superior Street on the other side of town. The hand-hammered aluminum Communion sets for the Lutheran Church were made by Edward B. Deniker and Robert Glessner, when both worked at Arthur Armour's workshop in the Alley behind the former Grove City Hospital.

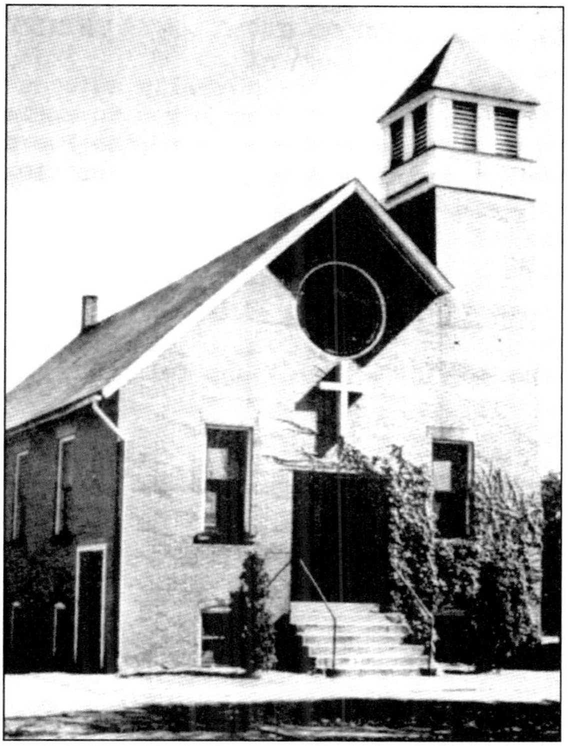

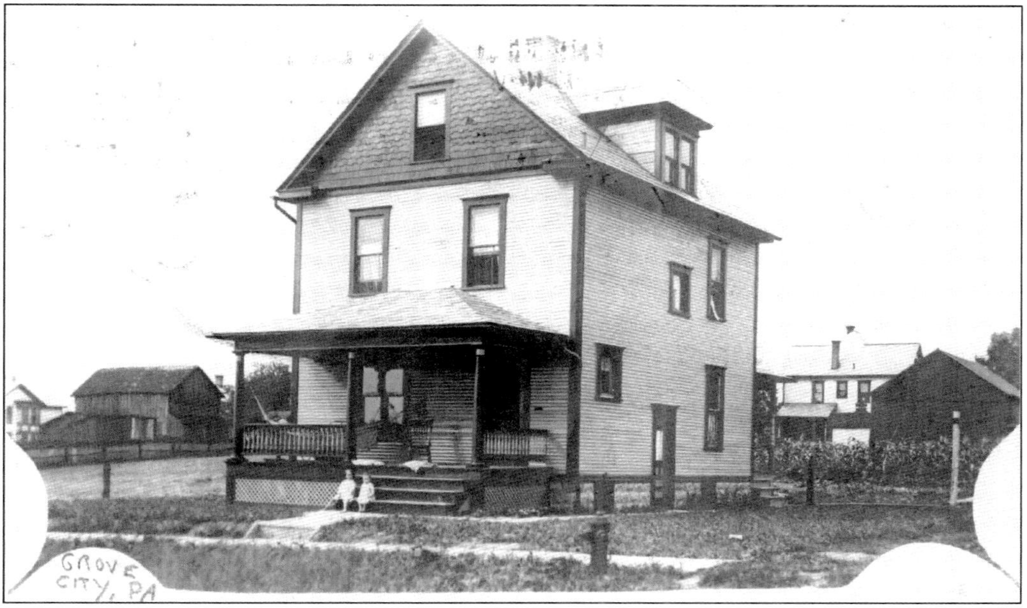

This house is typical of homes built in the early part of the 20th century in Grove City. It has a porch with a hammock, a slate roof, and a dormer that made the third floor usable space, and was painted at least three colors. Judging by the height of the corn growing in the garden behind the house, this picture was taken in August. While it is not known if this house is still standing, many similar to it are still in use in Grove City.

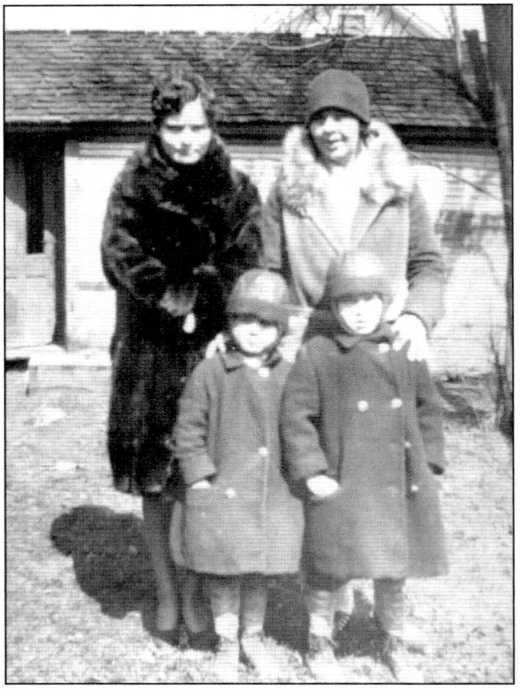

Farther up North Broad Street was the home of author John Hummel Jr. Pictured here are his aunt, Connie Jones Jiles (left); his mother, Mae V. Jones Hummel (right); his brother Don (left); and John (right). As the Bessemer plant expanded its workforce, new employees moved to Grove City from other parts of Pennsylvania. John Hummel Sr. found a job in the plant in 1925. The family moved from Phillipsburg when John Hummel Jr. was two years old. Originally living on McConnell Street, the family later moved to a home on North Broad Street. After a career at the Bessemer, the elder Hummel became a police officer for the growing town.

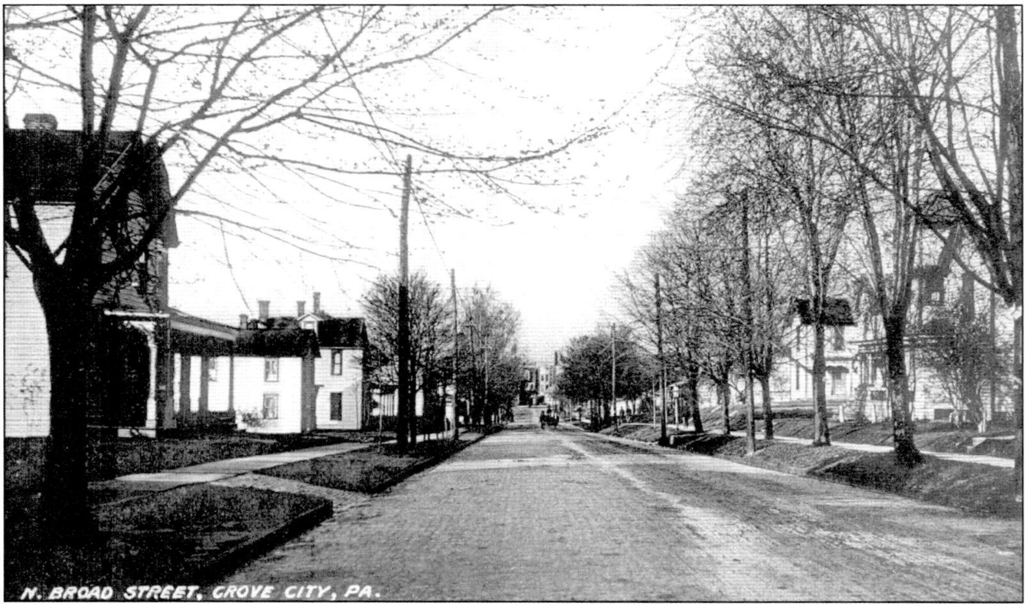

This view looks south from Spruce Street back toward the center of town down North Broad Street. The home of Lt. Oakley Kelly is just out of the picture to the left. Lieutenant Kelly and Lt. John A. Macready were the pilots of the first transcontinental flight, in 1924. The plane they flew resides in the Smithsonian Institute today. The home of Dr. Allen, a dentist, is barely visible to the right through the trees lining the brick-paved street. Broad Street connects the business area that first developed in the vicinity of Cunningham's Mill with the business area that developed around Shaw's Mill at the Upper Dam.

Eight

SHAW'S MILL AND SLABTOWN

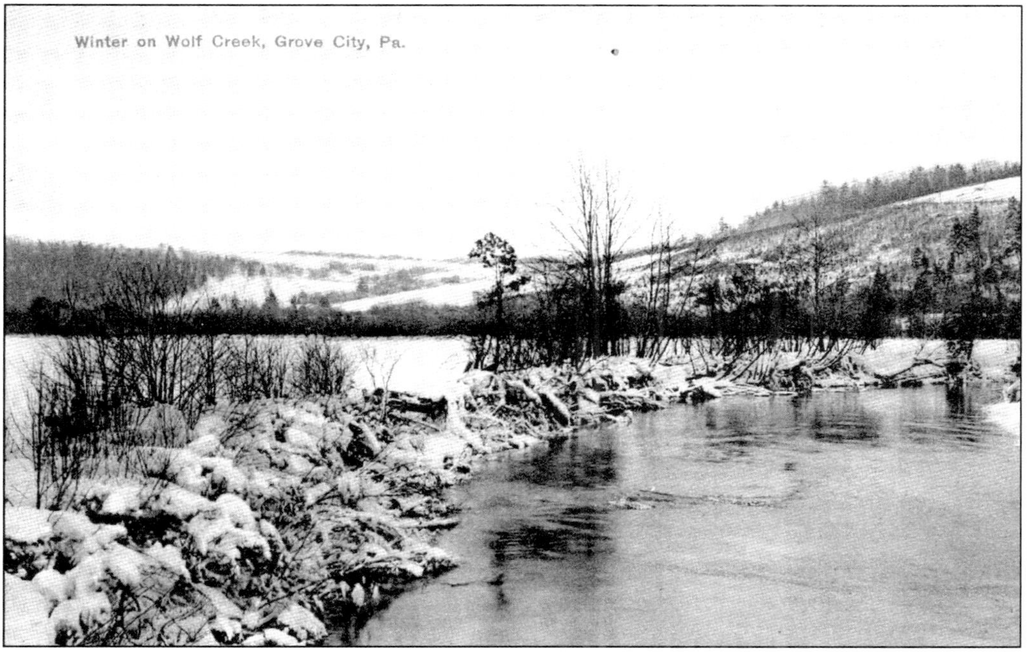

Winter on Wolf Creek at the turn of the 20th century provided the opportunity for skating. In a letter from Jennie Pearsall to her boyfriend Edd Reed on December 28, 1899, she wrote, "Will Ketler and Ida [Pearsall] and D.O.P (Deborah Olive Pearsall) and Mark [Graham] are skating this evening, while Frank [Pearsall] and I are keeping house. The ice is fine and you can skate four miles upstream from Shaw's, along the banks where we rowed so straight, Edd."

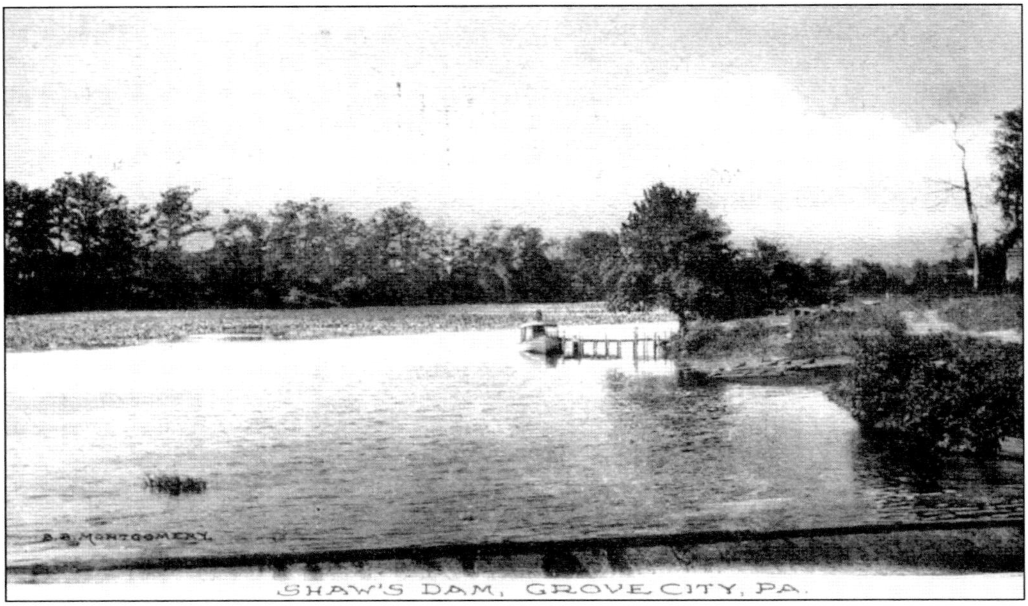

The first Upper Dam was built by James Graham in 1806 to provide water power to his gristmill. The mill site had many owners but was known as Shaw's Mills at the time this postcard was created. When the gristmill and sawmills were in operation in the 1800s, a small town was forming around the Upper Dam. Known as "Slabtown," at the time, it had a shoe shop, a store, a blacksmith shop, a school, and churches. The Methodist Episcopal church later moved downtown and was built on the hill overlooking Shaw's Mill. The crest of the dam appears along the bottom in this picture. In the distance, a steamboat can be seen docked at the eastern shore. The boat ferried vacationers and fishermen to camps and summer cottages upstream to the "Third Island." The lake that creates the islands and the two-centuries-old marsh and wetlands will be drained with the removal of the Upper Dam, scheduled for the summer of 2004.

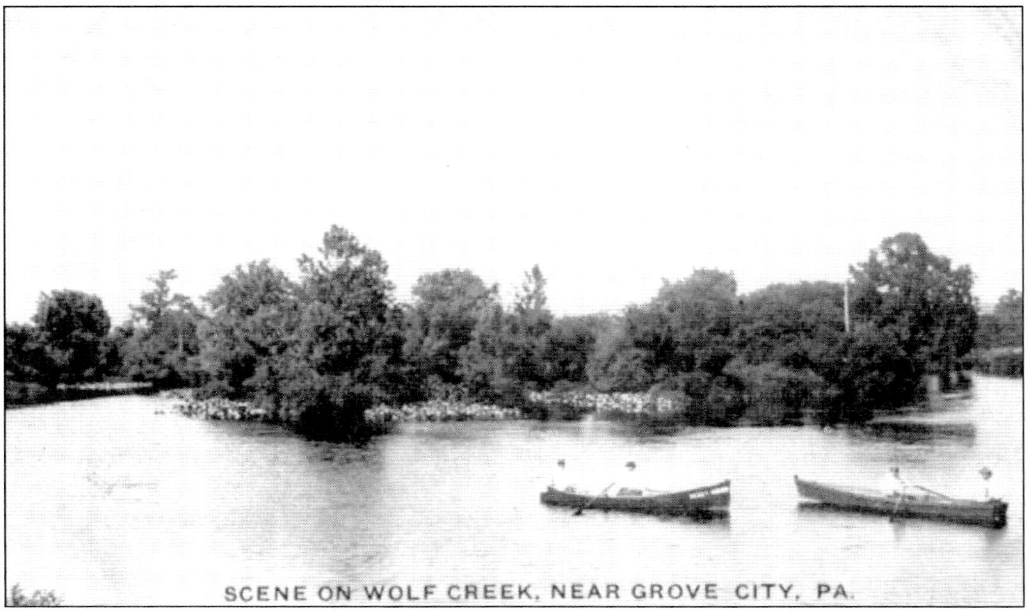

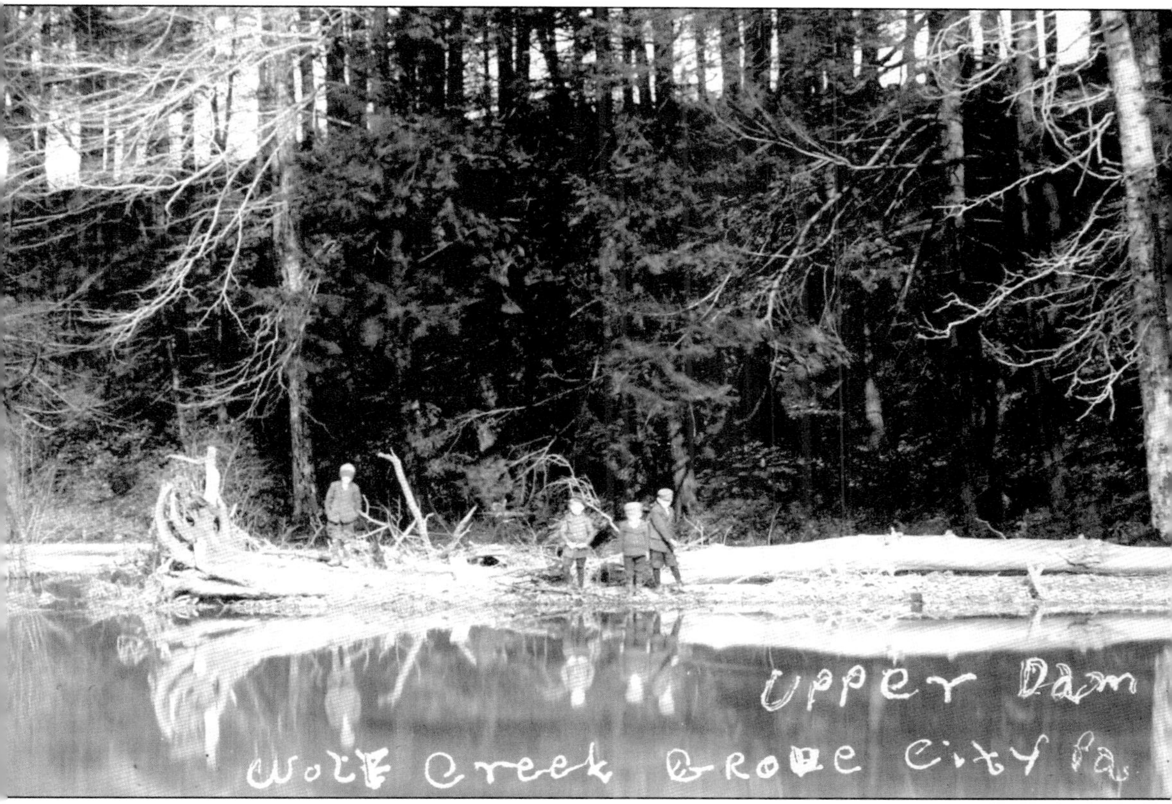

In this scene along Wolf Creek in the area around the Third Island, boys play along the bank near where water from Hallville and Slabtown coal mines drained into Wolf Creek. Upstream, near where Daugherty Road is today, John Daugherty, Esq., operated a sawmill where he produced 100,000 feet of board lumber yearly, sawn from the dense hemlock forest that was used to build the homes and businesses in the expanding town.

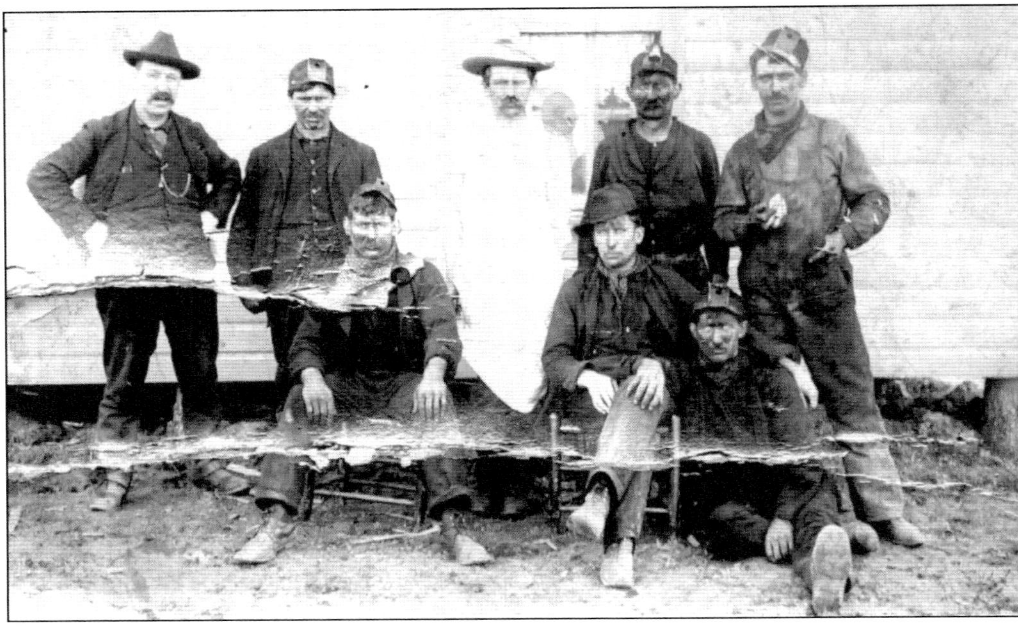

Coal mining at the turn of the century was a dangerous business; there were many injuries and deaths. In the photograph above, only the foreman and the cook are not covered head to foot in black coal dust. Several miners have handkerchiefs tied around their necks to pull up over their mouths to try to keep out dust. Coal was excavated beneath the entire town of Grove City during the 19th and 20th centuries. Currently, mine subsidence is an occasional problem as these old mines collapse deep beneath the surface. Miners in the picture above have hats equipped for carbide lights, which were lanterns that burned a gas produced by mixing carbide and water. The miner to the right of the cook still wears his lantern. The same miners are seen dining below at a table set with china and goblets and seem oddly out of place. Typically, the miner's lunch pail was round like a bucket or oval shaped and had a tray for pie and another for coffee. The coffee was ice-cold by mealtime.

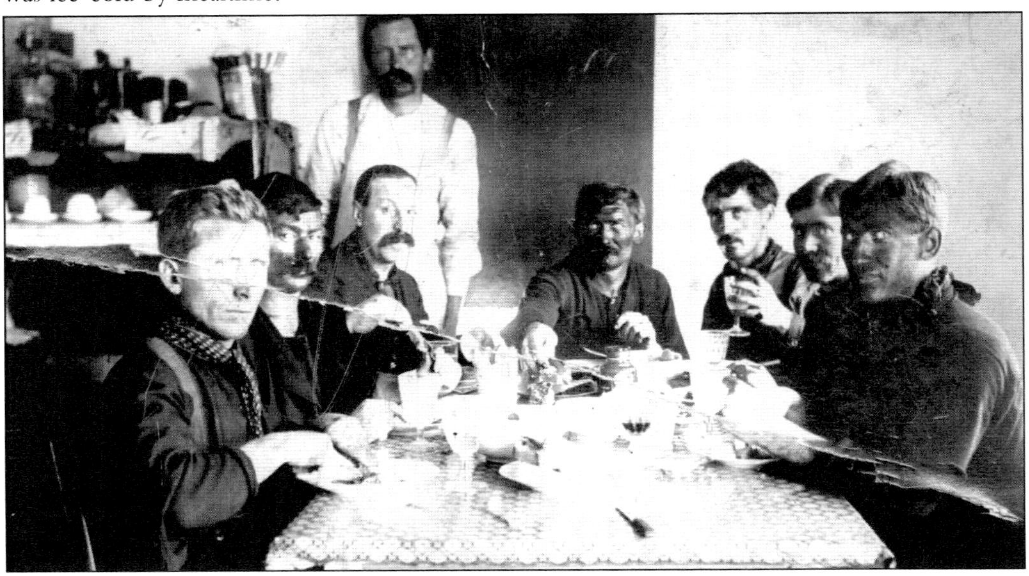

Immigrants provided much of the labor to the developing mining industry. Many were Catholics who settled in the vicinity of the Church of Our Lady of the Sacred Heart of Jesus near the Upper Dam in Hallville. Visible in the background of the picture below, the church stood across from Gill Road. W. A. Keller poses with his championship horse Prince Charlie. Keller delivered milk to homes and collected garbage in the same wagon. Especially in a small town, the people who know the most about you are your priest or minister and your garbage collector.

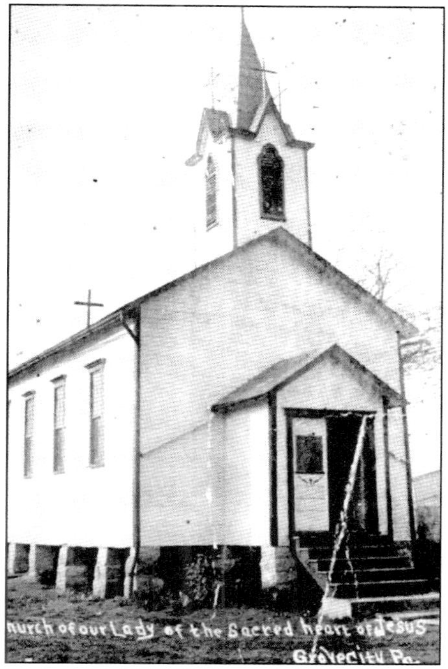

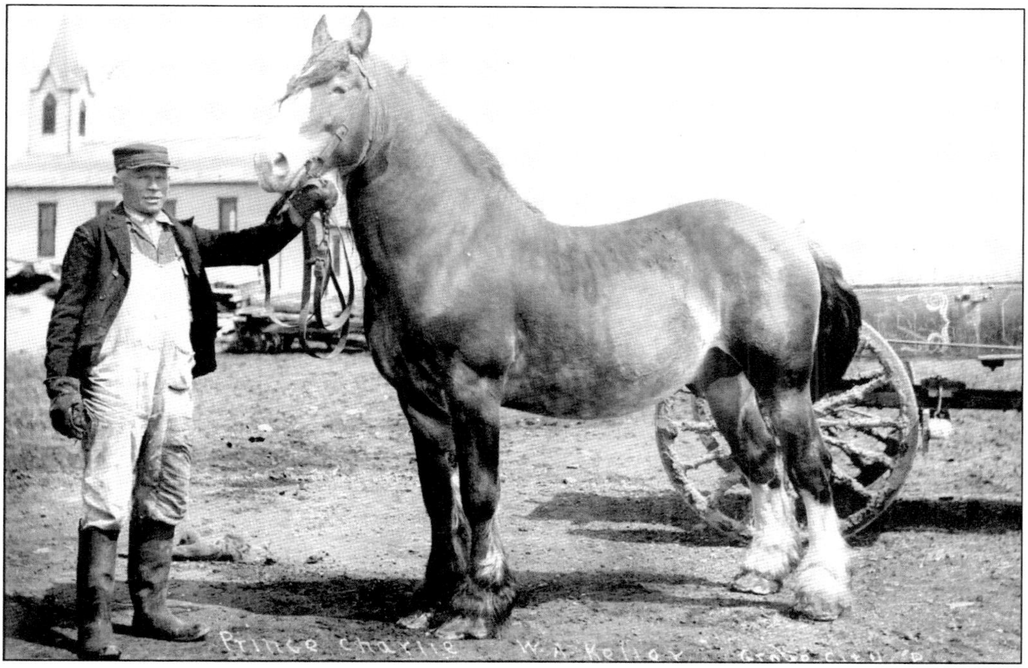